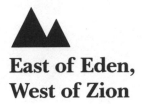

East of Eden,
West of Zion

Wilbur S. Shepperson
Series in
History and Humanities

East of Eden, West of Zion

Essays on Nevada

Edited and with an introduction by Wilbur S. Shepperson

University of Nevada Press   *Reno • Las Vegas*

WILBUR S. SHEPPERSON SERIES IN
HISTORY AND HUMANITIES NO. 26
(formerly Nevada Studies in History and Political Science)

Series Editor
Jerome E. Edwards

The paper used in this book meets the requirements of American National
Standard for Information Sciences—Permanence of Paper for Printed
Library Materials, ANSI A39.48-1984.

Library of Congress Cataloging-in-Publication Data

East of Eden, west of Zion : essays on Nevada / edited and with an
    introduction by Wilbur S. Shepperson.
        p. cm. — (Wilbur S. Shepperson series in history and
humanities ; no. 26)
    Includes bibliographical references.
    ISBN 0-87417-149-0 (alk. paper)
    ISBN 0-87417-150-4 (pbk.: alk. paper)
1. Nevada—History. 2. Nevada—Economic conditions. 3. Gambling—
Nevada—History—20th century. 4. Tourist trade—Nevada—History—
20th century. I. Shepperson, Wilbur S. (Wilbur Stanley) II. Series.
F841.E27   1993
979.3—dc20   93-10074
                                                CIP

University of Nevada Press, Reno, Nevada 89557 USA
Copyright © 1989 by Wilbur S. Shepperson
"The Melting Pot" is reprinted from *Nevada, A History,* by Robert Laxalt, by
permission of W. W. Norton & Company, Inc. Copyright © 1977 by the
American Assocation for State and Local History.
"Buckaroos" is reprinted from *Owning It All,* by William Kittredge.
Copyright © 1987 by William Kittredge.

05 04 03   7 6 5 4

Contents

The land between California and Salt Lake City was a virtual Land of Nod—east of Eden and west of Zion's religious settlements. It was held in low regard as a place for serious settlement, even unfit for habitation, possibly a place of exile.

William D. Rowley, *Reno: Hub of the Washoe Country*

So it is with Nevada now, a land that explorers shunned in the beginning, a territory that, with the discovery of silver and gold, became a crossroads of humanity, a plundered state that "didn't deserve to be" when the fortune seekers departed, a desperate state that broke with moral convention to sustain its very existence, a rediscovered region of America in which economic soundness and quality of life have caused a rebirth that will be a long time ending.

Robert Laxalt, *Nevada*

Preface

East of Eden, West of Zion is not designed to denigrate or overshadow Nevada by signaling worthy neighbors. Rather, its aim is to suggest the differential geography and the historic and contemporary contrasts between vast regions of the West. California and Utah have always been highly defined in the popular mind, but Nevada has evoked a less substantial and consistent image. This study makes reference to states north and south, as well as east and west, as a way to gain a broader perspective and to better illuminate the subject. In choosing topics for discussion, the contributors have thought less as historians or literati per se and more as "free spirits," who choose and pursue their individual pathways across the Nevada landscape. The study ignores the dramatic soft-core exposés that titillate with Comstock prostitutes or Las Vegas mafia. And although the state's places and customs are no more than a tiny piece in the national mosaic, like William Faulkner in his Yoknapatawpha County, Mississippi, we "will never live long enough to exhaust it."

Chapters take the form of either personal, scholarly, or impressionistic essays much like the style of Michel de Montaigne of four hundred years ago. They are trials and experiences: a journal of responses to Nevada. Like Montaigne, writers sometimes drift off on tangents and often question those who claim easy answers. Like him, they hope that through pain and pleasure and long observation they can gain some little guidance into the conduct of their lives and into that of the community. But most important, all have enjoyed working on the book because, as the novelist Reynolds Price has said, "The essay is the place where you get to say what you mean."

While every essayist hopes to achieve accuracy, the work is not totally objective, and, conversely, while the subject is colorful, the purpose is not to create a vision. In presenting their thoughts and focusing the essays, authors have tried not to linger too long on the flesh, on historical detail, thereby dissolving the spirit. Yet Lincoln's angry comment about Stephen A. Douglas is remembered: "He has no right to mislead others, who have less access to history." The work is at times an open panorama and at times a personal account; it is less aca-

demic than accessible. The articles are intended to add up to a co-
herent survey that will help explain Nevada's turnstile life-style.

Basically the book is the result of two publishing experiments. First,
in *Forty Years in the Wilderness* (1986) James Hulse issued a critical dis-
section of Nevada's major industry and of the state's social and cultural life. Hulse graciously invited me to add a brief introduction. I
have reflected often on *Forty Years* and have decided that my good
friend was on the right track but at times headed in the wrong direction. Second, for the past ten years, I have been managing editor of
Halcyon: A Journal of the Humanities. Among the over one hundred articles presented to the public, a few of those on Nevada can be given
increased clarity and purpose if pulled together in book form and
carefully focused on contemporary issues. Finally, the essays will high-
light the complexity and the rapidity of Nevada's growth and change.

Five of the twelve essays were first presented in *Halcyon* between
1979 and 1988. Five articles were written especially for this study;
"Buckaroos" appeared in William Kittredge's 1987 collection, *Owning
It All,* published by Graywolf Press, and Robert Laxalt's "The Melting
Pot" appeared in *Nevada: A History,* 1977, published by W. W. Horton
and Company. In general, Part One is designed to offer a background, a place, and a historical look at Nevada. Part Two, with its
emphasis on population growth, notes the state's urbanization. However, many of the essays do not neatly fit into a single category; several
emphasize the old heart of Nevada as well as the new urban reality.
Each article represents more of an individual statement than part of a
composite whole. Four of the twelve essayists are native sons and five
of the others have lived in the state for some twenty years or more.

For a century Nevada was washed over, but not truly settled, by
waves of migrants; it barely survived repeated economic recyclings.
Finally, out of a land of space and isolation there evolved two major
population centers, two cities which, to use anthropologist Claude
Levi-Strauss's idiom, are "masterpieces of bricolage." A number of
writers, moralists, environmentalists, and ideologues suggest that
there has been heedless destruction of nature, as well as the debase-
ment of tradition, learning, and the sacred texts of society. They argue that Nevada's famed entertainment palaces are a mere extension
of our blunted and base corporeality. They suggest that in pursuit of
the good life we interpreted the wrong passages, took the wrong

turns, and failed to understand the true secrets of either the land or our forebears.

Most contemporary students of the society agree that from the days of the Comstock Nevada's chief centers have been strikingly international and cosmopolitan. Most also agree that, while there has been temptation and illusion, the cities have provided a refuge, a new human frontier, where many of the dispossessed have moved upward into economic sufficiency and have become contributors to public life. Citizens generally find Nevada cities neither immoral nor artificial, but rather real business, commercial, and manufacturing centers, which double as places of entertainment. They are only in part patterned after Europe's Monte Carlo and Baden-Baden or America's giant amusement parks like Disneyland, Old Tucson, or Astroworld. All concede that Nevada's tourist-oriented institutions are in no way camouflaged, that they are a network of references and influences that have infiltrated both the private and the public sides of our institutions, and perhaps of our character.

Throughout recent decades, an economically prosperous Nevada has faced relatively minor conflict between labor and management or between expansionists and preservationists. With a population of only 110,000 in 1940 and over 1,000,000 today, the state has readily "extended the open door." But most surprising, the natural and climatic limits once thought to preclude spectacular expansion in a semidesert land have thus far proved to be illusions. Since World War II Nevada has steadily closed the gap between what she was, poor and underdeveloped, and what she may become, rich and highly developed. The state seems to have crossed a "critical population threshold."

But as a translator of Nevada society, the study deals with culture as well as with economies, with tradition, faith, cohesion, and purpose as well as with rapid population growth. The building of myth around charismatic figures, heroic deeds, or tragic events is a common human impulse and a necessary cornerstone for the formation of any culture. In this invention of tradition, Nevada has been singularly unfortunate. The stuff of legends has too often collapsed into tawdry tales of only cracker-barrel proportions. Stories worthy of becoming an epic have been either ignored or reduced rather than enhanced in the telling. The culture of Nevada has profited little from the presence and antics of Mark Twain and Dan De Quille and none from the observations of celebrities like Clare Booth Luce and Simone de Beauvoir. Indeed, the state has been badly served by the itinerant observers. Nor has it enjoyed founding fathers with Brigham Young's power and vision or Father Junipero Serra's abiding grace and zeal.

Of course, in a land dated by bristlecone pines, cui-ui fish, and petroglyph drawings, European arrival is as of yesterday. And it is much too soon to know if current Nevada Man will survive nature's rhythms from the basement of time. But in focusing on individual and contemporary concerns, these essays inquire whether Nevada can use the ever-present human friction between acquisition and preservation, quick wealth and refined sensitivity, carnality and creativity, to build a more humane and enlightened society.

Wilbur S. Shepperson

Acknowledgments

Four persons have made particular contributions to this book. The idea that Nevadans could discover and rediscover their heritage through a collection of individualized essays was first suggested to me by Judith Winzeler, director of the Nevada Humanities Committee. William Rowley provided the title and helped in restructuring several of the articles. John Stetter, former director of the University of Nevada Press, was consistently sympathetic to the idea and supportive of the process. Cliff Segerblom graciously offered his 1982 watercolor *Whistle Stop* for the book cover and jacket. The Nevada Humanities Committee assisted financially with printing and production. I am personally indebted to each of these special friends and to the NHC.

W.S.S.

The West is a region of extraordinary variety within its abiding unity, and of an iron immutability beneath its surface of change. The most splendid part of the American habitat, it is also the most fragile. It has been misinterpreted and mistreated because, coming to it from earlier frontiers where conditions were not unlike those of northern Europe, we found it different, daunting, exhilarating, dangerous, and unpredictable.

Instead of listening to the silence, we have shouted into the void. We have tried to make the arid West into what it was never meant to be and cannot remain, the Garden of the World and the home of multiple millions.

Wallace Stegner, *The American West as Living Space*

Introduction

Toward
Century's
End

Wilbur S.
Shepperson

At the end of the nineteenth century Nevada was mired in a deep and prolonged depression. Both the boom-camp optimism and the Gilded Age sophistication of the Comstock era had faded. No new mineral deposits had been developed after the late seventies. Falling prices, expensive railway transport, and the "white winter" of 1890 had cut livestock production by more than two-thirds. During the two decades before century's end Nevada lost over 1,000 persons per year, reducing the state's minuscule population to some 42,000 by 1900. Nevada's right and ability to be a state was under question. Legislative attempts to attract settlers through the creation of an immigration agency failed, and the new University of Nevada at Reno could boast only 10 instructors and 127 students by 1890. Some faculty even argued that Nevada provided none of the cultural and little of the economic base necessary for a sovereign state or for an institution of higher learning.

In the world outside Nevada's depressed and dusty window, the American West grew by a third from 1880 to 1900, America's great cities were rising, and beyond its shores western Europe enjoyed a gaudy and somewhat artificial fin de siècle mood. This clever and creative, yet faddish and fluid European vagary of a hundred years ago can be compared to the rich, plush, and sometimes deviant Nevada motif of our own era. It has been argued that Nevada today, as Oscar Wilde said of Europe a century ago, is "vibrantly decadent" and a "creation of fantasy." As we approach another century's end, perhaps we are, as Tom Wolfe noted, "America's first unconscious avant-garde . . . arising . . . out of the vinyl deeps."

We will evaluate the Wolfe and other insinuations as they apply to Nevada character and study the transformation of a dilapidated mining community of late nineteenth century into a prosperous society of late twentieth century. We will note how the anemic young state has, within recent memory, developed a robust economy and become the arbiter of a new entertainment culture.

During the first hundred years of Nevada's history, the human ebb and flow, while confused and colorful, is relatively easy to map. Historians have often noted that Congress granted statehood in 1864 with little foresight for the resource base necessary to create economic growth, cultural life, or a political system capable of true sovereignty. Fortunately, rapid innovation in mining techniques allowed for the quick exploitation of the Comstock Lode, and the growth of California fostered a rapid expansion in railroad transportation across the state. For some two decades it seemed that Nevada could sustain itself as a mining and ranching society. However, technology without a continuing rich ore base and a rail line without major commercial centers failed to provide economic stability, hence the population decline after 1880.

At the beginning of the twentieth century new discoveries of precious metals, along with copper mining in White Pine County, brightened the state's fortunes. Although the copper endured long after the collapse of the major gold and silver boom camps, the mining strikes occurred in isolated desert areas and gave birth to rude and dusty towns that, like their predecessors, quickly collapsed into ghostly ruins. Not a single mining-based community went on to become a significant economic center on the scale of Reno or Las Vegas. The state had to await yet newer technologies, a more refined system of transportation, and a shift in American population and social attitudes before it could tap the bountiful human resources that were to bring it prosperity.

Nevada long remained the most sparsely settled area of America and for almost a century was perplexed by a fluctuating economy and a transient population. Under such conditions it was difficult for traditions, folk cultures, and well-knit institutions to mature. In the most arid state in the Union extensive agriculture proved to be impossible, and it was not until mid-twentieth century that Nevada could boast a town with as many as thirty thousand people. Having only one poorly funded college and no professional schools other than mines-engineering, culture and refined ideas were not a major concern. Like things indigenous to the state—its mines, its land, its streams—culture and creativity required much energy and ingenuity before prospering.

To sensitive observers Nevada's geography suggested the image of man contesting with the elements. Sometimes as in Mark Twain's *Roughing It* man was depicted as a humorous oddity, sometimes as in Harry Sinclair Drago's twelve Nevada westerns he was set adrift by the isolation, sometimes as in George Stewart's *Sheep Rock* his despair was tied to the broader cosmos, and sometimes as in Robert Laxalt's ode to a Basque sheepman he appeared as humble and determined. But whether zestful or nondescript or timeless or serene, man was always pictured as engaged in a constant struggle with desolate nature. Nevada became the story of small figures against large vistas—a land inhabited but never quite settled, where the American continent took the measure of all things. Rural society had to contend with the brutal and the pragmatic forces that decreed a marginal survival. The ideal of virgin frontier that molded the psyche and symbolized the natural beginning of new life was always problematic. It was a country where settlers did not meld and blend into the natural surroundings, nor could they slowly and lovingly shape the land to provide a new way of life for their children and their children's children.

No one who arrived in Nevada to found a settlement pointed with robust faith to the Ruby Marshes, Vegas Valley Wash, or Truckee Meadows and declared, "This is the Place." The state was not seen as a promised land. It had neither milk nor honey. The beehive ethic of Utah and the sun-kissed image of California did not take root. Perhaps five hundred towns and communities sprang into temporary prosperity only to collapse in on themselves like miniature black holes. Indeed societies emerged and flourished rather like life at an active beach on a pleasant July weekend. All the paraphernalia of civilization would miraculously appear, but only barren sands would remain by late November. Few towns lasted a single human lifetime. In Nevada, as elsewhere, the phenomenon of building and collapse, start and failure, caused a dearth of ideas and a sameness; stability would have permitted the evolution of social uniqueness. The older things grow, the more different they become. Most children at five months are similar, whereas fifty years later they differ greatly.

But despite the cruel geography and the pattern of economic failure, the state was not devoid of variety, originality, and cosmopolitanism. Nevada pioneered in mining law, industrialized mining, the effective movement of water, federal reclamation, cooperative colonies, free silver, and socialism. During its first fifty years the state attracted the largest per capita foreign influx to be found in America.

During the first half of the twentieth century, 85 percent of the fiction writing on Nevada introduced foreign-born characters: in one out of six novels, colorful European or Asiatic immigrants emerged as leading figures, giving a catholic cultural tone to the oft-repeated "boom and bust" settings.

Starting in the 1920s and 1930s and rapidly unfolding after World War II, a new technology and changing American mores rescued Nevada from its mining past. The legalization of gambling and the construction of Hoover Dam—followed by fast automobiles, interstate highways, air conditioning, sophisticated air transport, the largest westward movement in American history, rapid social democratization, and a vast media promotion—brought a major migration to the far reaches of the Nevada deserts. Finally, technology or business acumen or human avarice, coupled with massive social change, had provided Nevada with the wherewithal to construct an economic base that attracted an ever-mounting inflow of both tourists and expectant residents.

Professor William Rowley argues that in the two decades between the world wars Nevada made the conscious choice "to open itself on an official and public basis to types of naughty fun that were banned for social reasons in other states."[1] Nevada laid the foundations for a society and an economy that were much more than a mere continuation of the past traditions of western permissiveness. Rather, the state reshaped the vices characteristic of an isolated male frontier society into a tourist attraction of major proportions (see the Rowley essay). The new activity quickly came to be known locally as the "gaming industry." Nevada had long been noted for easy divorce, but it was not until after World War II that divorce, marriage, gambling, and similar institutions were transformed into businesses that brought financial stability and marked economic growth to the state. To some degree the mid-twentieth-century success story was based on reorganizing and effectively advertising many of the forms and pastimes of the Old West. But the western motif tended to fade quickly during the fifties, and Nevada became a model postindustrial, consumption-oriented, tourist-directed society.

Since the state has few natural resources, residents during the late twentieth century have come to rely more and more on a rather basic utilization of their human resources. Historically, western societies that depend on the exploitation of natural resources, whether mines, forests, fisheries, or even agricultural lands, experience drastic fluctuations in their economies, as Nevada did in the nineteenth and early twentieth centuries. Gambling and tourism, while not high on a creative scale, utilize human resources and exploit the whims and fantasies of a mobile society. Only by such means has a dry, barren area with few gifts from nature been able to build prosperous communities and support a rapidly growing population. Japan, Singapore, and the Silicon Valley are differing examples of the employment of human resources to create spectacular prosperity.

Nevada, in its own peculiar way, has transcended its environment. The deposits in the state's sixteen federally chartered and state-chartered banks are among the fastest expanding in the nation. As of the mid-eighties the state's 4.11 percent annual rate of job creation was third, surpassed only by Arizona and Tennessee. Since 1980 Nevada has attracted some three times as many new businesses per capita as the national average. New foreign trade zones are being opened, while the population for the third consecutive decade continues to expand at the fastest, or near the fastest, percentage rate of any state in the country. During the decade of the seventies, Las Vegas alone gained more new residents than New York and New England combined. By 1980 only three states, Wyoming, New Hampshire, and Connecticut, had a lower poverty rate than Nevada's 8.7 percent. In terms of families in poverty and children under 18 years of age in poverty, only Wyoming and New Hampshire could boast a better record. Poverty levels among minority groups are substantially lower than in most states. The black population increased by 85.3 percent and the American Indian by 94.5 percent during the decade of the seventies. Asians and Pacific Islanders, as well as Mexicans and Cubans, flooded into Nevada during the same period, raising the total ethnic-minority population to 17 percent by 1980.

Nevada now enjoys the largest per capita increase in senior citizens of any state. Although the area is becoming a major retirement center, the death rate is well below the national average. In 1985 about 1 percent of the work force nationally was declared artists (painters, actors, dancers, novelists, poets, musicians). Nevada hosts the fourth largest per capita number of general artists in the United States and is the leader in the disciplines of dance, music, and photography. Persons in these cultural fields have tripled in number during the past twenty years. Many citizens do not consider the Atomic Test Site a plus for the state; however, it has become the hub for much personal and industrial expertise in southern Nevada. The Desert Research Institute, the National Judicial College, and the National Council of Juvenile and Family Court Judges also provide unique intellectual and research opportunities.

The major cities of Reno and Las Vegas allow for plumbing the depths of human experience; at the same time they reflect many of the secret ambitions of, and provide for the fullest expression of, the American bourgeoisie. For example, while the criticism of Las Vegas has gone unchecked, its position as an American showplace and glamour city is unchallenged. Homegrown millionaires have emerged to fund cultural events, medical facilities, and universities. It could be argued that behind Stanford University, the Huntington Library, the Rockefeller Center, or the J. Paul Getty Museum there was the accumulation of wealth by questionable means. Be it amassed by business acumen or historical accident, money tends to beget culture. Following in this great American tradition, Nevada has become the home of the Max C. Fleischmann Foundation, the Robert Z. Hawkins Foundation, the Steve and Elaine Wynn Foundation, the E. L. Cord Foundation, the Nell J. Redfield Foundation, the Grace Dangberg Foundation, the Margaret Elardi Scholarships, and an impressive list of educational and cultural entrepreneurs like Artemus Ham, Judy Bayley, Marjorie Barrick, Thomas Beam, Leon and Jacqueline Nightingale, and a score of others. Numerous Nevada financial institutions like the Hilton Corporation, the Summa Corporation, the First Interstate Bank of Nevada Foundation, and the Nevada Gaming Foundation for Educational Excellence are also making substantial contributions to the aesthetic and humanistic life of the community.

According to an old Dutch Calvinistic proverb, "For every good there is an accompanying evil." Nevada is still haunted by many of her traditional and long-standing problems and perhaps blessed by a few tenacious Socratic gadflies, who emphasize the state's social and spiritual failures. In the early decades of the twentieth century, reformers repeatedly cited Nevada as the "ugly duckling" and the "weak sister" among the states. Most progressives who had condemned "cronyism" and "political bossism" and "rotten boroughs" found the state's social deviations even more objectionable.

The late-twentieth-century acceptance of show girls, gambling, quick divorce, easy marriage, and legalized prostitution as part of a prosperous Nevada would have been incomprehensible to the earlier critics. They had predicted a doubtful future for the state and had argued that not only religion and education but also the arts and humanities could not prosper if social immorality continued to be tolerated.[2] But instead vice was democratized and transformed into economic virtue; the old plea for morality was swept away by a new prosperity. The reformers had hoped that redemption and purification were to come. How wrong they were and how ironic that the state's national success grew in part from an expansion, not an elimination, of the perceived evils. In short, Nevada defied both the economic guidelines and the moralistic overtones of the early-twentieth-century reform era. The state became prosperous by ignoring the progressive formula for greater production of capital goods as well as by rejecting the idea that a legislative mandate could uplift and purify society.

Nevertheless, Nevada's economic successes have not totally eclipsed either the problems or the criticisms of the early twentieth century. If the reformers (several of whom Hulse notes in his essay) were alive today, they would bombard the public with an impressive list of troublesome and detracting statistics. Of course, statistics can mean whatever the manipulator wishes. They are often weighted, fudged, misinterpreted, or misapplied. Still, statistics collected by environmentalists, social service personnel, students of health care and prison reform, educators, and religious groups forcefully suggest that Nevada ranks poorly in human services and that its permissive institutions seem to have high social costs.

After several studies between 1981 and 1986, the Secretary of Education, William Bennett, ranked Nevada last among all states in nine separate educational categories. Nevada has also been ranked last in its per capita support of higher education and lowest (at 14.4 percent, contrasted to Colorado's high of 23.0 percent) among the thirteen western states in the percentage of population completing four years of college. The state's suicide rate, at double the national average, is the highest in the nation. Rates of teenage suicide, teenage pregnancy, and teenage venereal disease are consistently among the highest in the country. Alcoholism and the sale of both hard liquor and wine are above those of any other state, and the unusual number of deaths from cirrhosis of the liver suggests that not all the alcohol is carried out of state by tourists. The incidence of lung cancer is high; both Reno and Las Vegas are among the top ten cities in the country in carbon monoxide pollutants. Nevada ranks first in divorce and violent crime. Health care costs are the highest in America, and a special congressional committee ranked Nevada's nursing homes last in meeting federal standards for patient care, diet, and condition of buildings.

The state is last in the registration of eligible voters and has the lowest voter response in both national and local elections. The populace pays one of the highest interest rates in the nation, and during the mid-eighties Nevada ranked seventh in the cost of car insurance. It has one of the lowest rates of payment to dependent children and is the second lowest in the country in per capita welfare payments. Nevada is last in agricultural production and, despite the wide open spaces, the Environmental Protection Agency in 1987 named it one of the five states not meeting air quality standards. With 422 persons incarcerated per 100,000 population, Nevada has more than double the national average in prisons. And, equally as significant, Nevada's expenditure per inmate is the lowest in the West. (For example, a prisoner costs the state $26.97 per day, whereas New Mexico spends $64.66 per day.) Both church and synagogue membership and attendance are lower in Nevada than in any other state. Salaries for teachers and others involved in cultural activities are generally well below the national average despite a high cost of living that equals that of Washington, D.C.

For many critics, Nevada's basic problem is simply defined. Tourists and residents are more interested in the quick gain inspired by gambling than in traditional business practices. (Capitalism, however, is not above reproach. The art historian, Jonathan Brown, has contended that from its seventeenth-century founding in Holland, "the difference between the stock exchange and the gambling casino was largely a matter of interior decoration.") The state proudly boasts each quarter's increase in gambling tax revenues. When these revenues do not rise at the projected rate, a blue pall descends upon the offending community. Few questions seem to be asked as to the purpose, meaning, and direction of, or the natural resources required for, growth. The critics argue that in Nevada, as in the new west in general, there is little personalizing of possessions. As in much of the Sun Belt, wealth is symbolic and functional. For example, a Mercedes is something that shows how successful you are and also gets you around. It is not like a teacup, prized because your grandmother carried it across the plains. (In Steinbeck's *Grapes of Wrath,* Ma Joad's happy memories are in her little souvenir from the St. Louis World's Fair of 1904.) Humanism, cultural appreciation, love for the object because of what it represents in emotional terms have, according to the reformers, often escaped the Nevada mentality.

Clearly, Nevada has not been one of those special visionary places like the "old sod" of Ireland, the Green Mountains of Vermont, or the Shenandoah Valley of Virginia that are dear to people who have never visited them. W. B. Yeats could brag that every river and mountain in Ireland were associated with at least one legend. New England, the South, and, to a lesser degree, the Midwest have stories and yarns associated with the meadows, the hedgerows, the streets, the old decaying houses. There are Indian tales, military defeats, monuments, ballads, cemeteries, and moving fiction. Memory and imagination require being stabilized and implanted in a way not yet experienced in Nevada.

Nevertheless, the state is filled with paradoxes and high contrast. There is the "other Nevada" of Robert Laxalt; a Nevada which boasts ancient bristlecone pines, spectacular desert lakes, and the majestic Ruby Mountains and the Sierra Nevada. In Nevada traditional crafts such as horsehair reata braiding, Indian beadwork and basketweaving, and cowboy storytelling still survive. Branding and buckarooing, Basque sheepherding, ethnic festivals, and stone farmhouses built by Italian masons add texture and richness to the landscape. Conversely, the traditional lack of an established societal structure has promoted easy relationships in which foreign immigrants and local migrants have discovered few obstructions to upward social and economic mobility. With no single group dominating the society, most new arrivals have found avenues for opportunity fairly wide and inviting.

Someone has said that no place can exist in the consciousness, the mind, the soul, until something has happened to give the spot meaning. It must become a landmark where lovers loved, or writers wrote, or fighters fought, or headless horsemen rode. For example, rural Nevada has been given meaning and place and dignity by Robert Laxalt's *Sweet Promised Land* and the short stories of William Kittredge. Reno achieved character with Walter Van Tilburg Clark's *City of Trembling Leaves*. But Las Vegas, with its fast unfolding boomtown economy, has all but crowded out the memory of an older population and has plunged into the future without a history. A spate of contemporary novels (note Irsfeld's essay) is only beginning to give name and purpose to the city. Of course, the reputation of the state would be enhanced if it could boast of persons like New England's Robert Frost, or Mississippi's William Faulkner, or Utah's Wallace Stegner.

Yet Nevada is beginning to preserve and create its own brand of worthy artifacts. In addition to government-supported cultural facilities, the Liberace Museum of Las Vegas, the Wilbur D. May Museum of Reno, the Green Valley Sculpture Garden of Henderson, the Las Vegas Museum of Natural History, the Stardust Museum of Gaming, and even the Ethel M. Chocolates Cactus Garden of Southern Nevada suggest the many private contributions that enrich, feed, and enlarge the public imagination. Of course, tradition requires time. The frontier was declared closed only one hundred years ago, and Nevada had fewer than 150,000 people less than forty years ago.

It can be argued that pop art and entertainment from Elko's annual Cowboy Poetry Gathering to the Las Vegas neon shows have made a tangible contribution to contemporary Nevada culture. Popular forms of music, drama, literature, and design are regularly converted and evolve into meaningful humanistic forms; they stimulate reflection, raise the consciousness level, and are slowly adopted by "genteel tradition." Lineage and credentials quickly follow. Through his clever art Andy Warhol is said to have given "the Brillo box the same stature as a totem pole." American culture, like American life, is fluid, upwardly mobile, and constantly being recast and rearticulated. We are entertained, but we also learn from a performance by Charlie Chaplin or Garrison Keillor. Old quilts have become tapestries on our museum walls. Stephen Foster became a master of ballad and song, transcribing the southern vernacular into musical expression of deep meaning. Walt Whitman in his essay "Democratic Vistas" demanded that a whole new "programme of culture" be formulated and promulgated for America, not for "the parlors or lecture rooms," but rather "with an eye to practical life, the West, the workingman." If we of Nevada can wisely guide what Alexis de Tocqueville called America's "virtuous materialism" and allow the wealth to enhance and not diminish the soul, and if we can make pop culture reflective and not deadening to the imagination, the state may achieve new meaning and purpose by century's end.

NOTES

1. Russell R. Elliott, with assistance of William D. Rowley, *History of Nevada*, rev. ed. (Lincoln: University of Nebraska Press, 1987), 374.

2. For classic examples, see Jeanne Elizabeth Wier, "The Mission of the State Historical Society," in *First Biennial Report, Nevada Historical Society, 1907–1908*, and Anne Martin, "Nevada: Beautiful Desert of Buried Hopes," *The Nation*, July 26, 1922.

Part One   From Frontier to Hinterland

The country is new and the population heterogeneous—you see every grade of every nationality represented—Americans from everywhere that have been everywhere . . . Castilians with their fierce mostachios and jingling spurs—Frenchmen, Englishmen, Prussians, Russians, Poles, Swiss, Dutch, Jews, Irishmen and Scots—Indians with their blankets and half naked squaws. . . . You can live as you please, dress as you please, eat as you please, make money as you please, or lose it as you please, go where and as you please and die and be burried or not as you please. . . . Everybody, women as well as men, ride at full gallop up hill and down—almost everybody gambles, plays faro, monte rondeaux or billiards, checkers, chess and dominoes.

Marvin Lewis, *Martha and the Doctor*. Excerpt from a letter, Martha James Galley, Austin, Nevada, to her brother, George James, and sister-in-law, Lilla Cabot Lodge, of Boston, April 17, 1865.

The warmest days of summer are modified by soft south-west winds, laden with the sweet odor of wild flowers and the aroma of the indigenous sage, while the nights are seasons of transcendant loveliness, rendered so by the gentle mountain breezes that waft health and vigor to the sleeper.

Brochure of the State Immigration Bureau, 1888.

Sense of Place in the Great Basin

C. Elizabeth Raymond

To a country that prides itself on being a land of beauty and abundance, the Great Basin is a serious and disturbing geographic anomaly. One of the last American regions to be thoroughly explored, the Great Basin first entered the national consciousness as an obstacle, a terrible stretch of desert that had to be crossed in order to reach the mecca of the California goldfields. Nothing that weary travelers learned of it during the overland journey encouraged them to tarry and try the area further. In the heartfelt words of one 1850 traveler, "The whole country appeared so dreary and dismal, so forsaken and cursed of the Almighty, that it reminded me every day of the curse pronounced against Babylon, and I cannot now look back upon our hardships, and sufferings, on the Humboldt without shuddering."[1] Even explorer John Frémont, who was aware of successful Mormon cultivation in eastern parts of the Great Basin, was adamant about its limited productive capacity: "Sterility . . . is the absolute characteristic of the valleys between the mountains—no wood, no water, no grass; the gloomy artemisia [sagebrush] the prevailing shrub."[2]

Frémont set the prevailing tone of comment about the region, whose characteristic feature of inward-flowing drainage he first identified in 1844. Bounded on the east by the Wasatch Range of Utah, and on the west by California's Sierra Nevada, the Great Basin is a unique geographic province, distinguished by extreme aridity, high elevation, and numerous basin-and-range formations. Agriculture is limited to areas that can be irrigated, which, given the paucity of water, are necessarily few. Historically, the economy of the region was based on exploitation of limited natural resources, in the form of ranching and mining.[3] These natural resources were so limited, however, that regional population remained low. Despite the discovery of major deposits like Nevada's Comstock Lode, mining boomtowns came and went with depressing regularity, and the Great Basin was never permanently or convincingly prosperous. For all but the Mormons, it remained a barrier to be crossed, or a temporary way station on the trail to somewhere more promising.

Ambivalence about its purpose and value for the rest of the country is reflected in written accounts of the region extending from the first records of white intrusion up to the present. One of its earliest chroniclers, Jedediah Smith, summarized its physical features as early as 1827: "The general Character and appearance of the country I have passed is extremely Barren. High Rocky hills afford the only relief to the desolate waste for at the feet of these are found water and some vegetation While the intervals between are sand barren Plains."[4] This extensive, mountainous, sterile landscape is positively un-American in its lack of productive potential. Some confidently predicted that it would never be permanently settled. Others campaigned for Nevada's removal from statehood, on the grounds that it had too few people and resources to responsibly exercise the privilege of self-government. General disparagement of the Great Basin West was summed up in the early twentieth century in no uncertain terms: "The mean ash-dump landscape stretches on from nowhere to nowhere, a spot of mange. No portion of the earth is more lacquered with paltry, unimportant ugliness."[5]

Despite its open challenge to American environmental faith, however, the Great Basin also attracted a coterie of admirers. From the very beginning, there were some who celebrated its distinctive, if difficult landscape. As unlikely as such praise might have seemed to the horrified overland travelers, some of their contemporaries actually found things to *admire* in the wilderness around them. Celebrants like reporter Albert Evans in 1869 remarked breathlessly on its beauty:

The sky above is gloriously blue; the snow fields on the mountains that bound the wide horizon glitter dazzlingly in the full flood of the light of the declining sun. Almost beautiful seem the barren valleys, seen through the soft, blue haze which mellows all their outlines. This strange, weird land never looked so attractive to our eyes.[6]

They praised its serenity, the mystical calming effect of the scenery, and, ironically, its potential for future development.[7]

These desert admirers mostly shared a variant environmental ethic;

they admitted that the Great Basin was a desert but appreciated it for those very qualities of aridity, limited population, and deeply etched topography that others viewed as ominous. In the words of modern traveler William Least Heat Moon, "There's something about the desert that doesn't like man, something that mocks his nesting instinct and makes his constructions look feeble and temporary. Yet it's just that inhospitableness that endears the arid rockiness, the places pointy and poisonous, to men looking for its discipline." [8]

Collectively, these variant accounts of the Great Basin West evince a distinctive sense of place, but one that is strangely contrary to the national environmental mythology. The Great Basin West emerges from contradictory descriptions as a region of permanent environmental poverty, rather than created abundance. To admirers and detractors alike, the region remains a desert.

Almost *all* observers, whether or not they appreciate the Great Basin scenery, agree that it appears dismal. Many would approve historian W. Eugene Hollon's remark, in his 1966 study *The Great American Desert,* that the consignment of large sections of Nevada to a military bombing range was appropriate, because "at least it serves some useful purpose." [9] A strikingly similar argument was used a few years later to justify selection of Nevada and Utah as the site for the massive MX missile installations. [10]

The aridity of the Great Basin makes it a physical desert, but its inherent hostility to human life renders it even more menacing. Newcomer Helen Viets describes her sensation of displacement in Nevada in 1936:

> At dusk, when the sage is gray and the colors have gone off the peaks, you can hear the peculiar low whine of the wind coming down the canyon. You turn up your collar and hurry for home, trying to buoy your sagging spirits as you go. . . . I can't help but think: What are we doing here, children of the cities that we are; aliens in this lost and forgotten land? [11]

Numerous accounts of the Great Basin agree about human irrelevance in such a harsh landscape. Its tremendous scale and apparent timelessness diminish human purpose and defeat human technology. Those who venture out on it are appropriately fearful, whether they travel in ox-drawn wagons, in air-conditioned railroad cars, or in modern automobiles. In the words of contemporary essayist Rob Schultheis, the Great Basin is a kind of "geographic purgatory":

From a speeding car (and you drive as fast as you can) the landscape looks dull: the sullen hills, the endless repetition of sagebrush sagebrush sagebrush, rabbitbrush, bitterbrush, coyote-
brush. On the passes they call the summits, the trees are scrub,
barely head high. Here and there where someone has tried to
mine is a hummock of corrosion, yellow, ocher. . . . The cities—
Las Vegas, Reno, Winnemucca, Sparks, Lovelock and the rest—
are convulsions of febrile activity: the kind you find in a maze full
of rats fed on cocaine-infused nutrients.[12]

Earlier, more benign American lands had simply awaited the beneficent hands of energetic pioneers, who could fulfill their natural destiny by making the wilderness productive. But the Great Basin, "sinister, cruel, and capable of horrors,"[13] actively discourages human
incursion. Its destiny is to remain unchanged.

Nonetheless, there are some exceptions to the desolation. The desert is virtually absent from descriptions of the Mormon agricultural
settlements of Utah and eastern Nevada. Thus a contemporary short
story by Lynne Larson takes place in an astonishing Utah valley,
where "sap dripped finally, bees droned, ripening fruit bulged and
burst and fell heavy with the season and the surfeit."[14] And 1930s bus
traveler May Winn describes the approach to Salt Lake City in terms
reminiscent of paradise:

Through its center wandered a clear mountain stream, on whose
banks grew clusters of green poplars, scarlet elders, and golden
cottonwoods. Fields green with alfalfa made a checkerboard on
the valley floor, and dotted here and there on little farms were
sturdy, simple houses, such as one sees in rural New Hampshire
or Vermont. . . . Mountains closed in the valley with tawny, pro-
tective arms, drawing apart only toward the south to let us glimpse
the distant range of the Wasatch, mauve and pink against an
azure sky.[15]

Winn explicitly ties this country to more congenial agrarian land-
scapes. The fact that she is not in New England, however, is pointedly
recalled by the presence of the tawny mountains in the background.

These agricultural paradises in the middle of the desert are shock-
ing. Winn and other travelers who remark upon them stress their implicit contrast with the barren landscape surrounding them. Green
fields are not natural in the Great Basin, however. They are achieved

only at tremendous cost in terms of the resources committed to build and maintain the irrigation systems. They exist as an environmental monument to the cultural imperatives of Mormonism.

Intense cultivation, as Wallace Stegner suggests, is a peculiar characteristic of the Mormon subculture in the Great Basin:

> Especially you see the characteristic trees, long lines of them along ditches, along streets, as boundaries between fields and farms. . . . These are the "Mormon trees," Lombardy poplars. Wherever they went the Mormons planted them. . . . they make the landscape of the long valleys of the Mormon Country something special and distinctive. . . . There are Lombardy poplars elsewhere in the world; there are few places where there are so many, and there is no place where the peculiar combination of desert valley and dark lines of trees exist as it does in this country.[16]

Visual contrast between areas of Mormon and non-Mormon occupancy in the Great Basin has always been pronounced. Frémont first remarked on it in 1848, and Mary Mathews noted it in 1880, as she traveled west by railroad:

> In Utah we find the first cultivated field since we left the eastern part of Colorado. We also see fine fruit trees, most every farm having a large orchard and nice gardens. Poultry of every description is raised in abundance: also large flocks of sheep, cattle, and horses. . . .
> Passing out of Utah we enter the great desert of Nevada. . . . Nothing grows on it but sagebrush.[17]

The *explanation* for the contrast, as Wallace Stegner describes it, lies in the particular cultural assumptions of Mormonism. Broadly defined as a system of shared symbols and meanings by which a society organizes and gives significance to its experience, culture affected both perception *and* behavior among the Mormons who settled the Great Basin:

> The Gentiles who had driven the Saints from Ohio and Missouri and Illinois were contemptuous both of the Mormons and the arid desert they had settled upon. It was necessary to love these valleys of the mountains as the fairest land on earth, because they were sanctuary. And it was unthinkable that the gathering-place

of the Saints should be a barren desert. It should be made to blossom, and it was. [p.28]

The Mormon newcomers already had a strong agrarian tradition, and they were prohibited both by lack of capital and by presidential directive from other undertakings. So they set about to transform the Salt Lake Valley in the image of the Midwestern farmland with which they were familiar. Through massive communal efforts and without federal government assistance, they physically modified the desert environment. They irrigated it and established numerous small, diversified farms, finding both personal and social fulfillment in making the arid land blossom.[18] In classic American fashion, they redeemed the wilderness, against all odds. Mormon pride in this undeniable achievement runs deep, and is reflected in contemporary fiction:

> Now the water arrives, a finger-size trickle swelling to fill the ditch and start spilling on the lawn. He stands, steps back near the house, and follows its spread by silver flickerings in the grass. . . . He did not think he'd like gardening . . . but to have something grow by his own labor, something they can eat even if not at much less cost than buying, feels good.[19]

Yet this epiphany to growing things is informed in part by the recognition that successfully cultivating anything in the arid Great Basin is a minor miracle.

The Mormon farms implicitly defy the desert's environmental constraints, but even the industrious and energetic Mormon farmers cannot completely overcome the Great Basin's sterility. The fragrant valleys remain surrounded by tawny hills. Indeed, it is the presence of those barren hills and dry valleys that makes the occasional lush patches so striking. As traveler Zephine Humphrey notes of another, somewhat different oasis, it is the surrounding desert counterpoint that defines it:

> The sudden unexpected verdure of Las Vegas had a most gratifying effect. We had almost forgotten what trees looked like; deciduous trees, that is. . . . I daresay, if one were to go straight to Las Vegas from an elm-shaded New England village, it would look bare. But Christopher and I shall always remember it as the place where there were so many trees.[20]

Her insight is confirmed by anthropologist Richard Poulsen, who observes the prevailing Great Basin pattern of ranch houses ringed by carefully planted and nurtured trees. Poulsen speculates that the trees in this case serve a symbolic as well as a practical function. Not only are they a windbreak, but they also symbolically wall off the intruding desert beyond them and symbolically create an artificial oasis of non-desert space within the boundary they describe.[21]

Lyrical accounts of successful environmental transformation thus inadvertently reinforce the preeminence of the desert in all other areas. Mormon culture, for a variety of reasons, predisposes its members to prefer an agrarian landscape, and they set about creating it to the best of their ability. The familiar American theme of taming the wilderness is once again played out; but the vast, silent sterility of the desert continues to lurk just beyond the boundaries of their irrigated land.

The contemporary Nevada economy, based on tourism attracted by legalized gambling, is similarly motivated to defy the environmental reality of the desert, but by different means. This second kind of transformation is not physical but mental, banishing the desert by modifying its image. Advertisements for the state selectively emphasize those natural recreational features that visitors are known to appreciate—mountain trout streams, winter and water skiing—rather than the more distinctive and predominant desert environment. As 1930s tourist May Winn sardonically observes, such promotion only confuses the naive tourist:

> The beautifully illustrated literature of the Reno Chamber of Commerce . . . has picked out the few wet spots in the dryest [*sic*] state in the Union and photographed them again and again, until the reader gets the impression that the only thing he really needs in Nevada is a bathing-suit. Since returning from our motor-bus Odyssey, I have studied the map of this state and have been overcome to discover that after leaving Winnemucca I traveled almost continuously within sight or actually by the shores of "rivers" and "lakes," although to my Eastern eyes they looked like the dreariest alkaline marshes and stretches of stagnant oose [*sic*] imaginable. [pp. 69–70]

Nevada's tourist industry promotes casinos as glittering playgrounds surrounded by areas of unsurpassed recreational potential. Those large areas of the state that don't conform to the chosen images of fun and sun are rather lamely promoted as oases in time, genuine outposts of that mythical "Old West" that tourists are presumed always to

be seeking. Where the physical conditions of aridity, slight population, and great distances cannot be transformed by image makers,
they are relegated to the past, marketed as quaint artifacts of a time
when people were less skilled at manipulating the environment to
overcome or disguise such inconvenient realities. They become outposts on America's "loneliest road." Or else, in the case of the Nevada
Test Site and the proposed nuclear waste dump, such spaces are given
over to destruction, relegated to distasteful national purposes because, in Hollon's haunting phrase, at least then they serve some
useful purpose. Despite this manipulation of beguiling regional imagery, however, reality invariably intrudes. Even casual tourists like May
Winn eventually discover that Nevada, for all of its undeniable beauties, is not simply a land of rivers and lakes.

Ultimately, neither kind of modification of the desert is entirely successful. Neither the physical changes made by the Mormon farmers
nor the seductive imagery disseminated by Nevada's tourist industry
can overcome the sheer physical intransigence of the desert. Those
who seek to know and understand the Great Basin must still confront
the fundamental fact of its barrenness.

Reactions to that barrenness depend in large part on the individual
circumstances of the observer. People passing through on their way to
California hate the desert's heat, monotony, and ugliness not just for
its own sake, but also because it impedes progress toward a desired
goal. Those who stay to make their homes in it, however, evaluate the
same landscape much differently. They know and appreciate subtle
changes, modest improvements. They are fully aware, in the words of
Nevada rancher Molly Knudtsen, that "it takes a lifetime of hard work
to create a ranch, and only a few years for it to slip back into the sagebrush of the wild." [22] Land that looks barren and unappealing from an
automobile may be cherished by an environmental initiate, someone
who can recognize the difference between wasteland and ranch land.

Residents are more likely to be defensive about the desert, justify-
ing their decision to remain in an apparent wasteland on the grounds
that it has hidden splendors that remain forever unknown to casual
passersby. Thus Nevada mining promoter and novelist Mark L. Requa
finds the untamed desert inexplicably seductive:

> The heat of the day had given way to the inexpressively pleasing
> coolness of a desert night in summer. Overhead the Milky Way
> shone with a brilliance unknown to dwellers in eastern States. . . .

The distant mountains even seemed to be surrounded with an indefinable something that attracted and held the attention of the onlooker. About everything was the fascination and spell of the desert, which, once experienced, can never be entirely forgotten.[23]

One must experience the desert, must get to know it, before it can work its magic. Similarly, the mediated experience of viewing the desert from a rapidly moving railroad car or automobile cannot possibly reveal the full range of its beauties. As Israel C. Russell pointed out in 1888, time is of the essence in appreciating the Great Basin:

Under the intense light of the midday sun, the soft mingling of gray and brown on the deserts, and the brilliantly contrasted colors of the mountains, are alike obscured and deadened by the glare of lights. At such times the mountains seem wanting in relief and are not attractive in form or color; one may ride for hours among gorgeous hills and not be aware of the grandeur surrounding him. But as soon as the sun approaches the western horizon, and the shadows of the serrate range begin to creep across the plains, each mountain becomes a complete picture and reveals every shade of color that its rocks possess.[24]

And the Great Basin landscape itself affects perception. Essayist John McPhee remarks bemusedly that neon does not look out of place in Nevada, where "the tawdriness is refined out of it in so much wide black space."[25] The Great Basin's tremendous distances and open vistas render the neon inoffensive, almost cheery, because neon symbolizes human presence in an eerily empty place.

Environmentalist Edward Abbey, on the other hand, exults in human *absence* when he seeks to enlighten a misguided tourist from Ohio:

"This could be a good country," a tourist says to me, "if only you had some water."

"If we had water here," I reply, "this country would not be what it is. It would be like Ohio, wet and humid and hydrological, all covered with cabbage farms and golf courses. Instead of this lovely barren desert we would have only another blooming garden state, like New Jersey. You see what I mean?"

"If you had more water more people could live here."

"Yes, sir. And where then would people go when they wanted to see something besides people?"[26]

As Abbey has discovered but the errant tourist seems unable to grasp, lack of water is the very essence of desert. If one is to comprehend the desert, one must accept its aridity. Otherwise, it is no longer desert at all but something quite other.

Despite the sparse settlement and transiency that disrupt life in the Great Basin, it has a distinctive regional identity that is based on a long history of confrontation with its arid desert conditions. Although individual observers vary tremendously in their responses to the intractable physical space of the place, the points of agreement among them are finally most significant. Common to all the images is the enormous, stark, and empty land of the Basin, despised by many, esteemed by few, but making a deep impression on all who pass through it.

It is the harsh reality of the desert which endures. Notwithstanding the heroic efforts of the Mormon colonizers, only very limited areas are amenable to irrigated agriculture. Alkali soils and the omnipresent spectre of American agricultural surpluses make farming highly impractical in most of the Great Basin. The desert does not simply evolve into farmland. Nor, despite numerous attempts, from railroad land companies to irrigation promoters to modern casinos, does the desert mysteriously dissolve in a cloud of beautiful images.

This fact—that the Great Basin's desert environment is fundamentally unchanged in spite of all the psychic pressures and technological developments brought to bear by those eager to modify or exterminate it—is finally the basic truth about the region. It is also the foundation of the Great Basin's unique sense of place, which is characterized by the insistent presence of a stark and forbidding landscape, against which human beings continually and often uneasily measure themselves.

Many have never made their peace with the Great Basin landscape. Like the disillusioned 49ers on the overland trail, they continue to flee its open spaces and its appalling indifference to humanity, either physically or psychically. Extractive industries that treat the land purely as potential profit take whatever advantage they have come for and then move on. And although the modern population of the region grows rapidly, most of the residents live isolated from the land in urban oases described by journalist Charles Bowden:

> The fantasy of the inhabitants of the Old West and the New West
> is that they have built a culture rooted in the land. Of course, this
> was, and is, hardly ever true. Here people have largely lived iso-

lated from the land in cities, mining camps, retirement communities, and irrigated agricultural districts. It would be difficult to find a region where more people worshipped the look of the landscape or hated and feared walking through the very landscape they admired. The desert is always the backdrop to the lives, but the lives are always lived in the pit.[27]

Aside from the tenacious Mormons, no one puts down roots into the hardpan of the Great Basin.

Even those who come to appreciate this stark landscape do not romanticize it. Its essence is not productivity or comfort, but fierce and unyielding resistance to human domination. Despite the onslaughts of generations of people eager to change it, large portions of the Great Basin remain today much as they were before "settlement." Here, to a considerable degree, wilderness has obdurately refused to be tamed and controlled.

Americans seeking to come to terms with the Great Basin must change their own attitudes instead of the land. Only small portions of this place can be physically subdued, so most residents must simply manage to adapt and survive under difficult circumstances. Admirers agree with desert detractors in emphasizing the severity of a remote and outsized land, but they modify their environmental expectations and learn to see it with new eyes, on its own terms. The greatest achievement of those who come to value the Great Basin landscape is to bring not water, but meaning to the desert. They learn to see the looming mountains as magnificent, rather than sinister. They learn to treasure water for the natural oases it creates, however limited. They learn to understand a complex ecology of scarcity. And in the process they help to create a unique regional sense of place, based not on love for a beneficent, humanized landscape, but on respect for a formidable and enduring natural environment.

NOTES

1. A. M. Williams, in *California Emigrant Letters*, ed. Walker D. Wyman (New York: Bookman Association, 1952), 121.

2. John Charles Frémont, "Geographical Memoir Upon Upper California, In Illustration of His Map of Oregon and California," in *The Expeditions of John Charles Frémont*, vol. 3, ed. Mary Lee Spence (Urbana: University of Illinois Press, 1984), 508.

3. Areas of Mormon crop farming and Nevada's reliance on tourism attracted by legal gambling are two major exceptions to this generalization that will be considered below.

4. Jedediah S. Smith, *The Southwest Expedition of Jedediah S. Smith: His Personal Account of the Journey to California, 1826–1827* (Glendale, California: Arthur H. Clark, 1977), 178.

5. Quoted in William E. Smythe, *The Conquest of Arid America* (New York: Macmillan, 1905), 214.

6. Albert Evans, "Among the Clouds," *Overland Monthly* 3 (July 1869): 66.

7. For a more complete summary of variant descriptions of the Nevada desert, see my article "Desert/Paradise: Images of Nevada Landscape," *Nevada Public Affairs Review* (1988, no. 1).

8. William Least Heat Moon, *Blue Highways* (Boston: Little, Brown & Co., 1982), 160.

9. W. Eugene Hollon, *The Great American Desert: Then and Now* (New York: Oxford University Press, 1966), 203.

10. Edwin B. Firmage, "M-X: National Security and the Destruction of Society's Values," in *That Awesome Space: Human Interaction with the Intermountain Landscape,* ed. E. Richard Hunt (Salt Lake City: Westwater Press, 1981), 123–37.

11. Helen Borden Viets, "Wind in the Sage: Journal of an Amateur Pioneer in Nevada," *Saturday Evening Post* 208 (February 16, 1936): 11.

12. Rob Schultheis, *The Hidden West: Journeys in the American Outback* (New York: Random House, 1982), 138.

13. Albert W. Atwood, "Wealth in the Outdoor West," *Saturday Evening Post* 199 (January 8, 1927): 149.

14. Lynne Larson, "Original Sin," in *Greening Wheat,* ed. Levi S. Peterson (Midvale, Utah: Orion Books, 1983), 191.

15. May D. Winn, *The Macadam Trail: Ten Thousand Miles By Motor Coach* (New York: Alfred A. Knopf, 1931), 50. Further references to this source will be noted by page number in the text.

16. Wallace Stegner, *Mormon Country* (Lincoln: University of Nebraska Press, 1970; reprint, Duell, Sloan and Pearce, 1942), 21–22. Further references to this source will be cited by page number in the text.

17. Mary M. Mathews, *Ten Years in Nevada, or Life on the Pacific Coast* (Buffalo, New York: Baker, Jones & Co., 1880), 32.

18. Dan L. Flores, "Zion in Eden: Phases of the Environmental History of Utah," *Environmental Review* 7 (Winter 1983), raises the point that the Mormon impact on the fragile desert ecology was not uniformly beneficent and that large areas were overgrazed and/or eroded by the late nineteenth century. Flores also points out that the Salt Lake Valley, being well watered, was chosen by Brigham Young as a particularly favorable site for settlement. It was not irredeemable desert to begin with.

19. Bruce W. Jorgensen, "A Song for One Still Voice," in Peterson, 5.

20. Zephine Humphrey, *Green Mountains to Sierras* (New York: E. P. Dutton, 1936), 193.

21. Richard C. Poulsen, "Circumference and Center: The Enigma of Sacred Space," in *The Pure Experience of Order* (Albuquerque: University of New Mexico Press, 1982) 116–36.

22. Molly Flagg Knudtsen, *Here is Our Valley* (Reno: College of Agriculture, University of Nevada-Reno, 1975), 20.

23. Mark L. Requa, *Grubstake: A Story of Early Mining Days in Nevada* (New York: Charles Scribner's Sons, 1933), 171.

24. Israel C. Russell, "The Great Basin," *Overland Monthly* 9 (April 1888): 422–23.

25. John McPhee, *Basin and Range* (New York: Farrar, Strauss & Giroux, 1981), 54.

26. Edward Abbey, *Desert Solitaire: A Season in the Wilderness* (New York: Ballantine Books, 1968), 129.

27. Charles Bowden, *Blue Desert* (Tucson: University of Arizona Press, 1986), 112.

The Melting Pot   Robert Laxalt

*You would call it a real international settlement these days, but
there were some other words, not so nice, for it then. It was a
copper company town, and the whole population only amounted
to a few thousand people. But, Jesus, was it divided! There was
Greek Town, Hunky Town, Jap Town, Wop Town, and Mid
Town. That meant the middle of town, and it was where all the
"white people" lived. The rest of us were cheap labor for the
copper mines and the smelter. The "foreigners" stuck together for
the most part, but once in a while, you could get a scrap if you
were a Hunky and you crossed the line into Greek Town. Our
common enemy was Mid Town. Anytime you crossed that line,
you were in for big trouble. I was a Serb, and my mother had a
cow in Hunky Town. It was my job to sell milk to houses in Mid
Town. The first couple of times, I went alone. And sure enough,
there would be a gang of "white" kids waiting for me. They
would take the milk pail away from me and spill it on the ground,
and then they would beat me up. So I went to my father and said
"I am tired of getting beat up because I'm a Hunky." And he
said, "I don't care how many times you get beat up. You are a
Serb and you got to be proud of it. If I ever hear of you running
away from a fight, you will get a worse beating from me than
them." So I went back and I got beat up a thousand times, but I
won a few, too, when I could get some of my Hunky friends to go
with me.*

Then a funny thing happened. When we got into high school, we were all together—"whites" and "foreigners" alike. When the "foreigners" showed they were good at sports, the people of Mid Town began to look at us differently. And when we won a few state championships, it changed altogether. That was when all the barriers broke down. They finally accepted us as human.

I guess it's the way life is, but now I go back there and some of my best friends are the guys from Mid Town. We can laugh about it now, but it was sure nothing to laugh about then.

All of us together were of a generation born of old-country people who spoke English with an accent and prayed in another language, who drank red wine and cooked their food in the old-country way, and peeled apples and pears after dinner.

We were among the last whose names would tell our blood and the kind of faces we had, to know another language in our homes, to suffer youthful shame because of that language and refuse to speak it, and a later shame because of what we had done, and hurt because we had caused a hurt so deep it could never find words.

And the irony of it was that our mothers and fathers were truer Americans than we, because they had forsaken home and family, and gone into the unknown of a new land with only courage and the hands that God gave them, and had given us in our turn the right to be born American.

And in a little while even our sons would forget, and the old-country people would be only a dimming memory, and names would mean nothing, and the melting would be done.

In the long light of historical perspective, probably no civilization is proud of the manner in which it has treated its minority peoples. At best, nations must inevitably fall back upon the rationalization that those early times operated under a code that numbers and might make right.

Of anyone, the native Indian has the most long-lasting complaint of shabby treatment by his white conquerors. But the Indian, too, existed by right of conquest over other Indian tribes. Wars, killing, subjugation, and the wresting of lands from the enemy fill the pages of Indian history as surely as they do the black, yellow, and white men's histories.

Before the coming of the white man, the primitive Nevada Indian had lived for thousands of years along the shores of prehistoric lakes such as Pyramid Lake in the north and the rare rivers of the south. In the northern summers, they either went naked or fashioned garments out of sagebrush fibers or the skins of pelicans, and in the winters, they made robes of chain-linked rabbit skins. They subsisted on seeds and nuts and roots of wild plants and pinenut trees, fish from lakes and rivers, reptiles, and the flesh of rabbit. Their weapons were obsidian-tipped spears and the hand-flung dart known as the atlatl. Until the bow and arrow were developed, Indians stood little chance of killing such fleet game animals as deer and antelope.

At first, they were cave dwellers. In later times, they learned to make temporary dwellings out of reeds and sagebrush, tightly woven storage baskets lined with pitch, nets for fishing and rabbit drives, and boats made from tules that grew in the swamps. They became nomadic in a limited sense, venturing into the mountains in summer in search for game, and retreating to the warmer deserts to wait out the long winters.

The Indian greeted the first white men in what is now Nevada with friendliness and almost childlike awe. There are no recorded incidents of warfare with American and Canadian trappers or Mexican traders in the first contacts between white and Indian through the 1820s.

Though Indian documentation of early contacts with white men is rare, one revealing description was written by Sarah Winnemucca Hopkins, daughter of the Paiute chief Winnemucca. In later years, after her marriage to a U.S. army officer, this remarkable woman become one of the first Indians to lecture and write about Indian grievances. In her book, *Life Among The Piutes,* she wrote:

> I was a very small child when the first white people came into our country. They came like a lion, yes, like a roaring lion, and have continued so ever since, and I have never forgotten their first coming. My people were scattered at that time over nearly all the territory now known as Nevada. My grandfather was chief of

the entire Piute nation, and was camped near Humboldt Lake, with a small portion of his tribe, when a party traveling eastward from California was seen coming. When the news was brought to my grandfather, he asked what they looked like. When told that they had hair on their faces, and were white, he jumped and clasped his hands together, and cried aloud, "My white brothers, my long-looked-for white brothers have come at last!"

The first trouble that was to set the pattern of hostilities occurred in 1833 near the Humboldt Sink. Mountain man Joseph Walker, who had separated from the exploration party of U.S. Army Captain Benjamin Louis Eulalie de Bonneville, encountered what he claimed to be nearly a thousand hostile Indians. Walker's party struck quickly, killing fourteen of them. Later, the Indians claimed they had approached Walker's party out of curiosity and without menace. Whatever the case, the stage was set for nearly three decades of intermittent warfare and recrimination.

The westward wave of pioneers served only to heighten tensions. Disregarding claims by tribal families to ownership of land, lakes, and the vital pinenut groves that provided main sustenance for the northern Paiutes, settlers took over the most fertile valleys and cut down the pinenut groves for firewood. Indians retaliated by isolated violence— shooting of horses and mules and oxen on the pioneer wagon trails, stealing cattle from ranches, and massacring small parties.

The discovery of Comstock Lode silver in 1859 was the end of Indian hopes of retaining their native dominions. They were relegated to uncertain reservations to thrive as best they could. Others became house servants or hangers-on begging for their existence on the fringes of the new mining towns. In a predominantly male white society, some Indian women had the choice of selling their favors or being raped.

When, in 1860, two girl children were taken captive by prospectors at Williams's Station on the Carson River, the final spark was touched to the major confrontation that had been so long coming. Indians killed the prospectors and rescued the girl captives. News of the killings spread in two directions—one to the white population and the other to an Indian council of war being held at Pyramid Lake between Paiute, Shoshone, and Bannock chiefs from as far north as the Oregon border.

The news arrived at the Pyramid Lake council just as a young

Paiute chief named Numaga was pleading for peace. Historian Myron Angel, who interviewed Paiute Indians in later years, recorded his eloquent plea:

> You would make war upon the whites. I ask you to pause and reflect. The white men are like the stars over your heads. You have wrongs, great wrongs, that rise up like those mountains before you. But can you, from the mountaintops, reach and blot out those stars? Your enemies are like the sands in the beds of your own rivers. When taken away they only give place for more to come and settle there. Could you defeat the whites of Nevada, from over the mountains in California would come to help them an army of white men that would cover your country like a blanket. What hope is there for the Pah-Ute? From where is to come your guns, your powder, your lead, your dried meats to live upon, and hay to feed your ponies with while you carry on this war? Your enemies have all of these things, more than they can use. They will come like the sand in a whirlwind and drive you from your homes. You will be forced among the barren rocks of the north, where your ponies will die; where you will see the women and old men starve, and listen to the cries of your children for food. I love my people; let them live; and when their spirits shall be called to the Great Camp in the southern sky, let their bones rest where their fathers were buried.

As Numaga finished, an Indian on a pony dashed into the gathering and told the chiefs of the killing of the prospectors at Williams's Station. Numaga gave up his effort towards peace. "There is no longer any use for counsel," he said. "We must prepare for war, for the soldiers will now come here to fight us."

In Carson City, a ragtail volunteer army of 105 men was hurriedly assembled under the command of Major William Ormsby. The volunteer army, already lacking military training, was further weakened by an attitude of brash confidence about "teaching the red devils a lesson." The assembled Indian warriors turned both lackings to their own advantage. When the volunteers penetrated the rocky terrain near Pyramid Lake, they were lured systematically into an ambush. Indians caught them between two flanking movements and poured a shower of arrows and bullets into their disorganized ranks. The volunteers who survived the ambush fled for their lives. Most of them, including Major Ormsby, were ridden down and killed. When the battle was over, seventy-six white men had met their death, and of those who managed to escape, most were wounded.

The Indian victory was short-lived, however. The news of what was to become known as the Pyramid Lake War was dispatched to California, bringing four companies of trained U.S. cavalry from California. They joined a volunteer force of more than 500 men from western Nevada. Together, they inflicted a major defeat upon the Indians, killing 160 of them in a single battle near Pyramid Lake. As Chief Numaga had predicted, his people were driven into nearly impassable mountains, there to linger in starvation and finally disband. Numaga sued for peace.

Though the peace treaty was meant to be enduring, there was really no way in which the idealistic Numaga could control the actions of independent bands of Paiute and Shoshone warriors. They continued to raid farms and isolated stations on the main travel routes.

A network of military posts was established by the federal government to protect the farms and stations and the continuing flow of fortune seekers. Indian troubles subsided, but it was not until 1878 that a degree of tranquility was reached. By then, reservation agreements were formalized and most Nevada Indian tribes finally abandoned their nomadic way of life. They became farmers on reservations, hangers-on in the vicinity of military outposts, and menials in the white settlements.

Nevada Indians have never been reservation dwellers in any substantial number. There are twenty-three Indian reservations in Nevada, but at most, only half of the Indian population has ever lived on them. Others have chosen to congregate on land set aside by the federal government in or near such towns as Reno, Carson City, Dresslerville, Lovelock, Winnemucca, Battle Mountain, Elko, and Yerington. Still others, who have prospered through jobs and small businesses, live in white neighborhoods that were formerly off limits to them.

Indian rights, even on legally constituted reservations, went through a long period of erosion at the hands of railroads, agricultural interests, and land speculators. Lakes, timber preserves, and potential farmland were lost to the Indians through political pressures brought to bear on governmental agencies. The history of the Nevada reservation Indian is one of broken treaties and arbitrary land seizures. In recent years, however, the reservations have become organized into self-governing entities capable of defending their rights in the courts.

As an example, the Pyramid Lake reservation today is locked in a three-way struggle with ranching and farming interests and the rapidly growing municipalities of Reno and Sparks. All three entities are dependent upon water from the Truckee River that flows from Lake Tahoe in the Sierra Nevada and empties finally into Pyramid Lake. Before it gets there, it must flow through the metropolitan centers and undergo diversion to downstream agricultural land. The Pyramid Lake Indians are claiming water rights under old treaties, protesting that the level of the prehistoric lake is dropping as each year goes by, and that their fisheries are being endangered.

The keys to the new status of the Nevada Indian have been education and citizen involvement. Both have been a long time evolving. It was 1891 before the first vocational Indian school was founded at Stewart near Carson City. In 1924 Indians were finally granted full citizenship. And in 1932 the right of public school education was granted to Indian children.

Even so, Nevada's Indians were slow in taking advantage of schooling and citizenship. Until the 1930s, Indian children rarely went to school beyond the sixth grade, and most Indian adults did not take advantage of their voting rights as citizens.

All that has changed now. Nevada's Indians are organized as never before, Indian children receive their full measure of basic schooling, more and more of them are going on to university levels; arts and crafts stores are flourishing on reservations; and nearly forgotten traditions of song and dance are being revived.

At Pyramid Lake, some 450 Paiute Indians live on the reservation, farming and ranching and working in construction to supplement their earnings. Their jade-green lake, twenty miles long and resembling a giant-sized mirage in a desert setting, has become a favorite boating and fishing area for the nearby metropolitan centers of Reno and Sparks. The tribal council charges fees for use of the lake and leases sites for construction of tourist motels, restaurants, and bars.

As for the Paiute Indians who control the Pyramid Lake reservation, they maintain one important vestige of their age-old tradition. There is no right of private ownership of land even for tribal members. And the right to fish and hunt where they choose is shared by all. This old relationship between Indian and the land is what the property-oriented white man could never understand from the beginning.

Western history and literature for too long a time perpetuated the myth that the frontier was settled by the American-born Anglo-Saxon. It is only in recent years that historians have dispelled the myth and shown that the frontier West was indeed a potpourri of nationalities from Europe and Asia.

Nevada was a classic example of that potpourri. When Nevada achieved territorial status in 1861, nearly one-third of its population had come from foreign lands. In fact, by the time the decade was over, the percentage of foreign-born had climbed to nearly half the population, or almost triple the percentage for any state in the Union.

They came from their homelands for myriad reasons—impending wars, religious persecution, restlessness, lure of adventure, and opportunity. The last reason was the main reason. Trapped by old-world economic caste systems that denied the opportunity to better one's station in life, most came in search of the one key to escape from unchanging station—money.

And they found it. Poverty-ridden in their old-world circumstance, they possessed in common the willingness to work at any job, no matter how demanding.

Chinese and Hindus labored at laying rails; Italians and Swiss burned charcoal for mine smelters, founded ranches and built dairy herds in the valleys near Reno; Cornishmen and Irish worked in the deep mines of the Comstock Lode and other mining booms; French-Canadians were lumberjacks in the deep forests surrounding Lake Tahoe; and Germans in fertile Carson Valley farmed the produce that fed the Comstock Lode. Later, Slavs and Greeks worked in the mines and smelters of Ruth and McGill in eastern Nevada, and Basques and Scots herded sheep in the deserts and mountains. Others drawn from the thirty-three nationalities that peopled Nevada became merchants, opened printing shops, worked as maids and waitresses in hotels and restaurants, or became itinerant laborers in mining and agriculture.

Landless for the most part in the countries of their birth, they shared a common passion for ownership of property. That, combined with the thriftiness that seemed to be inborn in them, was parlayed in the space of a few years into prosperous enterprises, many of which have lasted to the present day.

Though homesickness and loneliness were something else to be contended with in an alien land, the foreign-born compensated by forming social groups confined to their own nationalities, published newspapers in their native languages, and celebrated the holidays of their land of origin. During its heyday for example, Virginia City could count on a continuous round of celebrations ranging from the Chinese New Year to a Scottish gathering of clans to a Mexican Independence Day.

In a social structure where the American-born Anglo-Saxon usually formed the ruling class, all the foreign-born tasted discrimination in one form or another.

In the summer of 1879, Italians in the mountains of central Nevada were engaged in gathering wood to be converted to charcoal for the mining smelters in the boom camp of Eureka. A dispute over costs arose between the smelter operators and the "charcoal burners." The Eureka sheriff, claiming fear of violence by the charcoal burners, sent an armed posse into the mountains. In the one-sided conflict that followed, five Italians were killed. The posse emerged unscathed.

In eastern Nevada the company towns surrounding the copper mines and mills were a microcosm of separated nationalities. The town of McGill in particular was sharply divided into segments for Greeks, Slavs, Italians, and Japanese. These nationalities formed the "cheap labor" work force for the copper operations. They were looked down upon by "Americans," who commanded higher wages and better positions. Discrimination was rampant, and incidents of violence between the "foreigners" and the "whites" were frequent. Time alone solved the problem of company towns in constant conflict. As the young of the immigrants grew up, they showed marked athletic abilities and provided the core of teams that brought statewide recognition to the company towns, thereby breaking down the racial barriers.

In both World Wars, the industrious Germans and their descendants, who had played a major part in developing Carson Valley in western Nevada into a rich farming and ranching region, were forced to bear the sting of criticism, even to the point of allegations that they were sending money to the German enemy.

On the open ranges of Nevada, the Basques with their free-roaming bands were the cattlemen's common enemy. Though they had been early comers to Nevada in the years after the California gold rush, they began to emigrate from Europe in substantial numbers in the years after 1900. Vilified by politicians and newspapers aligned for the time being with the established cattle interests, they nevertheless refused to be run off what they considered to be free range. They fought back with a ferocity the cattlemen had never expected, even when outnumbered by marauding bands of buckaroos who shot their invaluable dogs, scattered their sheep, and took shots at the herders themselves.

But like the rest of Nevada's nationalities, the Basques were tenacious. In the classic immigrant pattern, they sent home passage money for brothers and nephews to help with the sheep, and sisters and nieces to work in the small Basque hotels. The small hotels, really boardinghouses, became gathering places where herders could rest in their off-times or between jobs, speak with their countrymen in a familiar language, meet their future wives, and keep alive the song and dance of their homeland in the Pyrenees Mountains between France and Spain. Out of the ambience of these little hotels was born the tradition of the Basque festivals held each year in such towns as Elko, Ely, Winnemucca, and Reno.

None of the minorities of Nevada were subjected to the indignities that befell the Chinese. Recruited first to lay the railroad tracks that were spanning the continent, they later became woodcutters, laundrymen, herb doctors, operators of tiny restaurants, and menials.

As much as color of skin, fear that the Chinese were taking over the economic underpinnings of small communities at the price of unemployment among white men led to the Yellow Peril movement. Chinese were literally driven out of one town after another, their possessions confiscated and their homes burned to the ground. When the purge reached the stage where it actually became formalized by legislative resolutions, most Chinese left Nevada and went to San Francisco's Chinatown, where they could be assured of a haven of reasonable safety. Others returned to their homeland. Only a handful remained to weather the storm and become respected citizens. Today, the Chinese of Nevada are prominent in professions and business circles, particularly in the Las Vegas area.

The black was a latecomer to Nevada. In the rich 1860s, Negroes numbered less than 50 out of the total population. Even by 1900 there were only 134 blacks in the entire state. The building of Hoover Dam and the World War II years brought the first major influx of blacks into Nevada. Most of them settled in an area called Westside Las Vegas, working for the most part as maids and groundsmen in the growing resort-hotel industry. By 1960 the black population numbered nearly 15,000, and by 1970 some 30,000 out of the state's half-million population.

With the enactment of the U.S. Civil Rights Act in 1964, the black began to emerge as both an economic and political force in Nevada. In 1971 the first black, Woodrow Wilson of Las Vegas, was elected to the Nevada legislature. His election marked the second time in Nevada history that a nonwhite was elected to the state's legislative body. And in 1974 Lilly Fong of Las Vegas became the first Chinese-American to hold important public office when she was elected a regent of the University of Nevada system.

Three decades earlier, in 1938, Dewey Sampson of Reno had become the first Indian legislator of his native state. His election was an event of no mean proportions. More than a century had passed since his forebears had welcomed the first white man to Nevada.

Nevada's Mining Heritage

Blessing and Burden

Russell R. Elliott

Nevada is a creature of the mining frontier. It was, as Morison and Commager suggest in their classic, two-volume *Growth of the American Republic,* "the most extreme example of a mining community; nowhere else in history do we find a society so completely and continuously dependent upon minerals."[1]

The mining frontier opened the Far West to settlement in the mid-nineteenth century. The progression of frontiers from the Atlantic Ocean westward, envisioned in Frederick Jackson Turner's famous essay on the closing of the frontier, faltered when settlement reached the Great Plains and the emigrants were faced with a large and hostile desert to the west. That barrier, of which the Great Basin was a part, disrupted Turner's progression where the buffalo and the Indian were followed by the fur trappers and explorers, the cattlemen and miners, and finally, the real heroes of the frontier essay, the farmers.[2]

The Basin did experience the initial stages of the westward progression when Peter Skene Ogden of the Hudson's Bay Company and Jedediah Smith of the Rocky Mountain Fur Company penetrated into its interior in search of furs in the late 1820s. It did not take long to demonstrate that the great semidesert was not worth exploiting for its furs. With that realization there appeared little real reason for anyone to settle, since there were few spots within the area where farming might be practiced successfully. Thus, the only reason for entering it for the next few years was to get across as quickly as possible in order to get to the more inviting lands along the Pacific coast, particularly to California after the discovery of gold there in 1848.

These attitudes changed abruptly when silver was discovered in Colorado in 1858 and in Nevada in 1859. The siren's call of silver and gold publicized the Mountain West in a way that no other could have, bringing thousands of people to the region that only a few years earlier had been considered solely as an unwelcome obstacle on the march to California.

The discovery of the Comstock Lode in 1859 brought the mining frontier to what was then western Utah Territory, in a mad rush of people somewhat reminiscent of the earlier 1849 outpouring of emigrants to California. This time, however, most of the newcomers moved east from that state, since this mining frontier not only disrupted Turner's sequence of settlement but also temporarily reversed its direction. The eastward movement opened the Great Basin to settlement as thousands of prospectors fanned out in all directions from the original mineral strike. Each new discovery acted, as had the Comstock, as a "mother" district in an ever-widening circle of mineral developments. As new strikes were made, it was soon apparent that impermanence was one of the unfortunate results of the mining frontier, for development always depended on the size and quality of the ore deposits being exploited. Thus, there came into being the cycle of discovery, boom, and bust—a cycle that became all too frequent, as the mining frontier spread from West to East across the Great Basin. The large number of ghost towns in present-day Nevada testifies to the destructiveness of this cycle.

Although depletion of the ore body and stagnation of the economy were the ultimate conditions facing the miners and the owners, the discovery and the boom parts of the cycle brought good and bad results, many lasting long after the mineral development had passed into history.

The Comstock Lode—because it was so big and so rich—provided an early example of the benefits and evils arising from the mining frontier. Immediately it created problems of law and order. The demand for some kind of stability in the society led to pressure for territorial status and then for statehood. Mining activity also forced settlement of the Indian problem, for miners had little or no respect for the rights of the Indians when a discovery happened to infringe on Indian territory or on the Indian way of life. In the case of the Comstock, that infringement helped to bring a confrontation with the Paiute Indians, which resulted in the Pyramid Lake War of 1860 and the subsequent establishment of Fort Churchill.

The Comstock operations forced the development of a better transportation system since cheap exploitation of the ore was the focus of the mine owners, particularly after large corporations started financing the expensive underground quartz mining. The basic problems of getting materials into the area and getting the ore to the mills and the metals to the refineries were solved with the completion of the Virginia and Truckee Railroad. As on other mining frontiers, the Comstock mineral activity stimulated the growth of ranches and farms in nearby valleys, particularly in Carson, Eagle, Washoe, and Smith valleys.

Another important result of the mining frontier in Nevada was the stimulus it gave to technological improvements in the mining industry. The Washoe Pan Process of ore reduction, the square-set timbering in the mines, and the wire cable were but a few of the developments that came from the Comstock boom.

A mining boom also brought banks and other businesses and, in the case of the Comstock, fostered the growth of corporate monopolies, such as the Bank Crowd and the Bonanza Crowd. As a boom stimulated the development of sophisticated corporate organizations, it also brought labor unions into the picture. The Gold Hill Miners' Union, formed on December 8, 1866, and the Virginia City Miners' Union, established on July 4, 1867, spurred the development of union labor throughout the mineral west.

The great wealth produced from the mining frontier helped to develop other areas, locally, nationally, and even internationally. It was Comstock wealth that changed the bustling, but small town of San Francisco into a modern city. Comstock money also stimulated the growth of Oakland, Hayward, Millbrae, Alameda, and even Santa Monica in southern California. That wealth also was seed money for such developments as the Pacific Commercial Cable Company, the Postal Telegraph Company, the Palace Hotel, and other real estate ventures on the Pacific coast, the establishment of the Bank of California and the Nevada Bank of San Francisco, the latter heralding in its name the unusual relationship between Nevada and California. The billions of dollars produced by the mining frontier helped to strengthen the national economy and to build a technological world in the twentieth century.

In addition, the mining frontier developed new political institutions, such as the "mining district," and produced a resource distribution system that gave right of ownership to the discoverer in the adoption of the National Mining Laws of 1866 and 1872, both of which came from the Comstock experience. It brought social development, with schools, churches, and lodges, to areas remote from so-called civilization. And, although no Nevada mining town survived as a major city, many small towns that were created have managed to survive to the present. The mining frontier also added to American folklore, language, and literature.

Mining dominated Nevada's economy for such a long period and was so generally associated with positive accomplishments that many Nevadans in the second half of the twentieth century have forgotten the negative aspects of that industry. Memories of the past, however, are often at variance with the facts, and it is time to refresh memories concerning the negative aspects of the industry that made Nevada the "best example of the mining frontier."

The introduction of twentieth-century legalized gambling to Nevada in March 1931 did not bring prostitution, crime, graft, corruption, and assorted other so-called evils to Nevada and Nevadans. Unfortunately, they followed in the wake of the rush to the Comstock. They rode into the area on the heels of the mining industry, an industry naturally susceptible to many forms of gambling, from the original risk involved in opening and developing a mine to the later wild machinations in uncontrolled stock markets. Speculation became the name of the game on the Comstock where "people were speculating on hope" and where it was unusual to find a man "who has not a certificate of stock in his pocket."[3]

A major culprit in the game of speculation was the stock certificate, which warned on its face, but in very small letters, that it was "fully assessable." Since nearly all of the Comstock stocks were "fully assessable," the holder found himself continually paying assessments in a futile attempt to save a stock that was no good in the first place. It was not uncommon for those who speculated in mining stocks to hold certificates that showed many dollars more paid in assessments than were paid for the original stock. Compulsive stock gamblers were not uncommon on the Comstock.[4]

Speculation by individuals was only a small part of the speculative picture. The Comstock was noted for a number of major stock scandals, particularly William Sharon's manipulations in 1874, the stock ventures of the Bonanza Crowd in 1876, and the so-called Sierra Nevada Deal in 1878. All kinds of tricks were used by Comstock mine operators to influence the rise and fall of their stocks. One practice that became so common as to lose its effectiveness was the keeping of miners underground when a new mineral strike had been made in order to maintain secrecy until the owners could buy up all available stock. Invariably, when the strike was made public, the stock soared in price and the owners then sold at a fine profit.

Closely related to the overall picture of speculation was the practice of levying assessments on stock already sold. In his *History of the Comstock Lode, 1850–1920*, Grant Smith points out how mine owners used the custom to fleece the small investors. He notes that out of 135 Comstock mines quoted on the San Francisco stock exchanges in 1876, only three, the Consolidated–Virginia, the California, and the Belcher, were paying dividends. All the others in that year were levying assessments. Further, he points out that ultimately only five companies, the Consolidated–Virginia, the California, the Kentuck, the Crown Point, and the Belcher, paid more in dividends than they levied in assessments. Most of the Comstock mines assessed millions of dollars while producing substantially less ore, sometimes nothing at all. The worst record in this respect was the Bullion mine, which produced nothing, yet levied assessments totaling $3,872,000. Even a well-known and profitable company like the Savage, while paying $4,208,000 in dividends, still levied $5,412,000 in assessments.[5]

The speculative fever was only one negative aspect of the mining rush, for the mining frontier brought with it the dregs of society—the prostitutes, the gamblers, the saloon keepers, and assorted other "seedy" characters. Some of these individuals were depraved and vicious people. The criminal elements produced so many problems for the Comstock society and for the societies of other mining boom areas that police forces often were unable to handle them.

The speculation and street crimes were minor, however, compared to the graft and corruption that followed the entrance of the out-of-state Bank of California Crowd in 1864. Under the leadership of William Sharon, that monopoly led to a more detailed and organized exploitation of the Comstock ore body, solely to satisfy the insatiable greed of the Bank Crowd, for no thought was ever given to the interests of the state or those of its people.

To insure their economic control, the Bank Crowd moved to dominate the Nevada legislature and Nevada's congressional delegation. Supported in the state legislature by such able lobbyists as Charles C. "Black" Wallace and Henry M. Yerington and by the liberal use of money that was paid to voters, to state legislators and other officeholders, and to politicians on the local and state levels, Sharon and the Bank Crowd were able to control the economic and political life of the state until the Bonanza Crowd took over the reins of power after 1875. Although more subtle in their methods, the latter group continued many of the economic and political tricks initiated by their predecessors. One of the most interesting of the financial payoffs, practiced by both monopolies, involved the use of "sack bearers" who carried canvas sacks filled with money throughout the state "buying" voters, legislators, or anyone else they thought might help to elect a state legislature sympathetic to their interests.

The dominance of Nevada by the mining interests and, to a lesser extent, the railroad lobbyists from 1867 to the end of the century produced the most disgraceful period in Nevada history with its record of speculation, stock scandals, false assays, and political shenanigans of every sort.

The latter included every kind of voting fraud imaginable, including the practice of naturalizing thousands of foreigners just before an election and then guiding them to the polls to insure their votes, and the practice of voting in the names of the dead. The custom of using the so-called cemetery vote was memorialized in the following verse about the Storey County graveyard that was used during the campaign of William Sharon for election to the United States Senate in 1874:

> I know a grave yard bleak and barren
> Where lie the friends of Wm. Sharon
> Who, although dead and may be burning
> Are often from the shades returning
> Up to the beck and call of Billy
> To knock the opposition silly
> At break of dawn those sons of witches
> Rise from their grave without their breeches
> Bereft of party ties and collars
> Still swapping votes for twenty dollars
> Dead, decomposed and gone to glory
> God bless the grave yard vote of Storey.[6]

Nevada's political history is filled with examples of graft and corruption during the period of Comstock dominance. Certainly, the senatorial campaigns of John P. Jones in 1872, William Sharon in 1874, and James Fair in 1880 established standards of corruption that unfortunately set the tone for local and state elections during those years. The depression in the mining industry after 1879 deprived the state of its economic base and left it a prey to the railroad corporations that exerted the same kinds of influence over Nevada politics as those established by the ruthless mining monopolies. Working together, the mining and railroad interests demonstrated in the 1898 election for the United States Senate just how far they were prepared to go in trying to insure a state legislature that would vote to send their candidate to the United States Senate. Without a doubt, it was the most corrupt U.S. Senate election in Nevada political history.

The contest pitted the incumbent, railroad and mining candidate William M. Stewart, against Francis G. Newlands, heir to William Sharon's Comstock fortune and Nevada's lone representative in the House of Representatives. The November election of 1898 had insured Newlands a fourth term in the House. It appeared, also, that enough pro-Stewart state legislators had been selected to return him to the United States Senate. Newlands had other plans and disrupted the flow of events by announcing on December 6 that he would be a candidate for the United States Senate when the state legislature met in January 1899. His announcement brought an immediate uproar from the Stewart camp, which maintained that Newlands had agreed to abide by the decision of the electorate, which, according to the Stewart faction, had selected a majority of the senator's supporters.

Between the time of the Newlands announcement and the meeting of the legislature, both forces fought to gain and hold their legislative supporters, mainly by the liberal use of money. Newlands had a great deal of that commodity, whereas Stewart had very little of his own, but he did have the backing of the old-line Comstock mining interests and of the Central Pacific Railroad officials. That backing was essential when it became clear that money alone would not be sufficient to insure Stewart's reelection. At that point the Central Pacific officials supplied Stewart with a group of "enforcers" whose main function was to make certain that votes once bought would stay bought. The enforcer group included "Colonel" Jack Chinn, formerly of Kentucky, who asserted that he was in Nevada solely to represent the interests of the National Democratic Central Committee. The fact that he was at the time an employee of the Central Pacific made that assertion appear to lack reality. It also was reported that Chinn had remarked that he was prepared to "give the fractious legislator anything he wants from an argument to a fist or gun fight."[7] A second and more dangerous member of the group was Dave Neagle, a left-handed gunslinger, an old friend of Stewart's and famous by now as the killer of Judge David Terry in the Terry–Field affair. A local newspaper referred to the group as a body of "hired gunmen" and suggested that Carson City citizens should organize a vigilante committee to protect themselves against the intruders.

It is obvious that Stewart's enforcers helped to neutralize the effect of the Newlands money, yet a test vote on a parliamentary maneuver the day before the scheduled vote for senator indicated that Stewart would control the Senate but that the Assembly vote might well end in a tie. That test vote set the stage for the most bizarre action of an already bizarre election. The next day, when the voting started, Stewart received a vote of 9 to 6 in his favor in the senate, but when the assembly met later that day it was discovered on roll call that Willard A. Gillespie, an assemblyman from Storey County, was absent. The Newlands forces tried to adjourn the meeting, but when that effort failed, the Assembly then voted 15 to 14 in favor of Stewart. On January 25, a joint session of the senate and the assembly, as required by law, formally elected Stewart to the United States Senate.

The question of what happened to Gillespie has bothered researchers ever since the 1898 election, and a definitive answer continues to elude them. Rumors indicated that he had been kidnapped or had been convinced by threats or by money to absent himself from the Assembly. Sam P. Davis, at the time editor of the Carson City *Morning Appeal*, later wrote that Gillespie had been offered a ride to the legislative building but was taken instead to Empire where he remained for two days at the home of State Senator Williams. Davis indicated that Gillespie had gone along willingly and had received $1,800 for his absence from his seat.[8] Gillespie's obituary in a Tonopah newspaper in 1907 reported that Chinn proposed that after the test vote, but before the official election, some member of the Newlands forces be kept from the vote and that Gillespie's absence followed. Whatever the exact reason for the absence, the result certainly assured Stewart's reelection. In spite of all the chicanery and corruption associated with the 1898 election, Stewart had the gall to write a friend a short time later that Newlands with all his money "failed to receive one vote in the Legislature. This speaks very highly for the honesty of Nevada Legislatures."[9] This is to say nothing of how it speaks for the state of Nevada politics while the remnants of its mining frontier and new railroad tsars held sway in the state.

The mining industry also was criticized for the manner in which it tended to destroy the environment. That term did not come into common use until the latter half of the twentieth century, but a number of observers of mining development in the West in the nineteenth century noted the damage being done to the mountains, rivers, lakes, timber, and other parts of their surroundings.

Of particular concern on the Comstock, particularly after square-set timbering became a necessary part of any mining activity, was the manner in which mining activity swallowed the timber resources of the area. One of the most pointed criticisms of that practice came from the pen of Dan De Quille (William Wright), Comstock journalist-historian, when he wrote: "The Comstock lode may truthfully be said to be the tomb of the forests of the Sierras." He went on to envision a time when the Sierra Nevada would lie "bare in the sun." De Quille also noted that the exploitation of the timber resources not only destroyed the beauty of the surrounding areas but led to erosion that created a flood at the "first spell of hot weather" and ultimately caused the Carson River to become dry in the summer.[10]

Another, somewhat ambivalent critic, John Muir, wrote, after visiting the mines in eastern Nevada in the 1870s, that "many of them do not represent any good accomplishment, and have no right to be. They are monuments of fraud and ignorance—sins against science." But having said that, Muir reverted to the more traditional attitude of industrial America when he added, "But, after all, effort, however misapplied, is better than stagnation."[11]

A few other critics deplored the pollution of rivers and lakes, the cutting down of mountains, and spoliation of valleys, but their voices were seldom heard in the enthusiasm of those who felt that exploiting the earth's natural resources not only was good business but also was a God-given right. It was easy for them to rationalize that what they were doing was in the name of progress. Probably most would have agreed with a dredge superintendent in a Colorado mining camp who remarked that "industry is always to be preferred to scenic beauty."[12]

The decline of the Comstock Lode in the late 1870s led to a twenty-year economic depression that came to an end in the early 1900s with the discovery of several other rich ore bodies in the state. A silver strike at Tonopah in south central Nevada in 1900 started the excitement. It was followed two years later by a rich gold strike thirty miles to the south at Goldfield. A third discovery, a major copper development near Ely in eastern Nevada, although started in 1900, did not come into production until 1908. Ultimately, however, the copper district proved to be the richest of all three and made possible the continuing dominance of the mining industry in Nevada well into the 1950s.

Nevada's twentieth-century mining boom, like the Comstock before it, gave wide publicity to the state. Similarly, it encouraged the development of railroads; helped to develop ranching and farming; brought law, order, and government to the new mining areas; introduced many technological innovations in mining, particularly new metallurgical processes in the reduction of copper ores and open-pit mining to the great copper deposits at Ruth in White Pine County; and stimulated the growth of banks and other businesses, as well as social institutions, in the new mining districts. The great wealth produced by these camps, much more in total than the Comstock, not only helped to stimulate mining activity in Nevada and elsewhere in the West, it also revitalized such cities as Reno, Nevada, and San Francisco, California, and contributed to the national economy.

The new mining boom in Nevada also brought with it some of the negative aspects of the nineteenth-century mining activity. Generally speaking, the new towns were quieter and less boisterous, not so vexed by problems of law and order as were the towns of the Comstock era, although prostitution continued to be of major concern. Political graft and corruption were minimized at first, owing in no small part to the Progressive Movement, which struck Nevada rather forcefully in the early 1900s. The new political and economic atmosphere in Nevada lasted only for the first few years of the twentieth century, for by the time the state entered the era of political and economic dominance by George Wingfield and the so-called bipartisan machine, it was clear that voters, legislators, politicians, and others were still being controlled and manipulated by the leaders of yet another great mining monopoly.

An interesting, but illegal practice, little heard of during the Comstock era, called *high-grading*, became closely associated with the Goldfield camp during the boom years. High-grading, the custom of taking rich ore from a mine without the consent of the owners, in other words, stealing, flowered at Goldfield during the so-called leasing period in that camp. Leasing encouraged high-grading, for the lessee was concerned with extracting as much rich ore as possible, as quickly as possible, so paid little attention to the high-graders so long as they did not interfere with his objective. By the time large companies moved into the camp, the practice had become standard procedure in most Gold-field mines.

Harnesses and other devices were invented to facilitate the stealing of the ore; they were even sold in some of the stores. The harness consisted of a double canvas shirt that contained stitched pockets between the two thicknesses into which the rich ore could be pushed. Another device was the large hat with a double crown, capable of holding five pounds of ore. In addition, there was a long canvas bag, known as the leg-pocket which hung down inside the trouser leg. Besides such novel systems, dinner buckets and sacks of all descriptions were used to carry the rich ore from the mines. Mine owners had little success in trying to combat the practice. Attempts to recover the ore by legal means were hampered by quick assays of the stolen ore that made it almost impossible to trace. Some high-graders were indicted, but no one was ever convicted, for no local jury would bring a guilty verdict against someone who was simply doing what most of them had done at one time or another. When George Wingfield and George Nixon formed the Goldfield Consolidated in 1906–07, the former vowed to rid the camp of a practice that he claimed took millions of dollars illegally from the Goldfield mines. His main attack came with the installation of "change rooms" in the fall of 1907. Calling these rooms and the procedure an indignity toward the laboring man, the Western Federation of Miners (WFM) called for a general strike. The event was settled rather quickly when the workers agreed to a rather innocuous system of change rooms whereby each miner was provided with two lockers (one for work clothes and one for street clothes) adjoining, rather than on opposite sides of the room as originally planned. The system lessened the amount stolen, but it did not eliminate the practice. Wingfield's objective was gained, however, when he and other Goldfield mine operators succeeded in eliminating the WFM with the help of federal troops, when that union called a strike over the use of scrip in November 1907.[13]

Wingfield's power in the state continued to grow and his dominance of the Nevada political scene was clearly demonstrated in the events that followed the indictments of Ed. Malley, the incumbent state treasurer, George Cole, a former state controller, and H. C. Clapp, cashier of the Carson Valley Bank, for embezzlement of $516,322.16. Wingfield was involved in the case immediately since his Nevada Surety and Bonding Company held Malley's bond, and the Carson

Valley Bank was one of a group of Nevada banks owned and controlled by him.

Wingfield's first move was to convince one of his political protégés, Governor Fred Balzar, to call a special session of the Nevada legislature. He then acted to control the session so that ultimately the state of Nevada assumed the major share of the loss. Under the final agreement, the state lost $361,425.51 directly from the settlement and an additional $52,000 indirectly for the cost of the special session, additional audits, attorney fees, and incidental costs.[14] The so-called Cole–Malley case was specific proof, if any was needed, that political chicanery was still alive in Nevada into the late 1920s.

In another area of abuse, that of speculation, the twentieth-century boom at least kept pace with, if it did not outrun, its predecessor in the nineteenth century. Stock speculation at Goldfield, Tonopah, and Ely, although similar in some respects to that during the Comstock era, added many innovations to that age-old game. Particularly prominent were the many speculative ventures which featured cheap stock. No longer satisfied with the familiar $1-per-share, million-share company, the Goldfield brokers, led by a very unusual person, George Graham Rice, centered their attention on the million-share company with stock at 10¢ per share. Rice might well be called the Henry Ford of the speculation game in Nevada for the emphasis he gave to the sale of cheap stock to a large number of prospective buyers. Rice was, perhaps, the greatest advocate in western mining of speculation for its own sake. He never offered mining stocks as a means of gaining capital to develop a mine. His profits were to come from speculation, not from the ore body.

George Graham Rice was born in New York City in 1870 as Jacob Simon Herzig. He arrived in Goldfield, Nevada, in 1904, carrying in his background, among other things, a prison record that included time spent as a minor in Elmira Reformatory and five years in Sing Sing Prison, both in New York.

For the next eight years after his arrival in Goldfield, Rice dominated the speculative game in Nevada, centering his attention on the three boom areas of Goldfield, Rawhide, and Ely. In each of these areas he operated behind the scenes, as he had in New York—at Goldfield under the banner of the L. M. Sullivan Trust Company, at Rawhide under the cloak of the Nat C. Goodwin Company, and at Ely with the B. H. Scheftels Company.

Although Rice used every conceivable trick of the speculator's trade, his real genius came from the unusual promotions he used to bring the necessary publicity to his schemes. At Goldfield, it was a championship boxing match on Labor Day, 1906, between champion Joe Gans and Battling Nelson; in the case of Rawhide, it was the visit of a noted British novelist, Elinor Glyn, and the funeral of a racetrack gambler, Riley Grannan; and at Ely, it was a fancy prospectus which emphasized the report of a prominent national mining engineer.[15] In all three instances, Rice's main concern was to publicize the boom areas so that he could sell his stocks to the widest possible audience. Such activities led the editor of the *Engineering and Mining Journal* to write that Rice was a "poet of surpassing imagination when it comes to promoting oil and other stocks that are warranted to make purchasers wealthy even faster than a jury can return indictments."[16]

Rice's promotions at Ely led to the end of his speculative career in Nevada. On September 29, 1910, federal officers made simultaneous raids on the B. H. Scheftels office in New York City and its branches in other large cities in the United States. The officers of the company were charged with misusing the mails to defraud, operating a "bucket shop," making false quotations, charging interest on false securities, and converting securities belonging to customers.[17] Rice avoided immediate arrest, but within a week was in custody, blaming his arrest on the always convenient "whipping boys," the Guggenheims. When arrested he stated, "wait until the true story comes out. I am the victim of a conspiracy. The Guggenheim people are after me. But they won't get me, I am innocent." The *Ely Record* remained steadfast in its support of Rice, adding to the above quotation that there must have been an ulterior motive in the unwarranted attacks on him by the *Engineering and Mining Journal*.[18]

While in jail awaiting trial, Rice put his talents to work writing a series of articles for the *Adventure Magazine*. These were later published in book form under the title, *My Adventures With Your Money*.[19] In the articles and the book, Rice insisted that he and Scheftels were honest brokers pitted against the "bad" Wall Street financiers, particularly the Guggenheims. His story would have aroused more sympathy if his own record had been cleaner.

After a trial lasting five months, Rice and Scheftels were convicted. On March 7, 1912, Rice was sentenced to one year in a federal penitentiary and Scheftels was given a suspended sentence.[20]

The mining frontier brought obvious blessings to the state of Nevada, not the least of which was the part it played in bringing territorial status and then statehood to the western part of the original Utah Territory. Equally important is the role mining played and continues to play in the economic development of the state. The ultimate benefits of mining dominance to the state of Nevada, however, are clouded by a legacy of burdens.

From the perspective of an outsider, one of the most significant of these evolves from the idea that mining conditioned the people of Nevada to a ready acceptance of legalized gambling when it returned to the state in the 1930s. One of the most recent expressions of the idea comes from John Findlay in his book, *People of Chance,* where he writes, "Of all of the states of the Union, only barren Nevada had a social history that made it the logical choice to legalize casino betting in the 1930s. . . . Chroniclers have often pointed out that gambling resembled the chancy pursuit of precious metals, which had defined the state's economy from its earliest days."[21]

More destructive, in many ways, is the legacy left by the mining and railroad interests in demonstrating how easy and effective it is to translate economic control of the state into political control of its government. James Hulse, in his 1986 book *Forty Years in the Wilderness,* recognized the fact that the gambling industry has learned that lesson well when he wrote, "But the state could not avoid the suspicion, early in the 1980s, that it had become the slave and hostage of this multibillion-dollar offspring of dubious reputation."[22]

Certainly, the mining crowd and their sometime allies, the railroad clique, served as the model in Nevada for the collusion between government and the chief economic industry of the state. Such collusion, if not the most easily identifiable, is obviously one of the most pernicious legacies left to modern Nevada by the mining industry.

NOTES

1. Samuel E. Morison and Henry S. Commager, *The Growth of the American Republic,* vol. 2, 6th ed. (New York: Oxford University Press, 1969), 10–11.

2. Frederick Jackson Turner, "The Significance of the Frontier in American History," in *Problems in American Civilization* (Boston: D. C. Heath, 1956), 1.

3. Grant H. Smith, *The History of the Comstock Lode, 1850–1920.* University of Nevada Geology and Mining Series 37 (1943): 33.

4. See J. D. Galloway, *Early Engineering Works Contributory to the Comstock,* University of Nevada Geology and Mining Series, 45 (1947), 1–25, and John

T. Waldorf, *A Kid on the Comstock* (Berkeley: University of California Press, 1968), 64.

5. Smith, *History of the Comstock Lode*, 62, 199, 292–93.

6. As quoted in George E. Peckam, "Recollections of an Active Life," *Nevada Historical Society Papers* 2 (1917–1920): 62.

7. Mary Ellen Glass, *Silver Politics in Nevada, 1892–1902* (Reno: University of Nevada Press, 1969), 150.

8. Sam P. Davis, *History of Nevada*, vol. 1 (Reno: Elms Publishing Company, 1913), 432.

9. As quoted in Russell R. Elliott, *Servant of Power: A Political Biography of Senator William M. Stewart* (Reno: University of Nevada Press, 1983), 215.

10. Dan De Quille (William Wright), *The Big Bonanza*. Introduction by Oscar Lewis (New York: A. A. Knopf, 1947), 174–80.

11. John Muir, *Steep Trails*, ed. William Frederick Bade (Boston: Houghton Mifflin, 1918), 195–204.

12. As quoted in Duane A. Smith, *Mining America. The Industry and the Environment, 1800–1980* (Lawrence, Kansas: University of Kansas Press, 1987), xl.

13. Russell R. Elliott, *Nevada's Twentieth Mining Boom* (Reno: University of Nevada Press, 1966), 103–44. The similarity of high-grading in mining to the practice of skimming in gambling is worth noting. In both cases, potential tax money is diverted from the government by thievery—in one case by the workers, in the other by the owners.

14. Russell R. Elliott, *History of Nevada*. 2d ed. rev. (Lincoln: University of Nebraska Press, 1987), 271–72.

15. George Graham Rice's career in Nevada is well told in Richard Lillard's *Desert Challenge*. Bison Book (Lincoln, Nebraska: University of Nebraska, 1942), 266–69.

16. *Engineering and Mining Journal* 107 : 19 (March 1, 1919), 542.

17. *Ibid.* 90 (October 8, 1910), 709–10.

18. *Ely (Nevada) Record*, October 7, 1910.

19. George Graham Rice, *My Adventures With Your Money* (Las Vegas, Nevada: Nevada Publications, 1986). There was an earlier publication in 1913 by R. A. Badger.

20. *Ely (Nevada) Record*, March 15, 1912; *Engineering and Mining Journal* 93 (March 16, 1912), 542.

21. John M. Findlay, *People of Chance: Gambling in American Society from Jamestown to Las Vegas* (New York: Oxford University Press, 1986), 118.

22. James Hulse, *Forty Years in the Wilderness. Impressions of Nevada, 1940–1980* (Reno: University of Nevada Press, 1986), 66.

Reformers and Visionaries on Nevada's Frontier

James W. Hulse

Every civilized society needs its people of conscience, men and women with a sense of social responsibility. America has had them in abundance, from the time of the Puritan fathers to the ethical preachers of our own era—Jonathan Edwards, Ralph Waldo Emerson, Susan B. Anthony, and Martin Luther King. But there may be some mysterious rule of demographic distribution for such Jeremiah-prone types. Nevada has been relatively short of such people, even for a thinly populated state. This essay seeks to identify a few of them from the early periods of the state's history and to invite a search for more examples of this species.

Where are the Nevadan leaders who have tried to summon the residents of this state to a higher calling, to more noble living, to a more responsible citizenship? Even the rhetoric of the Fourth of July orator, the itinerant preacher, the earnest commencement speaker has become unfashionable in the waning years of the twentieth century in this part of the country. It has always been a rare quality in Nevada.

Kevin Starr, the California cultural historian, produced an admirable book in 1973 entitled *Americans and the California Dream,* which dealt with the ideals and aspirations of some of those who lived in the Golden State between the middle of the nineteenth century and the beginning of World War I.[1] He searched for that dimension of California life, when the provincial society was young, in which missionaries, environmentalists, and social reformers struggled for a higher moral order among the gold hunters and exploiters. It is an intellectual history of high order, not only as a tribute to people of conscience of an earlier generation but also as a challenge to a contemporary society.

"This narrative," Starr wrote near the end of his manuscript, "is an act of memory, a gathering from the California past some inner strands, understood and obscure. California 1850–1915 mocks the blunders of the present and is partially responsible for them."[2] He commented on the ministry of Thomas Starr King, the eloquent Unitarian minister of San Francisco whose figure represents California in Statuary Hall in Washington, who "challenged them [i.e., Californians] to high-mindedness, to seek, as he put it, Yosemites of the soul." King had been "California's Moses, pointing the way to the Promised Land." And he was followed by Henry George, who became famous for the "single-tax" protest against the land monopoly that had emerged in California. The beauty and riches of California's natural resources were being turned to the private profit of a few, he argued, and the nation had missed a golden opportunity for true social progress.

In his book, Starr dealt with a hundred or so moralistic Californians of those pioneering generations. He awarded special places of honor to people like Josiah Royce, who "saw in the California experience an American parable concerning the redemptive quest for loyalty, community, and law," and to John Muir, the founder of the Sierra Club and "the prophet of conservation [who] warned Californians not to squander what the ages had prepared." He continued with examinations of the California dreams of people like Jack London, the adventurer; David Starr Jordan, the co-founder of Stanford University; Gertrude Atherton, the elitist novelist; Luther Burbank, the plant scientist; and scores of others. The book defies summarization: it is an encyclopedic survey of writers who have enriched the life of the Golden State and who have gained national—even international— reputations for their dreams.

No one from Nevada rises to this level of recognition. But it is fair for a native son to ask who, among the Nevadans of the first two or three generations, have been moralists in the broader meaning of the term? We do not mean here merely politicians who have fought for the causes that they believed would get them elected and reelected and upon whom the historians have expended so much rhetoric. Even if we were to include politicians within our spectrum—Senators William M. Stewart and Key Pittman with their battles for silver and Senator Pat McCarran with his anti-Roosevelt anti-Communist crusades—the political thrust of their efforts overpowered whatever moral intention they reflected. Francis Newlands of reclamation fame had a vision about how to make the desert bloom with the use of federal dollars, but he probably had personal financial interests in so doing, and, in any case, he offered little in the way of social philosophy.

Nevada governors, with a couple of exceptions, have not represented themselves as moralists. In general, they have not seen it as their role or mandate to offer communal guidance or to inspire social reform. And the historians who presumed to chronicle the state's achievements in the early years—Myron Angel, Thomas Wren, Sam P. Davis, and James Scrugham—were all in the *business* of history for the sake of gratifying the egos and singing praises to the accomplishments of their contemporaries.[3] In some cases, they recruited responsible, sensitive writers for their chapters. In nearly every instance, however, they were promoters of the state's supposed virtues—and those of the men who paid to have their biographies printed—rather than examiners of its soul.

The list may be expanded indefinitely: when we search for men and women who have been willing or able to pronounce or publish an ethical message from Nevada, we find the pulpits virtually empty. There were, to be sure, a few mavericks. Sarah Winnemucca Hopkins, "the Paiute Princess," made a national reputation in her own day for the protests against the officially sanctioned exploitation of the Indians, and her reputation is growing today within the women's movement.[4] But her cause, like that of her less noted contemporary, Jack Wilson, or "Wovoka" (the Indian Messiah), was confined to the redemption of the oppressed Native American tribes.

Where do we search further? Among the frustrated Socialists like A. Grant Miller or Martin Scanlan, who made a brief noise on the Nevada political scene in the early twentieth century? Their social cause was broadly egalitarian; their values were noble, but they left us no literature—not even any rhetoric of memorable quality.

Was it that the pulpits were never there in Nevada, or that there were never enough parishioners for the pews, or that enticements for the potential audience were too great across the street in the saloons and gambling halls—which have always been some of the alternative temples of Nevada society? Are these things the result of the fact that Nevada is and always has been an impoverished younger stepsister of the wealthiest commonwealth in the Republic? Can we explain the phenomenon by the theory that California has inspired utopian thinkers because of the natural beauties and abundance of its coastlines, forests, mountains, and valleys, because it has been perceived as a logical place for Utopia from the beginning?

Whatever the reason, there is very little moral rhetoric in the annals of Nevada history. Perhaps it is merely a matter of numbers. The population of California in 1920 exceeded that of Nevada by a ratio of more than 40 to 1. Even in the late 1980s, it is about 25 to 1. Perhaps it is unrealistic to expect that such an underprivileged state, subsisting as it has on extractive and exploitative industries that have little interest beyond the making of money, could produce spokesmen for the moral order to stand beside the eminent California dreamers. Certainly Nevada has never had the publishing outlets or the automatic national prominence that encouraged so many Californians to seek a continental audience for their moral themes.

But Nevada has been, after all, "California's Colony," as Richard Lillard wrote nearly a half-century ago.[5] Let us consider a few candidates who challenged the existing political values in favor of a better society.

Henry G. Blasdel

The most obvious Jeremiah among Nevada's early politicians, and one of the very few in that category, was Henry Goode Blasdel, the first governor elected after Nevada became a state. He served for two terms as chief executive in the early Comstock era, from 1864 through 1870, when Nevada was in its most relaxed frontier period.

Nevadans, in their century-long adventure with gambling, have frequently been ambivalent or dissembling about the nature of the questionable business that they have tolerated. Governor Blasdel was not guilty of double-talk or of doublethink on this score. In his 1867 message to the legislature, he recognized that although gambling had been pronounced illegal two years earlier it still flourished in the saloons, and he proposed stronger legislation to suppress it. He said:

> Gaming is an intolerable and inexcusable vice. It saps the very foundation of morality, breeds contempt for honest industry, and totally disqualifies its victims for the discharge of the ordinary duties of life. Every energy of the State should be invoked to suppress it.[6]

And in that year he vetoed a bill that would have made gambling legal, and his veto prevailed. Two years later, as a devout Christian, he again deplored the survival of the games of chance and pointed out some basic defects in the regulation of the business. Enforcement was a dead letter because the justices of the peace of the various townships had original jurisdiction, the law imposed no penalty upon anyone except dealers in a game, and the offense was treated only as a misdemeanor. Yet in that very session, the legislature passed the first Nevada law legalizing and presumably regulating gambling by requiring those who offered games to be licensed by the county sheriffs. Blasdel vetoed the bill, but both houses of the legislature voted overwhelmingly to override, and legal games became the law of the state.[7]

In his veto message, Governor Blasdel expanded on his ethical objections to gambling in trenchant, biting sentences that built to a crescendo:

> I know of no greater vice than gambling. It is against public morals. It saps the very foundations of society. It induces intemperance. It begets idleness. It fosters immorality. It multiplies crime. It leads to reckless extravagance, and unfits its unhappy victim for any position of business usefulness. In short it is the root of all evils—the highway that leads to immorality and crime. For centuries it has been the aim and effort of Christian men and women to uproot and destroy it; and to-day I believe there is not a State in this Union whose criminal statutes do not pronounce it a crime and punish it with heavy penalties.[8]

Blasdel had a vision of a social order that would be more considerate of the family values, more thoughtful of the plight of the Indians who were displaced, and more attuned to the virtues of citizenship. But his rhetoric had no impact. Two years later, in 1871, the governor made yet another impassioned plea for repeal of the gambling policy in language that has seldom been matched for eloquence by a chief executive officer of the Silver State. He seemed to sense that Nevada was embarking on an antisocial path unparalleled elsewhere in the Union:

> Shall this vice, the prolific source of every crime—bringing in its train all the monstrous and corrupting evils that scandalize religion and demoralize society—be not only tolerated, but encouraged and legalized in our midst? Shall we say to our youth that this, which has met the condemnation of all christian communities, is no longer forbidden but is dignified and made honor-

able by the State? Shall we encourage men to follow the downward course to ruin and sin, or shall we remove the temptation and arrest their footsteps before the vortex of destruction is reached? It may be impossible to entirely prevent gambling. So is it impossible to prevent murder, but both may be restrained. But however this may be, in the name of that home impoverished and made desolate by gaming; in the name of that soul blackened and blasted by its influence; in the name of that Savior whose garments were gambled away at the foot of the cross, I protest against its legalization.[9]

Blasdel is almost alone in Nevada history among those in political office who have spoken out against the business that the state has made its primary "industry." Only two or three governors since Blasdel's days have been willing to reflect in public on the social consequences of officially sanctioned gambling. One need not agree with Blasdel's categorical indictment of gambling as a pervasive vice in order to conclude that the state has not done well at controlling the social evils that often accompany it.

Anne Martin

The foremost pioneer for women's rights in Nevada in the first twenty years after 1900 was Anne Martin, born in a little town called Empire, near Carson City, in 1875. It is not often remembered that she became an advocate of a broader spectrum of social reforms once her primary goal—women's suffrage—had been achieved.

Martin was one of the most articulate voices ever to rise from the dust of rural Nevada to be heard on the national level on behalf of social justice. She had studied at the University of Nevada in Reno before the turn of the century, had gone off to Stanford for more training, and had come home to the infant university in Reno from which she had graduated. She soon had a quarrel with the president and moved on to become one of the most prominent leaders of the women's rights movement in the West. She traveled to England and made news there in the suffrage movement, which was from its early days thought to be a work of broad economic and social reformation.

Even though she led the successful drive for voting rights for women in a mining and ranching state where men outnumbered women more than two to one, she regarded her life as less than successful because

she personally never won political office and never saw any broader
social change occur as a result of suffrage for women. When women
finally won the vote, they failed to use their newly gained political influence to effect any conspicuous social reform, and historians of the
state did not attach much significance to the achievement in her time.
She was one of the first women to run for the U.S. Senate, and she did
so twice. She gained a reputation as a troublesome radical, and only a
half-century later has history finally accorded her a small measure of
the credit that her contemporaries denied her.[10]

Although Martin was almost exclusively known as a suffragist, there
was a broader dimension to her social reform idealism. Near the end
of her active political career, she wrote a poignant article, which appeared in the liberal magazine, *The Nation*. The essay appeared in 1922
and was entitled "NEVADA" Beautiful Desert of Buried Hopes."[11] Its
theme was that the Silver State, because of its peculiar economic structure, exploited and stunted its predominantly male population and
restricted normal social and economic development. Much of its population was transient—miners, ranch hands, railroad workers, who
drifted from place to place without the civilizing amenities of home
and family.

In Martin's view, the villains in the picture were the oligarchs of Nevada's livestock interests. During the years of her youth, cattle barons
had managed to gain control of much of the state's water and rangeland resources. They were aided and abetted by short-sighted governmental policies:

> The live-stock industry, established as a monopoly in Nevada
> under very extraordinary conditions, is responsible. It has pre-
> vented the development of small farms, of family life, of a stable
> agricultural population, and has produced an excessive propor-
> tion of migratory laborers and homeless men, larger than any
> state in the Union.[12]

Martin's lament in this instance sounds like an echo of the Californian, Henry George, whose *Progress and Poverty* was widely known
during her youth. She had a vision of an economy based upon the
Jeffersonian ideal of rural self-sufficiency, and she thought she saw a
model to follow beyond Nevada's eastern border:

> Utah has shown our bosses both in Washington and Nevada
> how to manage large land and water holdings for the public

good. It was the policy of the Mormon church to divide good land into small farms. And Utah, with nearly equal agricultural resources, has a much larger population and greater economic and social stability than her neighbor. . . .

What is the solution of Nevada's problem? Undoubtedly the Government should end its long neglect of its vast public domain and administer these lands as it recently began the administration of its forest reserves, but in the interest of the small settler. The Government should extend its irrigation projects, providing credits and other necessary aid to settlers during the first difficult years, and, even more important, in cooperation with the State, should buy from the large stockmen tracts of land which control water for live stock.[13]

This neo-populism looks a bit naive six decades after it was written, but there was some rational basis for it. Martin obviously admired the achievements of the Newlands Reclamation Project, which put thousands of acres of arid land under cultivation by diversion of the Truckee River into the lower Carson River basin, and she had some familiarity with the Mormon experiment in eastern Nevada that led to the establishment of Lund and Preston in White Pine County.

In retrospect, it seems obvious that Martin's dream of applying a California- or Utah-style agrarian reform was misplaced in the "sagebrush state," but at least she had the conscience and the skill to articulate an alternate social program in a national journal. Perhaps her view of the problem was too narrow, perhaps the ills that she saw were less the fault of the livestock owners than of the fundamental economic poverty of the state. One can respect her critical spirit without accepting her analysis of the situation.

Martin did not live to see the unsuccessful struggle for the ratification of the Equal Rights Amendment in Nevada, which occurred approximately a hundred years after her birth and about twenty-five years after her death. Had she done so, she would have recognized a continuation of the patterns of political bias that operated in her active political years.

Jeanne Elizabeth Wier

Buried among the mostly forgotten addresses of Nevadiana is a noteworthy statement by Jeanne Elizabeth Wier, the

founder of the Nevada Historical Society, who directed that institution from its hopeful beginnings in 1904 until her death in 1950. The
successor of Anne Martin as history professor at the infant state university in Reno, she took it upon herself to teach virtually any field of
history that might be wanted and to chart the course for Nevada's historical preservation and writing for the future as well.

For Wier, history could and should be an instrument for social reformation: a society that forgets the past abdicates its responsibilities
to the future. She distributed her energies too extensively and her literary legacy is not strong, but the Society that she founded is thriving
nicely more than a half-century after her stewardship ended.

For her contribution to the literature of social conscience, the best
choice would be the address that she delivered to the Nevada Academy of Sciences in 1905, the year after the founding of the historical
society. She had embraced Nevada warmly as an adopted daughter
after arriving from Stanford, and she saw it as her role to help guide
the raw, impoverished, frontier state to develop a sense of worth and
justice. She loved the state enough to become its moral critic:

> You will understand me then, I believe, when I say that, to my
> mind, in but few other places in the United States is there to be
> found in the same space such poverty of ideals in social and intel-
> lectual life, and, perhaps I might add, in political life as well. The
> East never tires of girding at Nevada, denouncing her as a "rotten
> borough," scoffing at her so-called barbarism and uncouth ways.
> And I ask you to consider whether we, not as individuals, but as a
> whole, have not, in some measure at least, merited the criticisms
> which have been heaped upon us? Has not our development, as
> compared with that of our neighbor States, been in the main a
> materialistic one, so materialistic in fact that when men even to-
> day accumulate a competency they go elsewhere to enjoy a richer,
> more inspiring life? I leave you to answer these questions for
> yourself.[14]

Wier thought that Nevada had been "scarred" by history because of
its peculiar past; it had been ignored and bypassed during the westward movement until the Comstock's gold and silver had been discovered, and then it had been exploited for its mineral wealth without a
normal chance for the rise of a responsible society. "For it is a scar,"
she wrote, "not merely of scant population, but of retarded develop-

ment as well—the scar that comes from the lack of home-building instinct and from the absence of an agricultural stage in its proper time
and place" [pp. 66].

The remedy of this history professor was, of course, the use of historical study and reflection for the purposes of social improvement:

> The time has forever gone by when the writer of history has
> but to chronicle the deeds of kings, presidents, governors, or
> others who sit in high places. The history of to-day and that of the
> future must be the record of the masses, the events which have to
> do with human nature, with human hopes and ideals, and which
> point the way to the working out of the political and social order
> of the world. And if, perchance, here and there to one man or
> woman is given an extra page of the chronicle, the reason for
> such emphasis will be found, not in the strength of official rank,
> but in the heroism, the self-sacrifice, and the patriotism of the
> truly great individual.[15]

Wier was as mistaken about the uses to which history might be put in
the Silver State as Martin was to be about the rejuvenation of politics
once women had secured the vote, but her vision was of the same admirable material. "What we do need," she summarized, "is intelligent
organization of the forces, the passions, that are swaying the hearts
and lives of our people. We need, as some one has said, 'the primal
support of basal moral quality to insure success.'"[16] She envisioned
the newly created Nevada Historical Society and the Nevada Academy
of Sciences as being instruments for that redemption of the society.

When Martin and Wier were young professors at Nevada State University in that turn-of-the-century era, it had a president who was one
of the most articulate social activists in the history of the state, who
had a sense of social responsibility as keen as their own. He, like they,
has had little recognition in the history of the state, as it has been written in the intervening years.

Joseph E. Stubbs

Between 1894 and 1914, Nevada State University (now the
University of Nevada) was a small, struggling academy of learning
hardly worthy of the name to which it aspired. During most of that

time the institution served only 200 to 300 higher education students; only in one year did it exceed 400. By any standard, it was one of the weakest of the land-grant universities.

But Joseph Edward Stubbs was a man of considerable intellectual courage, and he personally brought the institution, by his personal stature, some national recognition. Stubbs assumed that the institution that he served should provide ethical guidance not only for its students but also for the state and that it would be stunted as long as the state tolerated social vices. And he assumed that it was a basic role of universities to provide ethical guidance for the communities they served.

In 1900, when he became national president of the Association of American Agricultural Colleges and Experiment Stations—an unprecedented honor for the head of a small western university—he delivered a presidential address at Yale.[17] A student of the classics addressing officers from other agricultural and technical schools, he sought to build a bridge between technical and liberal learning by referring to the moral responsibilities of the colleges.

"The test of every educational scheme, new or old," he said, "is found in the inquiry: *Does it give preeminence to ethical values?* We obtain, by this aim, substantial unity in all forms of education."[18] He did not see the university as primarily a place where students were preparing to make money or to gain power, but rather as a place where they were being made ready to render service to society. "From the higher education, therefore, we must exclude all over-particularizing and all over-specialization. Our first aim shall be to make men endowed with great social virtues."[19]

Stubbs not only spoke this way, but he tried to carry this message to the streets of Nevada. He risked public controversy by leading campaigns against legalized gambling and the prostitution that flourished openly in Reno. He was temporarily successful in the crusade against the games of chance but unsuccessful in his efforts to suppress the red-light district.[20] Prostitution continued to exist in many small towns and even in downtown Reno near the Truckee River until it was finally suppressed during World War II. Nevada continued to tolerate legal prostitution on a local option basis at the end of the 1980s, presumably because it had no social spokesmen willing to fight against the social disgrace.

Stubbs was a leader in the movement that resulted in a 1909 statute

of the Nevada legislature outlawing gambling, which had been officially sanctioned since 1869. The statute was moderately effective for
a short time, but gradually gambling resumed on a larger scale in the
back rooms of saloons, and eventually in 1931 it was again legalized by
legislative action.

The rhetoric and oratorical style of Stubbs is out of fashion in the
present age of mindless electronic entertainment and advertising
overkill, but it was influential in the early years of this century. When
he visited Goldfield in 1910, then Nevada's most prosperous mining
town, to address a teachers' institute, Stubbs took advantage of the opportunity to visit the plant of the Goldfield Consolidated Mining
Company, which was then at the peak of its prosperity under the
leadership of financier George Wingfield and Senator George Nixon.
He admired the gold refining capabilities of the mill, the most profitable of its kind in the West, and he immediately proceeded to draw
some lessons from the Book of Job, "which is as modern in its description of mining today as it was when it was written in the far off centuries of the early Hebraic literature."

He quoted some passages from the 28th chapter, in which Job put
the value of understanding high above that of gold and other precious metals and stones. "Where shall wisdom be found," he asked,
"and where is the place of understanding?" He obviously intended for
his audience—and not only the poorly paid teachers of Nevada—to
infer that there were or could be enterprises in Nevada that were
more durable than the gold mines and mills of Goldfield.[21]

Although he was a humanist by instinct and training, Stubbs threw
himself diligently into the challenge of leading a land-grant institution that was dedicated to offering training in "agriculture and the
mechanic arts." In 1900, when he was addressing the National Livestock Association in Fort Worth, Texas, he used the occasion to offer a
lesson or two on Caesar and the abuse of power, even as he was stress-
ing the importance of the cattlemen's work to a prosperous society.[22]

In a 1911 address in Reno he said, "The university keeps its eye
fixed upon the stars. . . . But, while it may sweep the heavens with the
glass of the astronomer, its work is upon the earth, and its purpose is
to make better the life of many by service, and to spread the knowledge of the brotherhood of man wherever its influence can reach."[23]

Stubbs died in office in 1914, and his name and service have virtually been forgotten in the commonwealth that he tried to redeem.

Walter E. Clark and *The Book of the Oath*

Resting, also almost forgotten, in the Special Collections Department at the University of Nevada–Reno is a large, handsome volume that reflects one more noble effort to commit education in Nevada to ethical and socially responsible purposes. It is identified as the *The Book of the Oath,* and it represents one of the typically symbolic efforts of a university president of the early twentieth century to define the main goal of the university as the betterment of humankind.

The man who conceived *The Book of the Oath* was President Walter E. Clark, the chief executive officer of the University of Nevada from 1917 to 1938. Like Stubbs, Clark was a graduate of Ohio Wesleyan University. He had earned his bachelor's degree in 1896 and had taught mathematics for several years. He later became a faculty member at the City College of New York and obtained his Ph.D. at Columbia University.

Clark was called to the University of Nevada three years after the death of Stubbs, following an interregnum in which there had been abnormal confusion in the fiscal management of university affairs. The regents selected Clark partly because he had an excellent scholarly reputation in economics: no President in the hundred-year history of higher education brought a better set of academic credentials and publications to his office. He had published books on economic history, on trusts, and on the rising cost of living.[24]

The Regents got more than an economist: they got a man who, like Stubbs, personified high ethical and social standards as well. In his third year as president (1920), he introduced *The Book of the Oath*. Its single page of text reads:

> I, about to be graduated from the UNIVERSITY OF NEVADA, ACKNOWLEDGING my great debt to the Giver of all life who has given me life in Nevada, the State whose people are most blest with pioneering strengths and whose land of all America is freshest from His hand, and most truly His cathedral, with mountain columns, star vaults and sage-incensed aisles, hourly urging me to reverent thinking and living,
> ACKNOWLEDGING my great debt to the race which has made me heir to civilization, wrought out by its centuries of toil and of thought, and preserved by the bravery of its heroes, the wisdom of its sages and the faith of its saints,

ACKNOWLEDGING my great debt to this Nation and to this Commonwealth, which, through guardian organization and through open school doors, have jointly made it possible for me to come into the full riches of my natural and my racial inheritances,
HERE AND NOW PLEDGE lifelong loyalty to the shaping ideals of American civilization:
    LIBERTY bounded by law drawn for the common weal,
    EQUALITY of opportunity for all, and
    JUSTICE administered in accord with the dictates of the common will, lawfully expressed.
I HERE AND NOW FURTHER PLEDGE that in all the years to be granted to me and to the fullness of my allotted strength
        I SHALL SERVE,
both alone and with others, to the high ends that uncleanness, greed, selfishness, and pride shall lessen, that cleanness, charity, comradeship, and reverence shall widen, and that this, my generation, shall bequeath an even better and nobler civilization than came to it.

If the language of the oath appears somewhat quaint and archaic in the waning years of the twentieth century, it is not merely because of the rhetoric in which it is cast. There is also the fact that in higher education generally and in the Nevada university system in particular, the emphasis on the university as a place for the development of social responsibility has declined. It was Clark's notion that each member of each graduating class would be asked to sign the oath on the occasion of the awarding of his or her degree. There were a hundred pages in the book: it was assumed that one page would suffice for each class and that the tradition thus established in 1920 would continue for a hundred years. Similar ideals had been pronounced for generations in Europe and in early America, so, of course, Clark would reasonably expect such ideals to be valued in the young and developing state that he had been called to serve.

Of course, we know better. Better? We have more cognizance, perhaps, occasioned by our later place in the historical chronology. But do we understand better? Universities have become the trade schools of the recent generations; the numbers of their students and faculties have increased beyond the fondest dreams of earlier academicians, and in the process, the moral content and the ethical expectations of the university have diminished. Clark's *Book of the Oath*, if it were to be called forth from the archives, would be an anachronism in this era.

This admirable tradition of *The Book of the Oath* did continue for nearly half a century, until 1964, when it was retired. A few of us signed it twice. No graduate has signed the book—presumably none has been invited to do so—for nearly a quarter-century. Perhaps this is appropriate because of the drastic change in the popular concept of what a university is and ought to be since Clark's time. Now there is much less emphasis on the university as a place to inspire ethical improvements of the individual and society and much more emphasis on it as a place to prepare to make money.

Clark, like Stubbs, became the president of a national association of university presidents, and in 1933 he delivered his last major address in Washington, D.C., to the National Association of State Universities in the United States of America.[25] There, in the midst of the Great Depression, he reaffirmed again his conviction that instilling in its students an ethical commitment to a better society was the primary responsibility of the university. He said:

> Is it not part of the greater job of the college to develop convinced and scientific and devoted and convincing democrats? "Democracy is deeper than liberty; it reaches responsibility." The four campus years do much if they help attune the student life to this key; they do little and ill except for such attuning. Craftsmanship, scholarship, even spirit mastery, worthy things in themselves, are superficial, pretentious, dangerous or injurious to one who uses them as means merely to get for himself more goods, better placement, higher prestige. All paths of selfish gain lead ultimately to discontent, pessimism, emptiness, despair, both for the individual and for the nation and the race.[26]

His speech was, in effect, an expansion of the sentiments expressed in the oath that he had introduced in the provincial little university in Reno. It was his vision that institutions of higher learning, dedicated to the cultivation of a "great army of new democratic leaders" would point the way to a world in which the disasters of war and depression could be avoided. Yet during the remaining years of his tenure as president of the University of Nevada, the Depression continued to stifle the efforts of those who wished to give the university a stronger economic base and, as he said, the institution merely marked time. After the Depression, the war, and the postwar boom, there was no invitation from the university's leaders to build the higher moral order on the foundations of education.

Where has this sentimental excursion through the antique prose and ideas of the early Nevadans brought us? Nowhere, obviously. But ruminations of this kind may be of some antiquarian interest to that small minority, in this generation or others, who, with Boethius, find consolation in philosophy, even if it is poorly done and if the contemporary examples are weak. It is the plain fact that no Nevada politicians since Blasdel's time, and few historians since Martin's and Wier's time, and perhaps even fewer university spokesmen since Stubbs's and Clark's generations have considered it to be their business to offer a moral statement to the constituency. These fragments of the rhetorical art are as quaint as the artifacts—the old dresses and the furniture of frontier days—that are on display in the Nevada Historical Society museum. But perhaps they are worth dusting off every generation or two as a reminder that Nevada did once, like California, have peculiar people who thought this state was also worthy of utopian dreams.

NOTES

1. Kevin Starr, *Americans and the California Dream: 1850–1915* (New York: Oxford University Press, 1973).

2. Ibid., 444.

3. Myron Angel, ed., *History of Nevada* (Oakland: Thompson and West, 1881; reprinted Berkeley: Howell-North, 1958); Thomas Wren, ed., *A History of the State of Nevada: Its Resources and People* (New York: Lewis Publishing Co., 1904); Sam Davis, *The History of Nevada* (Reno: Elms Publishing Co., 1913), 2 vols.; and James G. Scrugham, *A Narrative of the Conquest of a Frontier Land . . .* (Chicago: American Historical Society, 1935), 3 vols.

4. Hopkins's *Life Among the Paiutes: Their Wrongs and Claims* (Boston: 1883; reprinted Bishop, California: Chalfant Press, 1969) is now frequently cited in the feminist literature on the nineteenth century.

5. Richard G. Lillard, *Desert Challenge: An Interpretation of Nevada* (New York: Alfred E. Knopf, 1942), 55ff.

6. *First Biennial Message of Governor H. G. Blasdel . . . , January 10, 1867*, 14.

7. *Statutes of Nevada . . . 1869*, chap. 71, 119–21.

8. *Journal of the Assembly . . . ,* Fourth Session, 1869, 282.

9. *Third Biennial Message of Gov. Henry G. Blasdel*, January 3, 1871, 16.

10. Anne Bail Howard, *The Long Campaign: A Biography of Anne Martin* (Reno: University of Nevada Press, 1985).

11. Anne Martin, "NEVADA: Beautiful Desert of Buried Hopes," *The Nation*, 115, July 26, 1922, 89–92.

12. Ibid., 89–90.

13. Ibid., 92.

14. Jeanne Elizabeth Wier, "The Mission of the State Historical Society," *First Biennial Report of the Nevada Historical Society: 1907–1908* (Carson City: State Printing Office, 1909), 63.

15. Ibid., 61.

16. Ibid., 69.

17. J. E. Stubbs, "What is of Most Worth in Modern Education," reprinted in the *Biennial Report of the Regents of the State University and the Report of the President—1899–1900* (Carson City: State Printing Office, 1901), 63ff.

18. Ibid., 67.

19. Ibid., 77.

20. Samuel Bradford Doten, *An Illustrated History of the University of Nevada* (Reno: University of Nevada, 1924), 76–145 *passim;* James W. Hulse, *The University of Nevada: A Centennial History* (Reno: University of Nevada Press, 1974), 32–37.

21. J. E. Stubbs, "The Relation of the University to the Welfare of the People of the State of Nevada" (Reno: University of Nevada, 1910).

22. J. E. Stubbs, "Address Before the Third Convention of the National Livestock Association At Fort Worth, Texas," January 19, 1900.

23. J. E. Stubbs, "A Progressive State from the University Point of View," An Address . . . at the First Baptist Church, March 12, 1911.

24. Walter E. Clark, *Josiah Tucker, Economist: A Study in the History of Economics* (New York: Columbia University Press, 1903); *The Cost of Living* (Chicago: A. C. McClurg, 1915); *The Trust Problem*, with Jeremiah Whipple Jenks (Garden City: Doubleday, Doran, 1929).

25. Walter E. Clark: "A College Goal," *School and Society* 37 (January 28, 1933): 105–11.

26. Ibid., 109.

Buckaroos   William
Kittredge

One sure thing about us boys on those old dust-eating summery afternoons during World War II, out there branding MC calves on the high deserts, we dreamed of highways and rodeo. But that country of northern Nevada and southeastern Oregon is like an ancient hidden kingdom. Change and escape do not come easy there.

Owyhee. Sounds like Hawaii. In 1819 Donald MacKenzie brought one of the first brigades of fur trappers into the Snake River country, coming from the mouth of the Columbia, and he brought with him a few Hawaiians. He sent them off to explore the uncharted river that came into the Snake from the south, through the desert barrens. The Hawaiians never came back. The river and territory inherited their name.

This is a story of going back, on the road and seeking romance and Hawaiians in the desert, crystal fountains of my own making, and mountain-man hubris. What I wanted was Nevada, and *laissez faire,* hard-way sixes at four o'clock in the morning and then, if it should suit my fancy, a quiet drink on the terrace with myself and the sunrise, like a grown-up in the land where everybody gets to do what he wants to do.

Specifically, I was heading to visit the chuckwagon buckaroo outfit run by the IL Ranch, on the edge of the Owyhee desert north of Tuscarora, Nevada. The IL is an outfit run in the old and sensible way, four horses pulling the wagon, and no trucks and no town cars and no horse trailers. Just the men and the livestock and the countryside settling into a routine with one another amid the turns of the season.

The first branding of the spring season was to be the next morning, if the weather cleared. The smell of branding was one of the wistful things I had come looking for. But the storms had been driving in from the west, spitting snow and rain, and the prospects did not look good. The hot branding iron scalds and blots on the hides of wet calves.

Fearful that the desert would be all muddy roads and bad news, I skipped the Tuscarora turnoff and went on into Elko, one of those two-hearted Nevada ranching and gambling towns that grew up at the end of the nineteenth century after the Union Pacific traced the route of California-bound wagon trains along the Humboldt River. Up on the hill, in the shade of box elder, you have country people mowing their lawns and reading the *Western Horseman* magazine on their patios, while down by the interstate you've got gambling everywhere and bars that never close, and always, off on the exotic edges of what I knew from high school, the dangerous reek of prostitution.

Those whorehouses put me in a you-can't-go-home-again quandary of the most elemental kind. Back deep in the misty past there is this land inhabited by dreams and passions, and you love it—your daddy was rich and your momma good looking—and you want it to be all perfection, bronzed in your memory like baby shoes. And whorehouses, well, I just don't know.

There was a time I liked them fine. In Klamath Falls, Oregon, where we wintered when I was in high school, there were five houses, places with names like the *Iron Door* and the *Palm Hotel.* There was a whole crowd of us growing boys who ruined our athletic careers by hanging out in those homes for the misbegotten eros of the times. We were there a lot. And why not? Say it's Friday night in February and the basketball game is over, and the alternative is the sock-hop mixer down at the Teen Age Club. Lots of leaning against the wall and studying your look-alike basketball rivals from out of town while the girls dance with one another. Pretty soon somebody says "Let's go," and you nod in your cool-eyed way and all drift down to the Iron Door.

And there were summers, over in Lakeview, Oregon, near the ranch where I grew up. Riding with the wagon on the desert, or working in the hayfields, I was earning a man's wages by the time I was fifteen or so, and summers were a different ballgame. Out beyond the rodeo grounds there was a whorehouse district called Hollywood. And it was official—the houses paid taxes into a special city fund for streetlights. This was all part of the timeless rationale you would hear, the basic argument to do with ensuring the safety of decent women: sex-crazed ranch hands could work out their primitive lusts down in

Hollywood and not wander the streets, molesting wives and mothers. And besides, how about those streetlights? Hollywood, I guess, was a kind of civic sacrifice area.

The girls, some not much older than we were, would serve us boys with whiskey and take our money and smile and laugh with us so long as we could pay our way. Those houses sided with tar paper were not places to contemplate romance or running away with your darling, but they were where so many of us received our most formidable training for manhood, learning the most central message of western civilization: do not break your heart over anything resembling promiscuity; property remains. It was the same message my grandfather had been teaching me all of my life.

Sitting there in my Elko motel room, sipping at a wonderful little square pint bottle of Jack Daniel's whiskey, I could not bring myself to drift back down to the cathouses. Like Hemingway said in another context, and he is our patron in these matters, "the war was always there, but we did not go to it any more."

All of it, there in Elko, was like coming home. In the J. M. Capriola Company on Commercial Street I wandered around just touching the gear, rawhide reatas and horsehair mecates, rubbing my hands over the $1,500 working buckaroo saddles, eyeing the silver-mounted Garcia spurs and Spanish bits and belt buckles in their glass cases, feeling a pang of awe at the way prices had gone up.

At Capriola's, a complete gear-up for a desert horseback working man—saddle, bridle, Spanish and snaffle bits, chinks (the chaps they wear in the buckaroo north country, cut off at the knee), tepee camp tent, hobbles plus a pair of woolly sheepskin chaps for winter, bedroll and blankets—will run well beyond $3,000. Which is a load of money for a working cowhand, even if he gets board and room free. But the gear is built to accompany a working person through a good many seasons of serious endeavor, all up and down the road.

And downstairs in the Commercial Hotel were the crap tables and the mounted upright figure of what is reputed to be largest white polar bear ever killed, taken by native hunters off Point Hope, Alaska. At midnight the Commercial was Point Hope for everybody; the last stand of your most basic American fantasy, if you could cloud your mind and write off a $276 run of bad karma in the midst of those hard-way sixes. Which was an art I was practicing, along about midnight in Elko, the land of the free.

So when morning dawned bright, rain clouds gone, I was ready for my trip out past Tuscarora to the IL. For me it was like going back in time.

The headquarters of the IL Ranch is on the Owyhee South Fork, edged up on the sage hills above about 2,500 acres of native meadow hay land. Off west is the enormous rimrock flatland of the Owyhee desert, elevation always over 5,000 feet, reaching to the far-away Santa Rosa mountains, 70 miles by air, over 9,000 feet and still snow-covered in mid-May. About 20 miles east there's Jack's Peak, rising 10,000 feet in the Independence Mountains over the Columbia Basin, where the IL cattle and sheep run during the late summer and early fall.

If Elko smelled like home, this *was* home. Down in a cramped little office next to the cookhouse I met the ranch boss, Bill Maupin, and his wife, Wanda, and the sheep boss, Allen King, who was up from the sheep range, which is on the south side of the Humboldt River, far to the west between Battle Mountain and Winnemucca.

The IL Ranch runs about 5,000 mother cows and another 5,000 head of sheep on about 480,000 acres of deeded and government-leased land. And it is the smallest of the major spreads in that country. The Petan Ranch to the north, the Spanish Ranch, which headquarters over in the Independence Valley northeast of Tuscarora, and the Garvey Ranch to the west in Paradise Valley—they're all bigger, at least by reputation.

It's regarded as rude to ask a man how much property he owns. But there is one good story about a man named John G. Taylor, who was an early owner of the IL. Seems he was tired of hearing about the Miller and Lux Ranch. Around the beginning of this century it was claimed a man could ride from Burns in Oregon to the south end of the San Joaquin Valley in California and camp every night but one on Miller and Lux land. That's the version I always heard.

"Damn, I don't know about that," John G. Taylor is supposed to have said, "but I do know this. I can walk on the backs of my own sheep from Lovelock to the three forks of the Owyhee River." That would be maybe 150 miles.

A buckaroo at the IL Ranch, if he's been around long enough to build himself a reputation, might draw as much as $500 a month, board and all the room he wants for his bedroll. Those are standard wages in the country. Hard work, and you've got to respect it if you want the job. But it's a life to which a lot of people, in a complex variety of ways, are returning. Turning back to livestock and the long wheel of days, and some chance at self-knowledge, or at least some knowledge of who killed the cow you are eating.

On the way to where the IL wagon crew was branding, about 20 miles west from headquarters, Bill Maupin pointed out the ruins of an old stone house sitting grand and alone alongside a mostly wet-weather creek. The story is that a Mormon man built it around 1900 and brought his three wives to live there. Two of the wives died that winter and he buried them in the basement, since all the ground outside was frozen hard as metal. The joke was that those women winter-killed.

She is a wonderful country, go the intimations, but a good place to be careful every chance you get. If you are going alone—into your radical mountain-man independence and isolation and loneliness—think ahead and take precautions.

Winter-killed. Brings to mind another charming old saying: "She is a hard country on women and horses." Which means, I guess, that men and mules can make out all right and have a swell time digging graves in the basement.

This country fosters a kind of woman who never seems to bother about who she is supposed to be, mainly because there is always work, and getting it done in a level-eyed way is what counts most. Getting the work done, on horseback or not, and dicing their troubles into jokes. These women wind up looking 50 when they are 37 and 53 when they are 70. It's as though they wear down to what counts and just last there, fine and staring the devil in the eye every morning.

Bill Maupin pointed out a place where a dead man had been found with three silver dollars in his pocket, near the edge of a sandy wash through the sagebrush. One morning, years ago, the buckaroo crew from the IL had come across the fellow, dead of natural causes from what anybody could tell, sitting in a buggy, white eyes open to the new sun. The sheriff came out from Elko, looked him over and blessed him, and they buried him where they found him, the three shining silver dollars in his pocket for luck.

The country is thick with such stories. Unknown travelers. Bill Maupin was not so much telling me things about people whose lives he cherished as he was wondering if I shared his reverence for those old work-centered men and women who showed us how to live on the desert.

And, yeah, I did. Bill Maupin and I grew up knowing a lot of the

same people, and surely the same kind of people. The cow boss at the
IL, Tom Anderson, turned out to be a man I had just missed knowing
when we were both younger. Tom broke in buckarooing on the MC
just after I went away to the Air Force. Hugh Cahill and old man Ross
Dollarhide were running the MC wagon then.

In this memory, our kid is maybe eleven years old and catching
horses every morning before sunrise out on our high desert country
of southeastern Oregon. The remuda would circle in one of those old
stone corrals, and the alkaline dust would lift in a clear string to the
blooming bowl of sky. I was learning responsibility in a ranching
country of great distances and silences, where the history is a story of
ranching people and their dreams.

My grandfather, during the hard times of the Great Depression,
had yielded to one of those dreams and staked the property he spent
a lifetime accumulating in order to get his hands on one of the great
ranches, the MC in Warner Valley, out east of Lakeview and part of
the local mythology: some twenty-odd thousand acres of peat-soil
swamplands in the valley, and what seemed in those horseback days to
be endless summer range out east on the desert. A million or so acres,
that desert range was mostly Taylor grazing land leased from the Federal government, but my grandfather treated it like it was his own.

Before the end of World War II there was no asphalt within 35
miles of headquarters on the MC. No telephones; a Delco generator
for electricity. A great deal of time was spent in the company of animals, talking to yourself.

Which was fine. You would slow down and get used to the pace.
Going to the desert—that's what we called summering out there with the
cattle—ten or so riders, a chuckwagon and cook and no automobiles
until somewhere in the middle of the war. Clevon Dixon, who was cow
boss on the MC in the 1960s, said the quiet just took you over.

"First week," he'd say, "I always hate it, wondering what's happening somewhere. Second week I don't care so much. After that I can't
imagine anyplace else, and I don't ever want to turn back toward
town. If it wasn't for winter, you could stay out there forever."

That country I came from in southeastern Oregon and northern
Nevada is a land of great ranches: the IL and the Whitehorse, the
MC and the ZX and Peter French's great P Ranch, which has been
owned by the Federal government since the 1930s, miles of swamp-

land meadow along the Donner und Blitzen River, a wildlife refuge these days. History there is a story of ranches and dreams of empire, of land and cattle and great horsemen, but it is more a history of getting the work done, feeding cattle from a creaking hay wagon while the snow blows level to the ground in late January.

My education in such realities began with men like Ross Dollarhide, who lived to see 90 years, and died in bed, having endured. The way legends should end.

The MC was like a feudal kingdom in those days, not many neighbors you ever saw, nobody around for the most part but our family and the people who worked for them, a world centered on horses and cattle those years before the end of World War II, when everybody went to pickup trucks and tractors. When we lost the family farm in Montana, an old man told me, was when we went to the goddamned tractors. Maybe so.

Anyway, there I was, eleven years old, learning the business. It was late June, and we were branding calves alongside a little alkaline sink on the Gooch Plateau, right near the Oregon/Nevada border. Ross Dollarhide was wagon boss for the MC buckaroo outfit at the time, in charge of the riders, a cook, chuckwagon and 65 or 70 head of horses in the remuda, looking after the more than 6,000 Hereford cows and their calves, which my grandfather was summering in the desert. And maybe 500 head of bulls, purebreds, from places like Wyoming and Montana, shipped in on the railroad so there was no chance of inbreeding.

Dollarhide was as old as my grandfather, and he was my main example of how to live like a man in the world. Ross had been a legend in the country since he rode into the Whitehorse Ranch on a fat-tired bicycle the summer he was sixteen, around 1900, and announced he was looking for work, riding rough horses if there was a choice. Which is the way legends get started.

According to this one, the old hands grinned, and put him up on some Roman-nosed gray stud nobody had even thought about trying to ride. We know the rest, that devil horse bucked down to a stalled and sweaty, bloody-mouthed froth—even rode to death in some versions of the fireside tale—and young Dollarhide triumphant, the old-timers shaking their heads and smiling.

"We got one," they would say. "A real one." He was a real one to us, for sure, and we all believed some version of that story. Dollarhide was a great horseman, and he had earned and deserved any esteem the world might grant. We rode out each morning behind a legendary man, and we knew it. At least I did, when I was eleven.

So I was amazed to see him pulling leather like any greenhorn on that day in late June when we were branding calves out there on the Gooch Plateau. We had gathered maybe a hundred range cows and their spring calves out of the low hills off south, driven them down across a lava-rock flat, built a fire of greasewood and sage to heat the MC irons, and we were just getting started. A couple of the old roper hands, Dollarhide among them, would ride into the herd and hind-foot the calves with their tight-woven rawhide reatas and drag them to the fire where three or four of the strong young bucks were doing the ground work, the acrid smoke of burning hair and hide lofting around them and their hands bloody as they notched the ears and castrated the little bull calves with their thin-bladed knives. It was hard scab-handed work, and dangerous if you were new to it, or just awkward and given to daydreaming.

I was all of those things, so I was among the three or four who were left with the tiresome job we called "holding cows." We were stationed around the perimeter of the little herd, just keeping the cows and their calves together in a milling way until the ropers had done their work, and Dollarhide shouted, and another branding was finished. What we mostly did was sit quietly beyond the fringes of the herd on whatever horse it was that day, and wait to ride on and gather and brand another 70 or 100 calves before heading back in the late afternoon to the wagon, camped at Rock Spring or South Corral or one of those places, traveling at the long, jolting, killer pace Dollarhide preferred, all of us strung out behind, across the sage flats and going to our second and last meal of the day, hoping maybe the cook had opened a few cans of chilled tomatoes to go with the fried steak and milk gravy and chopped spuds and biscuits. Canned tomatoes were our main fruit dish on that desert, where a drink of spring water was a luxury and pancake syrup mixed with butter was our candy.

Maybe I was dreaming of some such thing when Dollarhide, right before me, got himself in quick and unimaginable trouble. He was riding a long-legged traveling horse, a black with three white stockings and not much in the way of brains, a big 4-year-old one of the young bucks had broken to the bridle that spring. The horse was just learning the rudiments of calf roping. There had been a lot of brainless skittering and crowhopping around, but nothing serious while the old man roped and dragged a couple of small calves. But then he swung a big loop, and caught himself a yearling bull calf that had been missed by this same branding crew the previous fall, caught that bull calf right around the middle, and the rodeo got started.

The yearling weighed close to 500 pounds, all quick bullish energy, and he ducked himself sideways and backwards just as Dollarhide dropped the loop at him—one of those things that happen every so often in a chancy world—and there you had the situation: that yearling bull calf caught secure around the belly and not by the hind feet at all, surprising the old man, who had maybe been paying more attention to this knot-headed horse than to his roping; the yearling cutting back in a wide swing, and Dollarhide already cursing as he spurred that long-legged horse, trying to get its head around to face the rope.

The rest of it was slow motion. The rawhide reata came cutting up under the black horse's tail, and the horse goosed it clear loose, just going straight up and coming down into a twisting bucking exhibition that would have looked fine in Champion of the World competitions. Dollarhide had seen what was coming, and already had turned loose his turns of rope on the saddle horn, getting clear rid of the reata, but he was halfways unseated by surprise, and they were out in the rocks and brush, the stocking-footed gelding plunging and nearly falling and then going high in another twisting leap. Looked like the old man was in danger of coming down hard, and this was no joke, not for anybody, out in those lava rocks. A young man might escape with bad bruises and cuts, but a man of 60 might likely break in two or three places.

Then I saw it: the old man got hold of the saddle horn with both hands, and he pulled leather, and he stayed up there, out of his stirrups and everywhere on that gone-crazy horse, but up there and not down. He made the ride, nothing clean and pretty and competition about it, his head snapping and his hat gone, those lava boulders with their etchings of lichen all around him if he should come loose, our legendary rider pulling leather like a child until the gelding wore down, and then Dollarhide was back in the saddle secure, the show was over.

The old man spurred the gelding, and came trotting back to us, the both of them breathless. A little whirlwind of craziness had gone by, leaving nothing much damaged but my belief in legends. Dollarhide got down off the gelding, rolled a cigarette, put his hat back on his head, and caught me staring, read my mind. "Boy," he said, "this ain't a time to get killed. Not for wages."

Rodeo memories. When I was a boy on the desert we dreamed of rodeos and those tight-bodied little buckle-chasing bunnies who used to hang around behind the bucking chutes, high-crowned white straw hats tipped back and wide purple ribbons trailing down to their asses. You know, the horn blows, the ride has been nothing but a rocking chair, and you kick loose and land running and then limp your way back to the chutes while the crowd goes on cheering. And there she is. Perfect teeth. Dreaming her own dreams.

We had a lot of those fantasies, late evenings around the cook fire after a back-breaking day in the scab-rock country between South Corral and Sage Hen Springs, where I served my horseback apprenticeship. "They're gonna put me in the movies, they're gonna make a big star out of me."

Or not. Maybe we always suspected, as part of our suspicion of anything eastern and citified, that any dream of rodeo always had at its center a sinkhole spiraling down toward night-town, drunk-man darkness and brain damage or moral failures of the most devastating kind. Or lost and pointless death, the kind that always happens to somebody else, like asphyxiation in the back seat of a second-hand car while it idles in a wintertime drive-in movie south of Bakersfield, California.

That happened to somebody I knew.

Even glory had its dark-side-of-the-moon aspects. Back at the IL chuck tent, sipping coffee and eating fresh-baked apple pie, Tom Anderson and I talked about old man Dollarhide and his son, young Ross, who is dead, too, and the night young Ross fought Beef Miller outside Hunters Lodge in Lakeview, and Tootie Gunderson, who was tending bar that long-ago night—wondering what had become of her. Last either of us knew she was running a bar down in Cottonwood, California.

That fight with Beef Miller had to do with Ross having been Champion of the World at bull-dogging sometime around 1953, with the huge silver buckle on his belt, and with him being white and Beef being Indian and the essential crookedness—racist and otherwise—of rodeo judging, and all the other resentments inherent therein. It wasn't any joke, and it isn't one in hindsight. Two large men, and they beat each other bloody. The next day I was sick drunk in the hayfield.

I only saw Ross Dollarhide one more time, ten years later in the summer of 1963. Imagine way off to the west there is a technicolor glow to the sunset scheme of things over Warner Valley, vivid pink shadows coming down into our valley and in the sky a crossing of feathery distintegrating jet stream contrails. I had watched my first Beatles concert on our only channel of television, and I sensed that uncanny things were beginning out there in the Great World. I was not taking part. I was home in the deep West, and because of that my life was lost.

This particular evening I was irrigating, which is a different process than may immediately come to mind, that art we called "balancing water," adjusting headgates and running pumps along our hundred or so miles of interwoven canal system, making sure nothing flooded before morning. None of that mucking around with a #2 shovel, no hip boots; but ramming along levee banks in a 1961 Ford pickup at 50 miles an hour, turning things on and off. Balancing water, and attempting to balance my perfect country life against desire. Barley coming up in long even rows against the sunset light and timothy in the meadows, water birds going north to their summer life on the tundra, my children and their horse, my wife in our home, and so much more, all against the burning of sour envy. I wanted to be somewhere else, nearby to that mysterious frenzy of energy echoing around those dim, grainy pictures of the Beatles and their manic hordes. I wanted to be riding and drifting into their high times.

And along comes trouble. Across the middle of our valley, a couple of years before, the state had built a highway that connected us to Winnemucca down in Nevada, and ran on to the west. "Winnemucca to the Sea," it was called, as if honoring some need to always think westward. After I parked and opened the wire gate into the Big Beef Field, I heard the soft humming of an oncoming automobile traveling toward me with all the speed built up on that long hundred-mile-an-hour voyage across the deserts of northern Nevada. With the gate open, I stood and watched it come at me out of the twilight.

It was a pink Cadillac convertible of that tailfin era, running without headlights. It began to slow and ended up coasting to a halt on the highway alongside where I stood. The top was down and the dark bareheaded man riding shotgun was someone I knew, but hadn't seen in years, Ross Dollarhide the Younger, a man who by that time was living his life mostly in Los Angeles, on the fringes of the movie business, near the heart of mythology. The driver was another rodeo cowboy whose name I forget, a compact little blond fellow who never seemed to say anything but "Damn straight." Otherwise, the cat had got his tongue.

But Ross was another matter. A huge and agile man, by that time he had broken one of his legs so many times, and ridden with it broken, that he was forced to wear a steel brace strapped on outside his Levis. That brace was like an emblem of courage and heedlessness.

Ross handed me a warm quart of Millers and climbed out to stand beside me in the twilight. He wanted to talk. Ross was maybe five years older than I, and an authentic rodeo hero. When I was a kid working summers around the desert chuck wagon, Ross was riding the rough string. So we knew each other, in the way little kids know the schoolyard big kids, and vice versa. And now here I was, working like a farmer for wages, and there he was, a former Champion of the World sporting that emblematic steel brace and wearing his silver-and-gold Champion of the World buckle, traveling in a pink Cadillac with no front windshield. The windshield was not broken out, but missing entirely, as if it had never been there.

"Looks like a windy sonofabitch," I said.

"Damn straight," said the driver, studying the road ahead.

Ross paid us no attention.

"If this is not pretty," he said. "Would you take a look at this?" Ross leaned close and the odor of lemon shaving lotion was fairly overwhelming.

"What's that?" I said.

"Bugs. I got bugs plastered all over my face."

Thinking back about Ross and the bugs, I am reminded of Gregory Peck in *The Gunfighter*, sitting under a clock in the glow of his barroom gunfighter fame, waiting as destiny gallops closer, knowing well that in the real West it was horsemanship, not skill with a six-gun, that defined a man. Knowing he had gone wrong.

"Thirty-four years old," Gregory Peck said, "and I never even owned a decent watch." He was seriously saddened by the fact, as Ross was by the mosquitoes.

The conversation never got beyond that, but I knew what Ross was telling me. Foolishness. He felt trapped by a foolish sport he had mistaken for a purpose. As I felt trapped in agriculture. They drove away and I went on about balancing my water, the warm quart of Millers between my knees as I drove, dumb with yearning to be along for the ride on that wandering adventure, if that's what it was. From the vantage of these later years I see that both Ross and I were mourning the demise of an older sense of what was proper, in which I would not have envied his venturesome skills, and he would not have looked at my foot-soldier life as anything he needed.

We were grieving for the world of his father and my grandfather. Although the elder Dollarhide, the old man, never owned an acre of ground anywhere I knew about, and my grandfather made a concerted effort to own them all, they were equal men before the world in a real and quite unromantic way. Property, in that old world, did not make the man, but rather something about being centered in life, in what was happening right at the moment. To understand, all you had to do was watch old man Dollarhide cutting dry cows from the cows and calves in the fall of the year on a quick little bay horse named Tinkertoy, the old man never suspecting the importance of anything beyond what he was doing, or at least never letting on. It was loss of such undivided minds and lives, nostalgia for work that mattered and a rangeland sense of proportion—those were getting at us both; loss of a direct knowledge of what to do next and who we were supposed to be.

Now I grieve for Ross Dollarhide the Younger. He died in Flagstaff, Arizona, killed while working as a movie extra. His horse fell, and Ross took a rib through a lung. Apparently Ross just roughed it out in that old cowboy way, and didn't say anything about needing a medical man, and went back to his motel room and drowned in his blood some time in the night, trying to sleep. The story goes like that. Confusion and things carried too far, and another ultimate loss.

When I was a kid we used to talk about those great silver and gold buckles, your name engraved under those magic words that will turn all the rest of your life just the slightest degree anticlimactic: *Champion of the World*. We used to guess at how much they would weigh, what they would feel like on your belt.

An existence thick with dreams. The young boys branding there that morning on the IL Ranch were like ghosts of what I most seriously wanted for a long time in my life. While they were roping and dragging calves, I cooked myself a half-dozen nuts—mountain oysters, testicles, whatever you know them by—on that juniper fire, right there nestling on the glowing charcoal. As I chewed them I got myself centered back into what I had once been. I found myself understanding what I had gone away hunting and why coming back here was not a sappy sentiment-filled thing to do.

In the summer of 1945 I was thirteen and we were haying the IXL, a little ranch my grandfather leased from the Charles Sheldon Antelope Refuge in Nevada, just south of the Oregon border in Guano Valley. Every summer the buckaroos had to hay that place. Took us maybe three weeks and kept us busy during the slack season. At least nobody had gone to tractors yet.

There were ten or twelve of us, counting the kids, me and my cousin and the wrango boy. As much as anything, this story is about the wrango boy, the kid who herded the horses and hauled firewood and water for the cook, sometimes doing a stint at peeling potatoes. Because that wrango boy, more than any of us, I think, had his eye on the Great World, those possibilities. All the past month we had been riding bucking horses after supper and most of the day on Sundays. Somebody had their bucking string running in the hills back of the IXL. We built a bucking chute in a stout round corral and the fun was on.

God, did I hate it. One thing I would never claim is any ability on horseback. Every Sunday I would get pitched into the fence or onto my head about three times. But this wrango boy was different. He rode those bucking horses as if they were a natural easy chair, and I've got no doubt that rodeo looked to him like a get-away route. From what, I don't know. Probably things to do with family and poverty.

But right then, in August of 1945, for that crew of men isolated way out there on the great highland desert, VJ Day must have looked like another kind of escape. Maybe just from the daily passage of commonplace life. An excuse for fun. Maybe from guilt at having taken an agricultural deferment from the Army and avoided the fighting. Those were grave matters.

Anyway, all of them, nine or ten men in old man Dollarhide's black V-8 Ford, headed off on the 85 dusty miles to Denio and the nearest barroom. They came back the next morning with cases of whiskey and beer, and soon we were all drunk, even the chuckwagon cook, an old man named Jack Frost. It was my first time, and I stayed drunk for two days.

About noon it was decided we should move camp to the Doherty Place, an old starved-out homesteader ranch up in the middle of

Guano Valley, just off from where the Winnemucca highway passes now. The men took the wagon, and we kids moved the horse herd at a long hard run for around twelve miles. For some reason there were no tragedies. I remember playing hand grenade with canned corn and dropping sacks of flour from the second-story windows at the Doherty Place like high-level bombers, watching them burst on the backs of horses. And finally we threw all the food into the open well and the men left again in the Ford.

The next morning we were alone, we three kids and the old cook. He was howling drunk in his bed, stinking of urine, and could not get up. We were still somewhat drunked up, but we managed to harness the teams and load the wagon, including old soggy Jack, who was still in his bed and muttering about dying, and headed for the MC Ranch headquarters; 50 miles across rutted desert roads to Warner Valley.

My cousin and I pulled chicken-shit rank. Because our grandfather owned them, we took the horses and left the wrango boy with the wagon. By midafternoon we were turning 100 saddle horses loose on the meadows near the ranch house. The wrango boy was two days getting there with the chuckwagon and that poor old cook in his bed, all the time lamenting and threatening to die. A little later, in Lakeview for the Labor Day rodeo, the last time I ever saw him, that boy looked at me with hot eyes and said, "That is it for you sons-a-bitches."

We were in one of those old double-duty barber shops, which are gone from the country now, where a man in off the desert could get himself shaved and his hair cut and then take himself an opulent two-hour bath, all the hot water you wanted for $1.50. And then get into fresh clothes from the skin out and be ready for town. That fellow, the former wrango boy, stood there looking at me slick-faced, his hair combed down and wet, wearing a new yellow shirt bought around the corner at the Lakeview Mercantile, and all at once he was a grown-up and I wasn't. He just shook his head and turned away.

What he was telling me was simple. At maybe 15, he was confirmed into an intention of never again being wrango boy for anybody, not ever.

But when my chance came, I got away from the ranch, too, looking for a way to be someone else than who I had learned to be, someone who was not the owner's kid—and that slickfaced youngster, his yellow shirt and his hair wetted down, glaring at me, got away to go rodeoing, and he was mildly famous for a while. Right then in America, at least in Lake County, the high desert country of Oregon, what all of us young boys wanted was escape and connection with the Great World we had just begun hearing about.

Over at the Doherty Place in Guano Valley, where we threw all the food down the well that afternoon in 1945, there is a raggedy pale oilcloth tacked to the bullpen walls. On it are written lists of names. Ross Dollarhide, Ernest Messner, Casper Gunderson, Hugh Cahill, Cliff Gunderson—maybe even Tom Anderson, who is cow boss at the IL these days. The lists began back before World War II: the names of men who rode for the MC. The lists are fading out pretty badly now. Half of the men are dead.

Heroes are defined as individuals who go out into the world, leaving home on some kind of quest, endure certain trials of initiation, and come home changed, seeing the world in a fresh way, bearing the wisdom of their experience as news that serves the stay-at-homes in their efforts toward making sense of themselves and of what they are attempting to make of their lives.

In my boyhood we all dreamed of going away to such heroism. And now it looks like things have changed. People are staying home, in that part of the country where they know how to live and what to care about. In some large blurry sense, there no longer seems to be too much currency in the idea that going away to seek your fortune is any sensible road toward anything that matters. Nobody imagines that either the Beatles or big-time rodeoing will save your life.

Not long ago some Hollywood people came out and shot part of a TV special starring Kenny Rogers up there in the Columbia Basin east of the IL. Sounds like it was fine for everybody, all the buckaroos getting in on the camera time and fun and action, but so far nobody has left for Los Angeles with acting on his mind.

Maybe it's just that the world has changed another turn, and life on the high desert looks better than it did in the old days. Maybe the wages are not much, but the food is fine. In my childhood, canned tomatoes all around was a big deal. At the IL wagon, the noontime I was there, they were finishing up with apple and raisin pie about three inches deep. An old-timer named Harold Smith was eating it with sweet canned milk. In that life you learn to wait for simple, specific pleasures.

After scraping their plates, they all went out to the rope corral and climbed up aboard their afternoon horses, which had been caught before the meal in a ceremony that must be ancient among horseback people—one man, the boss, in the center with a reata catching horses with names like Snowball and Snuffy, and each rider choosing his from the string. The white called Snowball was a trifle skittish, crow-hopping a little before he settled down. Then they rode away to another sweep across the sagebrush desert, another branding that afternoon. And I would have liked to have been along as they drifted away to their work, riding unhurriedly into the distance, and into an old horseback turn of life in which you can find some pride.

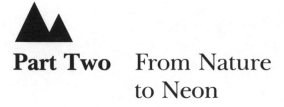

Part Two   From Nature
             to Neon

Denying the deep-rooting patterns of their culture, Americans became less anxious about work and more anxious about leisure. Certain that they must play, but unfamiliar with so much play and unsure about its benefits, Americans tended to exhaust themselves at leisure while seeking in it some of the personal fulfillment they had previously derived from their jobs. The result was the most unleisurely play imaginable, a sort of frantic leisure epitomized by casino gambling. . . .

Casino betting appealed to postwar society not only because it suited the new balance between work and leisure but also because it helped people develop a stronger sense of self. Finding individuality threatened by the rising economic culture of mass production, average Americans turned more and more to consumption of goods, services, and leisure time as a mode of personal expression.

John M. Findlay, *People of Chance*

The allure is most irresistible not to the young but the old. No one in Las Vegas will admit it—it is not the modern, glamorous notion—but Las Vegas is a resort for old people. In those last years, before the tissue deteriorates and the wires of the cerebral cortex hang in the skull like a clump of dried seaweed, they are seeking liberation.

Tom Wolfe, *The Kandy-Kolored Tangerine-Flake Streamline Baby*

Laughlin, Nevada, strings a half dozen casinos along the tame stream and is only a minute by boat from the Arizona shore. . . . Last night I slept in the hills overlooking the valley. Cottontails grazed around my head and hopped along the sides of my sleeping bag. All night the casino signs splashed color and form into the night sky and then at first light, lines of herons and ducks and geese slowly winged down the ribbon of river to the feeding grounds. In this big room of smoke, booze, and slots, sunrise and sunset count for nothing.

Charles Bowden, *Blue Desert*

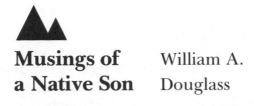

Musings of a Native Son

William A. Douglass

Times Past

My grandfather died in 1929, ten years before I was born. According to the headlined obituaries published on April 22 in the *Tonopah Daily Bonanza* and on April 23 in the *Tonopah Daily Times*, William James Douglass was one of the key founders of the town. He was born in Virginia City in 1867. His father was a mill operator from Vermont and his mother a pioneer in the mining camp of Aurora. Billy Douglass, as he was known, became an assayer in Candelaria in the 1890s. With the collapse of silver prices in 1893, he and some associates went prospecting for gold. They founded Douglass Camp in Esmeralda County, which enjoyed some initial successes. In 1900, when news of the Tonopah strike reached him, Billy immediately set out across the desert, becoming the thirteenth man to enter the fledgling camp. He secured a lease from Jim Butler, and throughout the leasing period of Tonopah's history (or until late 1901 when the Butler groups sold out to eastern interests), Billy Douglass ran the local assay office. He then became a principal owner and general manager of the Midway, West End, and Tonopah Montana mines. In partnership with H. C. Brougher, he founded the Tonopah Banking Corporation and served as its vice-president. He grubstaked Harry Stimler and William Marsh, discoverers of Goldfield, and was their partner in that district's Kendall, Sandstorm, May Queen, Nevada Boy, and Gold Banner mines. He was subsequently instrumental in development of the Tonopah Divide district and had interests in several Nevada and California mining camps. With Billy's passing the newspapers proclaimed the end of an era, the *Daily Times* even going so far as to publish a short list of the "Surviving Pioneers."

I have two mementos of the grandfather I never knew. I bear his name and I carry his gold pocket watch. The latter came to me along with a story that I cherish more than the remarkable timepiece itself. Its back is embossed with three figures—the intertwined initials WJD, a spider, and a wasp. Inside its cover there is a photograph of my grandmother, Kathleen McQuillan, herself a daughter of the Comstock, and my Uncle Bud, one of the first children born in Tonopah. Bud's real name was Belmont, which was my grandparents' way of honoring the community of Tonopah's discoverers and, not incidentally, Billy's business partners.

According to the story, the watch was a present from Philadelphia investors who, about 1907, sent their engineers to Nevada to look over potential properties. Billy Douglass had a reputation for grubstaking almost anyone in need, and in the process, he picked up interests in several hundred, mostly worthless, claims throughout the state. He was approached by the eastern engineers and provided them with maps and directions. About a month later, they returned from the desert to make him an offer. It seems that they were prepared to pay $100,000 for the group of claims called the Spider and the Wasp that he held in Wonder (between Fallon and Gabbs). According to Hugh A. Shamberger's recent book on that mining camp, the claims were indeed quite valuable and proved to be among Wonder's best. Billy said he wanted to think it over and would meet with them in the Tonopah Club that evening. There he opined that $100,000 was excessive but that he was willing to sell for $75,000! The deal was made and the buyers commissioned the watch in Switzerland as a token of their appreciation. Is the story true? Possibly.

I believe my grandfather's watch is an excellent example of both the wonderful quality and tenuous nature of Nevada history. It hearkens back to an era long since past but which in so many ways still dominates Nevada thought. It is rather axiomatic that we must learn from history in order to avoid its errors; however, for Nevadans this task is made more difficult because our heritage is as much a creation as a chronicle. Indeed, in at least a psychological sense, one might argue that our historical baseline derives from such works as *Roughing It* and the colorful vignettes from newspapers like the *Territorial Enterprise* and its subsequent mining camp emulators. The image that emerges depicts a world of self-reliant, independent entrepreneurs disposed to extraordinary risk-taking—whether raising livestock in one of the nation's most arid and hostile settings or scratching holes into bleak mountainsides in pursuit of elusive, unlimited wealth. Rather than

the product of pioneers seeking to sink roots permanently into virgin soil, the nineteenth-century Nevada settlement comes across as a
collectivity more than a community, a group of sojourners of questionable character hoping to make their fortune without breaking
too many rules before going elsewhere to spend it. Excepting a few
Mormon colonies and the servicing centers that emerged along the
transcontinental railway, most Nevada towns were as unstable as the
tumbleweeds blowing down Main Street, subject to abandonment and
dismantlement at the latest rumor that El Dorado exists and has just
been discovered somewhere "over yonder." That the state developed
permanent settlement was inevitable, yet viewed from the perspective
of nineteenth-century Nevada reality it seems epiphenomenal.

There is a sense in which Nevadans still invoke a spirit of "rugged
individualism" anchored in our past. Periodically, it is reaffirmed by
our best contemporary writers, as in Robert Laxalt's *Nevada* and his
National Geographic article "The Other Nevada" or James Hulse's *Forty
Years in the Wilderness.* Perhaps this is necessary catharsis for a people
who arguably share with Mississippi the dubious distinction of having
the worst national image (albeit for different reasons). Yet might we
not question whether this provides a viable charter and blueprint for
forging our place in the contemporary and future worlds? We were
both blessed and cursed by having Mark Twain, one of the consum-
mate writers (and notorious tale spinners) of world literature, among
our original interpreters. However, to my mind, Nevada's real challenge lies not in meriting his mastery but in transcending it.

Times Present

I attended Manogue High School when I was a boy growing up in the Reno area—not the present modern school next to the
university but the "Old Manogue" quartered in a made-over ranch
house situated along the Truckee River southeast of Sparks. Surrounded by miles of pasture, grazing livestock, fruit orchards and
fields of vegetables cultivated by Italian truck gardeners, the tiny
Catholic high school was truly out in the country. The rural atmosphere was not belied by an urban skyline hovering on the horizon—
at least not until the Mapes Hotel was constructed, prompting our
awestruck schoolboy imaginations to draw fanciful comparisons with

the Empire State Building. Reno and Sparks remained separate communities, linked by old Highway 40, rather than arbitrary divisions on the map of a continuous metropolitan area.

As I reflect back on my high school days, I realize now that I did not so much attend class at the Old Manogue as in the surrounding countryside. A true believer in the anti-intellectualism characteristic of my classmates (pervasive at rival Reno and Sparks high schools as well), I found little of interest within the confines of the curriculum. However, I soon discovered the wildlife inhabiting the Truckee River, the farmland sloughs, and the marshes of the nearby Nevada Game Farm. My interest and energy became focused upon the attractions of this magical world and its denizens.

The beginning of the school term meant fur prospecting within walking distance of the high school, as I staked out beaver colonies and muskrat slides and searched for signs of the elusive mink. Late autumn and early winter were devoted to running a trap line that ended at Vista. In the lowering dusk my partner and I would hitchhike back to Reno, entering the vehicles of our unsuspecting benefactors with a wet gunnysack filled with our gear and catch (few dared to ask). In springtime we pursued lizards and snakes, which we marketed by mail to biological supply houses and through our own auspicious sounding "Sierra Reptile Farm."

I gained my literacy during my Manogue years, but not through attentiveness to my teachers. Rather, I became an avid reader of works like Raymond Ditmars's *Reptiles of the World,* trapping and fur farming manuals, and the magazine *Fur-Fish-Game* (to which I contributed my first article—a description of trapping experiences in the Reno area).

Little remains of the world of Old Manogue. The Reno Cannon International Airport and a golf course now occupy the drained marshes of the Nevada Game Farm. A young boy's imagination could scarcely be fired by the asphalt and industrial parks that now cover most of the fields and sloughs that were once my kingdom.

While we were largely unaware of it at the time, the forces that were to convert Nevada into its present reality had already been unleashed. Between 1940 and 1950 the state's population had increased nearly 50 percent, or from 110,000 to 160,000 residents.[1] While northern Nevada experienced some of the growth (Reno gained a third of its 1950 population during the decade), the spectacular development was in Clark County. During the 1950s Washoe County was eclipsed demographically by the upstart to the south; however, for northern Nevadans there was still a qualitative difference between the two. Though only a third of Nevada's population resided in the Reno-Sparks-Carson area, our claim to political and, particularly, intellectual leadership remained unchallenged. Reno, with is 32,000 residents, was the largest city in the state and housed its only university. Carson was the seat of state government. Therefore, we *were* Nevada regardless of what some southern Nevada arrivistes might think. To the extent that we looked elsewhere for spiritual sustenance it was to northern California and "the City," and certainly not to our neighbors in the south with their obvious ties to southern California and "tinsel town." Our smugness might have allowed us alternately to patronize and to ignore the "cow counties" and southerners but, in retrospect, I believe that it was at our peril. For it precluded us from addressing meaningfully Nevada's real twentieth-century challenge—namely, growth and its prerogatives.

In the north, as the growth issue became more and more blatant, we turned against ourselves. Where once there was a degree of harmony and community spirit, we divided over such issues as the routing of Interstate 80 and the siting of the convention center and airport. The battles lasted for years and left a legacy of acrimony and bitterness. Suburbanization of commerce, as retail services moved to the shopping centers to be replaced in the downtown area by casino expansion, created new divisions between periphery and core, "residents" and "tourists." In short, public debate in northern Nevada increasingly acquired schizophrenic overtones as we split into "growth" and "no-growth" factions. There was also an element of illogicality and hypocrisy as we became increasingly dependent on the very tourist dollar that we damned and blamed for our environmental problems.

Another source of ambiguity in the public debate was the changing nature of the collective pronoun. With each new census, it became increasingly obvious that "we" referred to a shifting reality. Despite the fumbling attempts to rein in growth, the population of Washoe County almost quadrupled in the three decades between 1950 and 1980 (from 50,000 to 193,000 inhabitants).

Ambivalence best describes my own feelings about the process. I was saddened to watch my old boyhood haunts disappear pell-mell into the irresistible and insatiable maw of development. At the same time, I was pleased to witness the flowering of the arts made possible only by increased population—creation of the Nevada Opera, the Nevada Repertory Theater, the Nevada Festival Ballet, the Reno Philharmonic, the Sierra Art Museum, and the more than forty other arts organizations that now provide Reno with a variegated cultural landscape. This is in stark contrast with my youth when culture in Reno meant a ticket to the Community Concert Series, to the Reno Little Theater, and to San Francisco. I also cannot ignore the irony when I am exhorted by people who moved to northern Nevada, and thereby changed irreversibly "my" Reno, to make common cause with them against potential newcomers in defense of "our" way of life. How would they have viewed a similar campaign back in the 1950s, when it really might have been possible to opt for a future modeled after Monterey or Ashland? There are disturbing implications for such a process carried to its logical conclusion, for if I have the right to exclude people from Reno, I thereby confer upon someone else the right to exclude me from San Francisco or any other place that I might choose to live.

Meanwhile, the contrast between northern and southern Nevada could not be greater. The combination of disdain and myopia with which we northerners continue to view southerners allows us the delusion that we are still contenders in a contest over the state's economic and political hegemony. For the past four decades northern Nevadans have managed to consistently underestimate the south. For us it seemed axiomatic that the bleak and arid setting of Las Vegas would itself set natural limits upon its capacity for expansion. Who in their right mind would choose to settle permanently in the hottest corner of the continent? Each new Las Vegas project was greeted in the north with incredulity; each cyclical downturn in the southern Nevada economy was treated as a harbinger of imminent collapse. Yet Las Vegas, imbued with a "can do" spirit, not only survived but triumphed beyond the wildest dreams of its most sanguine boosters. In the process Clark County acquired nearly 60 percent of the state's population, or approximately two and a half times that of Washoe County.

Consequently, it is no coincidence that today the governor, lieutenant governor, and both of Nevada's U.S. senators are from Clark County. The reapportionment after the 1990 census will further consolidate southern Nevada's political base. In short, the south will enjoy an absolute majority in every statewide political arena. Consequently, Clark County is in a position to dictate Nevada's future social, economic, educational, and political agendas. Indeed, within a democracy is this not as it should be?

At the same time there is a challenge implicit in the new contemporary reality, particularly for northern Nevadans. One questions whether we can afford any longer the luxury of Las Vegas-bashing. I believe that to date southern Nevadans have displayed remarkable restraint in their dealings with the rest of the state. They have yet to flex their political muscle in arbitrary or punitive fashion. There may yet be time to bridge the hundreds of miles, and the even wider conceptual gulf, between the north and the south. One can only conclude that ultimately northern Nevadans have a greater stake in doing so than do our southern Nevada fellow citizens.

Times Future

Mother had a sense of the historic and momentous. When the all but moribund V&T Railroad was about to expire, she took my brother John and me out of school in order to ride the train to Carson City. As the virtually empty car swayed precariously, she lectured two mildly hyper boys, energized by the thrill of sanctioned hooky, on the importance of remembering what struck us as a simple outing.

It was in this same spirit that she awakened us about 4:00 A.M. one brisk autumn morning and bundled us into the car. We drove out of town towards Washoe Valley to escape the lights of the city and parked on a rise facing to the south. Mother made small talk trying to prevent her less than enthusiastic audience from lapsing into slumber. As she voiced her concerns about possible cancellation, the entire horizon exploded in a cold, white flash that lingered momentarily like a fleeting smile on the lips of an oracle and then was gone.

This atomic dawn, telegraphed to us instantaneously from hundreds of miles to the south, left us sobered and speechless. We drove back to Reno through the comforting cloak of restored darkness and stopped for breakfast at an all-night diner. I cannot recall Mother's exact words, but I remember their spirit. Subsequently, I witnessed other detonations from the flanks of Mount Oddie while visiting my cousins in Tonopah. From there we could see the cloud and then feel the tremor. Yet the mood was frivolous and festive as we watched a show that seemingly was staged by the federal government for our benefit in order to countermand the boredom of everyday small-town life. That morning in the diner, however, Mother told us that we had seen the future. It was clear from her demeanor that she was far from pleased.

Father was a gambler in both the figurative and the literal senses of the term. During my youth he was part-owner of a coin-operated device distributorship. Its place of business was on East Second Street, or a short walk from St. Thomas Aquinas grammer school where for a portion of each day I was forced to listen to Dominican nuns naively lecture the *cognoscenti* on the sorrows of purgatory. Once released from daily confinement, however, I could dash down the street to the Nevada Novelty Company and its wonders. There were pinball machines that passed through the premises for repairs before going out "on location" to some bar, restaurant, or bowling alley. If luck was with you, and you managed to be inconspicuous enough not to annoy the adults, you could spend the entire afternoon in an orgy of free games. Of equal interest were the jukeboxes, or rather the used 45 RPM phonograph records that they disgorged. My record collection was never current but it was complete.

The mainstay of the business, of course, was the slot machines. I recall being mystified at the attraction to adults of a device that provided neither interesting sights nor sounds, but I was under no delusion regarding its importance in the grand scheme of things. Indeed, from time to time Father would take me on one of his regular trips to rural Nevada to service his "slot route." We would visit such metropolises as Fallon and Hawthorne, linked by asphalt ribbons, before bouncing over the dirt roads that ended in places like Gabbs and Flanigan. It was there in ramshackle bars or general stores that the Nevada Novelty Company had its three or four slot machines. Usually, at least one would be "out of order" and turned to the wall, awaiting Father's less than polished mechanical skills. As likely as not, it was destined to be our companion in the back of the pickup truck on the trip to the slot-machine hospital in Reno. We would then roll and count the money. With our hand-operated coin wrapper, it took an hour to process even the meager proceeds generated by most locations. When all was ready, the proprietor was first reimbursed for any jackpots paid, after which the remainder was credited to county, state, and federal license fees. Once these expenses were met, the profits were divided fifty-fifty with the proprietor.

As we traveled along the desert tracks, we never discussed his business. It was a time when there were a few small casinos in the north, no Las Vegas strip, Jackpot, or Laughlin. Father was not prone to philosophize. While we counted nickels in back rooms in remote corners of the Nevada desert, it never occurred to him to tell me that I was glimpsing the future, although, of course, I was.

A nation's decision to explode its bombs in Nevada, on the one hand, and counting slot machine proceeds in the heart of the state's mining and ranching districts, on the other, encapsulate for me our dilemma as we contemplate the future. That is, for many Nevadans there is a feeling that we are somehow in the clutches of arbitrary outside forces—the federal government and gamblers, each sinister in its own fashion.

Germane to this view is the notion that the authentic Nevada lies somewhere east of Sparks and north of Las Vegas, is rural in character, and resulted when those rugged individualists referred to earlier gained a mining and ranching toehold in a hostile, frontier environment. As a boy I was taught that Nevada was the least populated of the forty-eight states, yet sixth largest in size. In 1940 our 110,000 inhabitants divided niftily into our 110,000 square miles, mathematics which seemed to give each Nevadan a privileged place on the planet, at least as measured in terms of elbow room. While the numbers have changed, the mind-set has not. Psychologically, the state's "wide open spaces" still constitute for Nevadans a redoubtable refuge in which to escape the crassness of twentieth-century materialism and modernity. More germane to the state's present and future reality, however, is another numerical coincidence. I refer to the fact that if 85 percent of our land, including most of the authentic Nevada, is under federal ownership, as of 1980 85 percent of our population resides in urban centers, largely outside the federal preserve. In terms of percentages, then, and despite our rural imagery, Nevada is the fourth most urbanized state in the nation!

I once lived for a year in Australia and was struck by the similarities between Aussies and Nevadans in this regard. Although a nation of coastal dwellers, of which the overwhelming majority live in five cities, the Australians' national images turn on kangaroos, koala bears, and the Outback. Few Sydney-siders have ever visited the Outback, or plan to, yet concur in the notion that somehow Australia's essence lingers there. As of 1980 approximately 650,000 of Nevada's 800,000 residents lived in the greater Reno and Las Vegas metropolitan areas.

As those of us who do frequent Nevada's interior in near solitude can attest, few Renoites or Las Vegans have ever experienced the Black Rock Desert, the Jarbidge country, or Monitor Valley.

Insofar as our rural imagery provides us with psychological strength and satisfaction, it is benign or even positive. However, when it is allowed to assume a critical role in debates over our future, it becomes a legitimate cause for concern. Stripped of their mythic properties, Nevada's ranching and mining traditions seldom proved reliable foundations for the state's economy. In strict ecological terms Nevada has much more in common with Afghanistan than with Iowa and, consequently, its agriculture can be viewed as only marginal at best. Lack of moisture and a short growing season alone set insurmountable limits upon it. This can be contrasted with our mining successes. Indeed, Nevada is one of the most mineral-rich corners of the globe, and individual discoveries such as the Comstock in the mid-nineteenth century, Tonopah–Goldfield at the turn of the century and, more recently, the "invisible" gold operations in places like Carlin provide the state with some of the most spectacular mining booms in the annals of human history. At the same time mining strikes are predicated upon a non-renewable resource and are, therefore, intrinsically ephemeral.

It is thought provoking to consider the demographics of the state when the economy was based almost exclusively upon ranching and mining. In 1880, or during the afterglow of the Comstock–Austin–Eureka mining discoveries and the homesteading that followed the Civil War, our population reached 62,000 persons. Twenty years later, with the mining industry in a deep depression and agriculture in the doldrums, it had declined by a third to 42,000, and the possibility of stripping Nevada of statehood was under serious consideration by the U.S. Congress. The Tonopah–Goldfield discoveries and their spin-offs essentially saved the day by doubling the state's population to 82,000 by 1910; however, the inevitable playing out of the mines and the vicissitudes of international markets for agricultural and mineral products conspired to reduce our population to 77,000 by the 1920 census.

The essential point is that Nevada's "traditional" economy was incapable of supporting a population of 100,000 inhabitants in the best of times and proved particularly vulnerable to periodic crisis. In its modern guises, it is even less capable of providing a livelihood to our citizenry. By this I mean that nineteenth-century Nevada agriculture and mining were labor intensive compared to their modern counterparts.

Last century small family ranches dotted the landscape, multitudes of hard-rock miners worked the diggings, and hundreds of prospectors roamed the desert. Today's ranch incorporates three or four of yesterday's abandoned homesteads, gigantic mining operations employ a few men versed in running state-of-the-art equipment, and a handful of geologists use satellite photos to pinpoint future prospects. Nor, for the most part, are these resources vested in the hands of native rugged individualists. Rather, today's ranch is likely to be owned by a movie star or a physician seeking a tax shelter, and the mines are controlled by multinational corporations.

It is therefore noteworthy that by 1980 rural Nevada's population (defined as everybody outside Washoe and Clark counties) approximates 150,000 persons, or almost twice that of the entire state during the palmier days of ranching and mining. Here, in fact, we confront the real Achilles' heel of the rugged individualist myth, since the bulk of rural Nevadans are employees of either the tourist and gaming industries or the government. Indeed, eliminate the jobs provided by the casinos and motels in Winnemucca, Jackpot, Elko, Wells, Wendover, and Ely; abolish those within the federal, state, and county bureaucracies; and dismiss the civilian employees of Nellis Air Force Base, the Fallon Naval Station, the Hawthorne Munitions Depot, and the Atomic Test Site, as well as those of the civilian defense contractors, and rural Nevada would become a vast economic wasteland. Whimsical "Sagebrush Rebellions" notwithstanding, rural Nevada is one of the most heavily subsidized and economically dependent regions of the nation.

We need only remember the anguished protests of the residents of Austin faced with the transfer of the Lander County seat to Battle Mountain and closure of the local offices of the U.S. National Forest Service, or the decision by Nye County officials to send a lobbyist to Washington, D.C., to argue *for* the national nuclear waste dump (thanks to urban Nevada they got Bullfrog County instead). Conversely, it is a bit ludicrous when Nevada ranchers ask to "get government off our backs." This appeal is by now a litany that is repeated with the same monotony of Tibetan monks spinning their prayer wheels. While it, too, invokes rugged individualism, it ignores the fact that through agricultural price supports and range use fees that are considerably lower than rates on similar private land, the average Nevada rancher is more heavily subsidized than a floor full of welfare mothers in a Detroit housing project.

Such, then, is the past and present reality of the authentic Nevada. By any stretch of the imagination can it inform our future, except by way of a warning? In short, can the approximately one million Nevadans who now call the state home find much that is relevant in this tradition, other than to esteem it for its historical quaintness?

This brings me to the question of Nevada's tourist and gaming economy, frantically promoted in the south while at best tolerated in the north. Many Nevadans view gambling as artificial, a hybrid phenomenon superimposed upon the state by outside interests ranging from the Mafia to Holiday Inns. There is a sense in which this is true, since it can in no way be contended that gaming's spectacular development is a homegrown product. On the other hand, I would argue that the concept is homegrown, and that it is but one manifestation of a broader survival strategy that was honed, beginning about the turn of this century, on the perception that ranching and mining were both fickle paramours. After riding the boom-to-bust roller coaster, which resulted in the demographic fluctuations considered earlier, Nevadans began to posture their state to take advantage of the laws of neighboring ones.

We were the first to legalize prizefighting, and our history as a divorce haven is legendary. When other states liberalized their divorce laws, we invented the quickie marriage, thereby substituting today's wedding chapels for the divorcée dude ranches of my youth. Legalized prostitution and gambling provided additional attractions to potential visitors. A more modern manifestation of the same mentality is the warehouses that banished my muskrats and that offer American industry a legal means of circumventing inventory taxes in California, Oregon, and Washington. Our most recent and possibly crowning achievement in shifting our civic responsibilities to others was the tax reform, which essentially insulated us from most of the onus of property tax (we dare not even brook the subject of a state income tax except, as happened in the last election, to banish the possibility through referendum). Thus, we have made our state coffers almost totally reliant upon the tourist trade (through the gaming and sales taxes) and federal rebates. As a consequence, our state government finds it difficult to set any kind of social or educational agenda that requires long-term planning. Rather, state officials are forced to engage in legerdemain with the ledgers, since all budgetary projections remain asterisked, subject to future results in casino counting rooms and merchants' cash registers.

One response to our essential ambivalence regarding near total dependency upon a single industry and its ancillary effects is to heed the clarion call of "economic diversification." While a worthwhile objective, it is fair to question our prospects and, consequently, the role that such aspirations ought to play in planning for the future. Realistically, our new commitment places us squarely in the pack with the forty-nine other states aspiring to host the next Silicon Valley. Without abandoning such initiatives, is it wise to assume in some vague sense that they really will reduce our dependency upon tourism and gaming? At the same time, it may even be relevant to ask whether they should.

By this I mean that, viewed strictly in economic terms, tourism and gaming have provided Nevada with its one unequivocal success story. The state is sometimes referred to as the "Gaming Mecca of the World." Despite the pretentiousness of the statement, it is scarcely hyperbolic since it reflects a certain reality. However, this very fact is a source of considerable ambivalence for some Nevadans.

This is particularly true of northerners who have somehow never quite lived down their shame over the conclusions of the Kefauver Report, which underscored the underworld influence in the state. Each new *Green Felt Jungle,* sensational feature article, or film depicting Nevada in such stereotypic terms only serves to feed the private self-loathing that results from dependence upon a disreputable activity. There are, of course, available defense mechanisms. It is common in the north to draw a distinction between "clean" northern casino operations and "hood"-operated southern ones, an exercise which might have had a certain validity at one time but has now been largely undermined by the progressively corporate nature of casino ownership at both ends of the state. Another ploy is for those who are not involved directly in the industry to maintain the illusion that they are not benefited, and thereby tainted, by it. Hence, some Nevada store clerks, physicians, and professors like to believe that they are insulated from gaming and could continue to pursue their careers here were the industry to simply disappear. Meanwhile, we have produced a cadre of critics, ranging from Cassandras to moralists, who decry the evils of gambling and the precariousness of a society built upon it. While this provides guidance for our self-flagellation and affords catharsis to the guilt-ridden, it also obfuscates many of the real issues as we chart our course.

To my mind, it is essential that we become at least resigned, indeed reconciled, to the future importance of tourism and gambling in the state's economy and image. No one would argue that gambling is a particularly noble enterprise, but neither is it the most ignoble human activity. The salient point is that it appeals to human nature and is therefore a fact of life. Having stated this, however, I would hasten to add that those who believe that Nevada gambling is merely a response to human greed are engaged in gross oversimplification. In such a view, unscrupulous gamblers load the dice against unsuspecting or reckless players blinded by avarice. This is at best a patronizing depiction of the millions of tourists who visit Nevada annually. Indeed, its plausibility is undermined by their sheer numbers. It is also akin to invoking sloth to explain the behavior of the same individuals should they choose to simply lie about on a beach instead.

In reality, Nevada gaming is no longer just about gambling. By this I mean that our resorts now have much more in common with Disneyland, Cannes, Maui, and Acapulco than they do with parlor poker or back-alley dice games. They offer an escape from the mundane by means of what Umberto Eco recently called *Travels in Hyperreality*. It is the Caesar's Palace that somehow eclipses rather than emulates the glories of Ancient Rome—the trip on the Mississippi riverboat without the mosquitoes.

There is a sense in which we have become so accustomed to our internal debate and self-doubts about the worth of the gambling industry that we have ignored its changing image. There was once a time in which virtually all the national press regarding Nevada gaming was negative. Actually, it ranged from the voyeuristic to the denigratory. We were essentially regarded as a gambling den and bordello, an aberration within national life. Of late, however, there has been growing recognition that Nevada gambling is actually part of a broader American tradition and that, in terms of architecture and design, it is a path breaker and pacesetter within the world's recreational industry.[2]

Finally, it should be noted that Nevada gaming is no longer unique and, hence, a virtually unchallenged monopoly. There was a time when we were the sole national renegade, at least with respect to casino gambling. This is no longer the case. Legalization of casinos in New Jersey is but the tip of an iceberg. Below the waterline several other states are considering a similar move, and most now have wagering in one form or another. The reality, then, is that Nevada gambling remains preeminent but far from unchallenged. It operates in a national and, increasingly, global market. While we draw some of our

visitors from abroad, it is also true that casino gambling has prolife-
rated in the majority of countries on every inhabited continent. In a
real sense, we presently compete not just with Atlantic City but with
Sun City, not to mention Macao, Monte Carlo, and Montevideo.

The very magnitude of our success, with the attendant per capita
income and life-style to which we have become accustomed, indeed
makes us vulnerable. One need only note the shiver that runs through
the body politic at the mention of legalized casino gambling in our
prime California market. Such a prospect is by far a greater problem
for the state than for Nevada's casinos. The New Jersey experience
has demonstrated clearly that expertise within the industry is at a pre-
mium. Just as much of the ownership and management of Atlantic
City casinos originated in Nevada, should California legalize gaming,
it might even prove to be an opportunity for many Nevada gamblers—
the same cannot be said of our state. If the casino business transcends
Nevada's boundaries and is no longer captive to our enabling legislation, as a state we have entered upon a new era of dependency upon
it, at least until such time as we develop a viable alternative. This dependency is increasingly like that of Youngstown upon the steel industry. Steel plants can be relocated, Youngstown cannot. Consequently, we might question the utility of incessant hand wringing over
what may be our ineluctable economic destiny.

Mirrors and Masks

Despite the critical tone in much of this essay, it is not my
purpose to be peevish or pontifical. Indeed, I declare unabashedly
that I love Nevada. In addition to being a native son, I am a returned
native, since I now reside here by choice after having lived in many
other parts of America and the world. In criticizing that which is so
much a part of me, I feel like the proud parent who seeks to appreciate the virtues without being blinded to the faults of his beautiful, yet
troublesome child.

There is a sense in which the analogy is particularly appropriate,
since Nevada may be regarded as an adolescent. By this I mean that
our recent growth is like that of the teenager whose physical maturity
suddenly begins to far outstrip his emotional development. As a state
our appearance has assumed adult form, yet we continue to have private doubts and fears regarding our future career. Given the fact that

we have increased our population tenfold in less than half a century, it is scarcely surprising that we suffer at this point in our history from what might be likened to raging hormonal imbalance.

The only "cure" for adolescent woes is the progressive development of a self-concept and hence self-confidence. In successfully forging an adult *persona,* the individual contemplates his childhood, largely in order to become reconciled with its passing, and assesses his present circumstances, in order to be realistic about his prospects. In this regard, both the past and present become the mirrors in which he learns about himself in order to shed the masks of youth in favor of assuming an adult role. Collectively, we Nevadans face a similar challenge. It is the purpose of this essay to suggest that it is only possible to transcend our adolescence if we are willing to remove our masks *before* gazing into our mirrors.

NOTES

1. All the population figures cited in this essay were adapted by rounding off the statistics provided in *Population Abstract of the United States, Volume One, Tables,* ed. John L. Androit (McLean, Virginia: Androit Associates, 1983), 502–5.

2. Cf. John M. Findlay, *People of Chance: Gambling in American Society from Jamestown to Las Vegas* (New York: Oxford University Press, 1986) and Robert Venturi, Denise Scott Brown, and Steven Izenour, *Learning From Las Vegas* (Cambridge: The MIT Press, 1972).

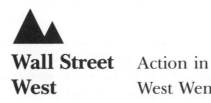

Wall Street West

Action in West Wendover

Charles R. Greenhaw

If you've made the Nevada Crossing you've seen the place. The image you have is a part of the westering consciousness: the forlorn Bonneville Salt Flats broken near Wendover by grassless knobs of hills lifting on heat waves; the onset of the interminable basins and ranges of the Nevada Crossing with Pilot Peak, the signal mountain that watered and guided the gold-frenzied forty-niners; and improbable Wendover itself, resembling a beached aircraft carrier at the edge of the salt desert. Wendover is wider and longer than in the Burma Shave era of westering. Gambling, the industry of Nevada borders, has lately quadrupled with the population growth in the Salt Lake Valley, and West Wendover, Nevada, has gained the strength of an adolescent. But like most things that change with gambling, the differences are really only of degree. For Wendover does not thrive on abundant resources or fresh ideas, but on the continual expectation of the quick buck and the passion for being free and being rich at the same time.

On Interstate 80 behind you on most any Friday night is a chain of cars linked by headlights back to Salt Lake City, 120 miles east. Most are headed for the brilliant promises of West Wendover, the place where the superlatives are thought to come true. No state marker announces Nevada on old Highway 40 at West Wendover. Everyone knows that Nevada begins and ends with a casino. The State Line and Silver Smith, the biggest of five casinos, hug the Utah line and slice the community in two. The small-town main street of motels and gas stations abruptly becomes a street of casinos and hotels and the Western Man, a colossal metal statue demarking "the place where the West begins." With Nevada begins the land of cybernetic revels, of hotels without lobbies and with thickets of slot machines and blackjack tables.

West Wendover has become the commoner's Monte Carlo. It has begun to challenge older, Mormon Wendover (Utah) for dominance.

The State Line, the landmark casino, seems to be constantly under-going remodeling and expansion. Its glassed-in skyway, passing over old Highway 40, connects with the brassy Silver Smith. West Wendover, a mere lean-to settlement of two hundred people a few years ago, has factory-new apartments, a park with tennis courts, a shopping center, and a new addition of fashionable homes. On the incline west of town a golf course—a pure oasis enclosed by the dun-drab rocks—is being built to lure more tourists. Old-timers speak of the millennium arrived. Newcomers, who may not know the desert's limits and moods, talk of a full-fledged city of twenty-five thousand in a decade—a minuscule Las Vegas of the north.

Yet it is hard to think of West Wendover as a community. It has many of the attributes memorialized by Americans—softball, bowling leagues, Scouts. Some churches are trying to establish services in a trailer village. West Wendover has the true-hearted neighbors whose sheer generosity and decency are the hallmarks of old-fashioned America, but the bedrock of West Wendover is not that upon which Main Street was built. You will not find many revered monuments or family albums dotting the community. To the world at large, West Wendover is about perpetual action and gambling and therefore about consumption and greed; it is about the illusion of pleasure, which in the eyes of Main Street must be practiced in secret or enjoyed only after great pain. As for the unseen inner world of Wendover, the town has all the usual community problems and then some: unpredictability, transiency, excessive mental depression, alcoholism, vagrancy, child abuse, and neglect. And its problems are magnified by the two Wendovers and their love-hate relationship.

Many of the newly arrived think of West Wendover as a new frontier and regard themselves as prototypical American pioneers following the primal command to build a new kingdom based on self-reliance and free enterprise. Skilled casino workers, weary of Atlantic City or Las Vegas or Reno, speak of the gentle manners of Utah gamblers and the virtues of small-town living. Even if their jobs are dull and repetitive, the poor and the unskilled celebrate the new life of intense living and intensive difference. Brown-complexioned illegals, speaking Mexican, polish the brass, make the beds, and bus the tables. Most of West Wendover's workers are refugees driven here by depression in substantial industry elsewhere. For poor youth, life in Wendover has more promise than drudgery on the declining farm, in the depressed oil fields, or the wasteland copper mine country. And for the illegals, West Wendover, even with the daily threat of an Immigration sweep, offers more economic reward in a week than Zacatecas does in a year.

The Wendover area has had its moments in the limelight. In World War II, Wendover Air Force Base was a training station for bomber crews and notably the airmen who dropped the atomic bombs on Japan. Some old-timers remember an age when twenty-five thousand airmen trained at Wendover. The Hiroshima bomb, which changed the world forever, was loaded onto the *Enola Gay* at Wendover. History of a popular kind has been made at nearby Bonneville Speedway, where numerous world land-speed records have been set. North of the speedway the disorganized Donner–Reed party, crossing the Salt Flats in 1846, had the first of their streak of heartbreaks when the soggy salt claimed some of their wagons and cattle. But these are mere curiosities of history, and little remarked upon, for there's no profit in it.

West Wendover is both a real place and, to use Herbert Gold's term, a purgatory of hanging loose. It is Salt Lake City and Circus Circus, Provo and Disneyland, Boise and Wall Street. It is a feature of our landscape and a zone of our character. Its symbolic meaning is much more complex than the dice and the slot machine or even the Big Bad Wolf playing with someone else's bricks and mortar. West Wendover is no mere variation of Main Street; it isn't a thoroughfare lined with the entertainment equivalent of factories and shops populated by people making and selling and building things. It is something else. It is the idea that life's losers should somehow improve the day by indirect taxes. Gambling is, after all, efficient taxation, and with it life comes down to a matter of discrete transactions. West Wendover is the symbol also of the now-rampant American notion that the quick buck—made on an inside deal on Wall Street or an inside straight in poker—is the ultimate and supreme measure of value and commercial truth.

Winter or summer, daytime or nighttime, it's all the same to West Wendover, which lives inside, collecting and dispensing money, looking for tourists and cheaters, and living strictly for the moment. The place is a study in contrasts between what we like to think we are and what we really are. The giant Western Man welcoming you to Nevada is a symbol combining John Wayne, the Marlboro Man, and perhaps a bit of Claude Dallas, too. He is the individual, rugged beyond compare, alone at the border of the West and the future. He is "I-can-do-it" self-sufficiency, the last hope of the world, the American victory over nature, regulation, and the desert. He is the changeless mythological boss-deity luring Americans ever westward. "The fast-growing states," John Naisbitt has observed, "share one similar characteristic: a romantic flashback to the days of the Old West. Americans are migrating westward toward the land of opportunity . . . where entrepreneurship is prized."

Yet the Western Man, the Adam of westering, does not preside over innocence, simpler times, or the free-roaming individualism of the myth. The casino world he guides you to with his swinging arm is not that of nature, but that of the Last-Chance Saloon, with its innate, tawdry flair. Here the South Dakota tourist, the Mormon experimenter, and the California traveler can touch the atmosphere of J. R. Ewing, where there's the hint of forbidden pleasures. But the seductive admixture of twinkling bars, red carpets, brass rails, and chandeliers makes it all okay. Inside the casino it is human against machine, and the bandit is a computerized slot. Nothing exists in the casino that is not an efficient utility of transacting and collecting money. Here exploiter and exploited become one.

A case could be made that the gambling halls once had a certain respect for history. Gambling had real people connected with it, and even if they weren't always entirely admirable, they were at least more open to appeal, if not a handshake, than are names like Peppermill, Holiday Inn, or Bally's. Before the gaming control regulators came on in force, gambling had some unspoken rules. A tragedy of losses at the tables would be no less a tragedy, but the loser could get the condolences of a square meal and a bus ticket back to Salt Lake.

Just a few years ago West Wendover was closer to our vision of 1900 than to our understanding of 1987, when a casino seems a high-tech purgatory, an arcade inspired by Hieronymus Bosch and Joe Orton. The casino was smaller, the lemon on the slot was a definite symbol, and not every operation in the house had to pay its own way. A certain friendliness (now studied in seminars of the hospitality industry) impressed the gamblers and distracted them from the casino counting cage, where the big winnings they envisioned were already being wrapped up.

Just a decade ago the microprocessor was still in the future and gambling machines were crude by the standards of the 1980s. The one-armed bandit of 1970, now a prized antique, meted out a pace more human in scale. Today, when the machines talk, grind out enthusiastic electronic music, and perform "instant art," the ways of

1970 seem archaic by generations. The slots of the primitive era were archaic compared to today's machines with their ability to dictate time and habits. In "the good old days" the machines did not seem entirely directed to taking everything.

But were they good? Was greed ever different, the urge to quick riches any less a driving force? I think not. Gambling is ever-changing, and yet it is always as old as it will be new. No amount of high-tech computing makes it any less an exercise of our base instincts, any more a ground of fresh ideas.

West Wendover incarnates action and changes that may be good and may be bad, but they represent central American passions. At the moment, gambling is much in favor because it is seen as a kind of tax shelter in which the poor and stupid help the clearheaded avoid the evils of government. In a similar vein, it is not a sin for the TV evangelists to exploit the poor and stupid because the money they engender betokens the puritan sense of God's nearness, and divine retribution strikes in nanoseconds. It is the perfect *deus ex machina*. West Wendover incarnates an extraordinary presence in the American soul. It is one of the most readily identifiable features of our self-understanding and the world's perception of us.

For eons, zealots and evangelists have predicted the end of the world and gained followers; historians, since Gibbon, like to find a moral thread in the decline and fall of empires. At a time when the nation is so obsessed with pursuit of money, many want gambling revenues and taxes to save their states. James Hulse, a native-born Nevada historian, would save them the trouble and the corruption. In his recently published memoir-like criticism of his home state, *Forty Years in the Wilderness*, he has written: "Nevada often seems to be a sick society, having got sicker as it got richer, and more disposed to neglect the humane values as it became more preoccupied with the millions and billions that it has taken in from the tourist." Hulse is hardly unique, even if he is on a different wavelength than the contemporary American mind. Hulse could have condensed his argument to the doomsday prophetics of Chancellor Kent, who, in 1836, may have better represented the more historically American moral mind. Kent, sure that American society was totally depraved, denounced it like a preacher of social jeremiads. Kent condemned the "rapidly increasing appetite for wealth . . . the vehement spirit of speculation, and the selfish emulation which it creates; the contempt for slow and moderate gains, the ardent thirst for pleasure and amusement; the diminishing reverence for the wisdom of the past." Hulse, wishing to decree more moral fiber, would call in the federal government to control Nevada's addiction to money. He would search out the symbols of self-sufficiency—the rancher of the Nevada outback, the Western Man—to return to Nevada sanity.

But aren't such keenings of despair merely futile oratories for the unrecoverable? Isn't the cure worse than the disease? Hasn't gambling become just a matter of the pragmatically useful? West Wendover in 1987 is geographically a mere blip on the landscape, but it is a major spot in the allegory of the American mind. The changes we regret are that things got bigger, the gold no closer to our grasp, the boss-deity less approachable, the equipment more able to require our conformity. Unlike humans, the computerized slots do not err. They are so mocking, so joyous in patience before human impatience, so perfect beside the imperfect. And the same trickster who directed humanity right from the beginning still commands through alternating rhythms of strife and love. It is so very difficult for people who have never touched the bauble not to go for the gold. People haven't changed much since they started trying to understand themselves. They have concocted an assortment of ephemeral self-help antidotes for their anguish, and they have often wept over their own inerrant machines. And our most adored machine—the human body—can nowadays appear younger for a while as it grows older. Nobody wants to halt progress on that matter. So it is with West Wendover and computerized gambling.

The microprocessor has increased the variety of combinations and capacity of gambling games to heights unimagined just a decade ago. The nickel slot machine is still there, but who can resist its multiple system for more nickels to cover all the bases before the action begins? So variety and volume have both multiplied. The marriage between the casino and the computer is one of the best of weddings. The silicon chip has abolished the need for the skills of adding, subtracting, and dividing in the casino and the need for players to make any mental effort at all. The more sophisticated the computer the fewer employees and the less real money needed. The computerized slot merely reduces everything, even randomness and fortune, to numbers. It speeds up the objectives and activities as it ever widens its sphere. Computer slots in bars, multiplier slots, poker slots, lottery slots, million-dollar pots . . . and there's talk of the billion-dollar jackpot. In the days of the mechanical slot, with its lemons and cherries and Bell Fruit

Gum bars, there seemed to be more to the game than mostly lose, rarely win. There was at least the thought that the machine had limits, that it could take only so much without bursting. It's different now. The computer is more in control than we thought, despite all the pro- testations to the contrary. There seems to be no limit to its taking and our spending.

The vibrancy of West Wendover is its wonder. Even with its naked, difficult terrain, it sparkles in the new commerce while all around is in decline and decay. The great copper mines of Magna, Utah, and Ely, Nevada, have gone silent; copper now comes from abroad. The great ranches are sad spectacles under the clouds of foreclosure. The Utah, Wyoming, and eastern Nevada oil fields sit near idleness. But West Wendover is an adolescent gaining strength.

I have come to depend on Wendover being there on the edge of the salt-bleak desert. Wendover is the midpoint of my trips from interior Nevada to Salt Lake City. I often think of it in terms of change. And what change! And some of the pleasure of the trip is to reflect on the unimaginable pluck with which people have managed to carve out an existence in a place that can't be much different from the moon- scape. The town does not evoke a particular fondness—say, like re- membering a trip with the kids to Fisherman's Wharf or Disneyland. Wendover is more the ambivalent curiosity, tinged with a sometime sadness, that defies all the prohibitions—prosperity without resources, immorality without illegality. Wendover is the place ever wished for and ever needed, the safety valve of Main Street.

Wendover is full of remembrances. I remember the State Line when it was a mere gas-station casino whose preelectronic, prevideo slots showed real nickels in a glass cage. The one-armed bandit crackled mechanically with every nickel lost, but on those rare occasions when you lined up the Bell Fruit Gum bars, the cage flushed its nickels jubi- lantly. I remember the half-asleep Greyhound riders, having a pit stop after the Salt Flat crossing, pointing to the slots and giggling and venturing a few tainted nickels as if they were doing the expected, prohibited thing. Welcome to Nevada! Things are not what they used to be in Wendover. People are still escaping to Wendover from their everyday world and seeking their fortunes here. More are spending and laying waste to powers . . . bragging of a few bucks lost here, a major jackpot won there.

In my impractical moments I agree with Hulse's suggestion of a moratorium on building casinos. He wants his state to be built on more rock and less sand. And one does get tired of the tentative feel of the state, of the transiency and lack of community. What would Wordsworth say to this getting and spending and seeing little in nature that is ours? How would Thoreau have tried to simplify life here? Could Prospero have woven more magic?

Just now a tour bus is unloading a group of ecstatic senior citizens at a casino entrance. A majority of them are women armed with social security. Not to linger on change and reality. This isn't a town; this is Wendover. No one lives here for long, but most of us do for a time. Somewhere there must be a purgatory of hanging loose. This is the place. Against all the house odds, even against change, the people still come.

Reno and the Desert of Buried Hopes

William D. Rowley

Nevada at the beginning of the century was an unlikely place for the seeds of social and political reform to flourish. Its largest city, Reno, barely 11,000 by 1910, the center of a burgeoning divorce industry and the place where railroad workers, miners, and cowboys sought fun and diversions, could hardly be looked to as a harbinger of moral uplift and social progress. Yet Nevada and its leading city by 1910 showed definite indications of falling under the influence of progressive reform. Reform-minded men and women "of good hope" worked to stamp out personal vices, bring more democracy to politics, and place reins upon the excesses of corporate business.

Nevada's lone congressman, Francis G. Newlands, emerged as one of several advocates of progressivism in the state. He put together on the ruins of the Free Silver crusade of the previous decade a Fusionist or Silver–Democrat alliance that worked for reform in the state. Nationally, Newlands's support of the National Reclamation Act of 1902 brought federal support to western irrigation projects. In his view, this was a personal victory and a major step in moving Nevada away from its "boom-and-bust" mining past into a stable agricultural and commercial future. Like others, he believed it was unfortunate for Nevada "that its youth was spent not under the open skies . . . but in the deeps of the darksome mines." On the basis of these achievements and his own personal wealth, he became Senator Newlands from Nevada in 1903 and a prominent spokesman for national progressivism.[1]

Newlands also saw himself as a focal point of reform in Nevada in the midst of an economic revival after twenty years of mining depression from 1880 to 1900. While Nevada could look to the benefits of federal irrigation programs, it also enjoyed the good times of its early twentieth-century mining boom in the Tonopah, Goldfield, and Rhyolite areas of southern Nevada. The southern mines brought as many as 50,000 people to Nevada from 1900 to 1910. Federal irrigation programs, the growing influence of national progressive reform, and the influx of population all gave Newlands and other state Progressives high hopes of building Nevada into a "model Commonwealth" that would erase Nevada's once tarnished image as a corrupt, empty Rotten Burough.

Newlands's considerable wealth, which came to him by way of marriage into the estate of the Comstock robber baron, William Sharon, placed a special burden upon him to make a mark as a reformer in the state. His commanding position enabled him to build a political following that served his reelection bids and promoted progressive programs in the legislature. These included state regulatory commissions to oversee and control the prices charged the public by electric, transportation, water, and telephone companies; more direct-democracy measures in government; protection of weaker members of society (children, women, injured workmen); and protection of citizens from their own weaknesses by calling for anti-gambling measures, prohibition of liquor, and attacks upon prostitution.[2]

The progressive program that Newlands and others fostered for Nevada saw increasing government regulation of business, greater democracy, and action against societal sin and vice. By 1910 the Director of the Nevada State Historical Society, Jeanne Wier, could write of Nevada: "The political progress she has made with respect to anti-gambling laws, primary election, referendum and recall, etc., would indicate that social consciousness is rapidly being developed in spite of isolation."[3] This was in sharp contrast to her earlier statements in 1905: "In but few other places in these United States is there to be found in the same space such poverty of ideals in social and intellectual life, and perhaps I might add, in political life as well." In 1911 Newlands wrote to Theodore Roosevelt, before his intended visit to the state, welcoming him to the "model democracy" of Nevada that had achieved so much in the way of progressive reform.[4]

Nevada's progressive record was impressive in the years from 1903 to 1918. The direct democracy measures of referendum, recall, and initiative were placed in the state's constitution. It enjoyed direct primary elections to choose the candidates for office from the political parties. In 1914, through the efforts of Progressive Anne Martin, it accepted women into the voting place. By 1912 its newly established Public Service Commission began regulating the rates of transportation, electric, water, and telephone companies. This fulfilled one of

Newlands's dreams that state government should play a role in establishing and controlling the monopolies that dominated the utility industries.

In the area of protecting the weaker members of society and in protecting people from their own weaknesses and vices, Nevada also achieved results. The 1909 legislature passed one of the strongest anti-gambling bills in the nation. Divorce, which had developed into an important industry in Reno by 1910, was temporarily curbed by the legislature in 1913, when it extended the residency requirement for a Nevada divorce from six months to one year. When businessmen and lawyers who depended upon the divorce trade began losing money, this reform was quickly reversed to the six-month period by the next legislature in 1915. Prohibition would not be accepted by Nevada's voters until 1918 and then only because many felt it was a patriotic measure to use food grains for the war effort rather than alcoholic beverages.

Reluctance to move rapidly against the presence of personal vices reflects an underlying weakness of the progressive spirit in the state. Little was accomplished against the open prostitution permitted in the communities of the state. No statewide ban occurred. Prohibition came late in 1918 as an afterthought to the progressive movement, and finally the legislature relaxed gambling restrictions in 1915, which promoted the growth of clandestine, back-alley gambling, especially in Reno by the end of the war and in the postwar years. Still, progressive dreams and hopes for the state ran high until World War I and the death of Senator Newlands in 1917.

During the interwar period Reno took a sharp turn away from the ideals of a progressive society. The progressive attempt to reform the Rotten Borough had come to naught as Nevada gained the reputation of being a wide-open state with respect to easy divorce, boxing matches, prostitution, available drink in a time of prohibition, and to some extent, gambling. Nevada and especially its leading city, Reno, failed progressivism. Nevada feminist and suffrage worker Anne Martin remarked in an article for the *The Nation* magazine in 1922 that Nevada appeared a "Beautiful Desert of Buried Hopes." Hopes had run high, during the enthusiasm for irrigation at the beginning of the century, for a sturdy farmer- and family-oriented population to bring stability and respectability to Nevada. Now with that image faded, Martin wrote, Nevada continued to be "the ugly duckling, the disappointment, the weakling in the family of states." The article insisted the political reform during the Progressive Era did not significantly uplift the life of the state despite an impressive list of reform legislation. Nevada's population, she contended, remained "boss ridden" and under the influence of monied corporations and personalities. By the end of the interwar period in 1940, Martin's contemporary, Jeanne Wier, would write that Nevada remained only "theoretically interested in progressive political ideas."[5]

Reno's history in the decades between the world wars highlights the abandonment of progressivism in favor of a headlong drive for commercial success that would ultimately lead the state to embrace methods of economic growth deemed socially unacceptable by most states. Ironically, growth and stability would come to Nevada in the form of some of the very vices that Anne Martin and other reformers abhorred. Until 1923 two choices were open to Reno. The first embraced the city's desire to improve urban life by restricting vice, with stricter regulations on gambling, drinking, and prostitution. The second fed upon Reno's desire for profits and commercial success. The fact that reform and commercial success could not coexist in the same town was probably a testimony to the poverty of Nevada's human and natural resources. But the choice that Reno would make was by no means clear at the end of World War I, as the 1920s began. The fires of progressive reform still glowed in the hearts and minds of many of the city's prominent residents, although the war and subsequent postwar depression did much to dampen the flames.

Many Renoites tired of causes that sought to protect people from the weaknesses of their own character—penchants for gambling, drinking, disorganized family life, and even prostitution. A sparkling pure city simply was not good business for a mountain and desert town that entertained miners and cowboys and enjoyed a growing divorce industry. At this point Reno confronted a crossroads in its history. It had been the focal point of urban growth in the state for the past twenty years and also of the state's fragile progressive reform movement. Reform in Reno as in Nevada had experienced rough sledding. Gambling had been curtailed, not abolished; divorce, prostitution, and drinking survived to taunt the reformers.

As the decade began, the U.S. census of 1920 revealed that for the first time in American history the majority of the U.S. population lived in cities. In Nevada, as on the mining frontier in general, the majority of people had always lived in urban settings. The rise of a newer urban America ultimately brought greater freedom to individuals. Movement away from many of the values of rural, white, Protestant America occurred. The moralistic side of progressivism tried to imprint these values on the cities in the form of opposition to alcoholic beverages, strict sexual and marriage codes, and a condemnation of games of chance. In the Nevada setting Reno life had never been greatly restrained by these values. As the new urban America sought greater freedom in marriage laws, and ultimately in drinking and gambling, Reno stood ready to respond with few qualms of progressive conscience.

Local politics often act as a barometer for impending change. From 1919 to 1923 city government was under the mildly reform leadership of Mayor H. E. Stewart. The mayor stood for civic improvement in the paving of streets, the acquisition of parks, and the building of schools. The city successfully acquired much prized parkland from 1920 to 1923. Prominent banker and mining entrepreneur George Wingfield deeded Belle Isle to the city, an island in the Truckee in downtown Reno, with some additional surrounding land. This would become Reno's quiet and green mid-city park known as Wingfield Park. Senator Francis G. Newlands, who had died in late 1917, became an indirect benefactor of city parks when his nephew, James Newlands, sold forty-nine acres along the Truckee that would eventually be named Idlewild Park. In the final year of Mayor Stewart's term, the Newlands Company gave one acre of land on Newlands Heights overlooking the city for an additional park.

Although both Wingfield and Newlands were benefactors of the city, the two men represented strikingly different traditions that would clash in the upcoming mayoral elections in 1923. Newlands, as early as the 1890s, had grand visions of Reno as the hub of an expanding agricultural and commercial region in western Nevada. Not only would the city nourish commerce, but also education, the arts, civic pride, and beauty. It would be the leader of a reform movement that would remake Nevada into Newlands's much-hoped-for "model commonwealth." Wingfield, on the other hand, was a self-made millionaire of Nevada's twentieth-century mining boom not unlike Newlands's father-in-law, Sharon, who was a leading robber baron in the Comstock era of Nevada history. Shrewd mining investments made Wingfield wealthy. He schemed and fought to increase that wealth and protect it from all challengers—labor, reformers, and state taxes. His investment sought out what Nevada had to offer—mining, real estate, hotels, and ranching. From his viewpoint, if an enterprise made money, it was legitimate. He had no yardstick of morality by which he measured the activities of society or the nature of his investments. As far as he was concerned, businessmen who were seeking returns on their money and efforts should be free of government interference or suggestions that their activities were inconsistent with the health and welfare of the community. His successes brought both admiration and envy.

It was from these two traditions that Reno would choose in 1923. The Newlands tradition represented community regulation of business, repression of vice, and open democratic politics; the Wingfield tradition sought freedom from rules imposed by society, no enforced public morality, and closed machine politics. Personally, he was a gambler, a drinker, and a divorcé. Certainly from his viewpoint Reno could accommodate all of these and profitably so.

The move that earned Mayor Stewart the "reform" label was his support of the "Redlight Abatement Movement" that sought to abolish Reno's "restricted district." Long a part of the Reno scene, the prostitution district briefly closed down during World War I but immediately reopened thereafter. Two months prior to the election, the mayor and his council closed down the "restricted district" and cracked down on the illegal sale of liquor in the speakeasies that operated almost openly in Reno. The mayor campaigned under the slogan: "Reno Beautiful, Not Reno Notorious." Generally, the press expected Stewart's reelection, but acknowledged that a word-of-mouth campaign against the mayor's reforms could be heard on every street corner in the business districts. It was also no secret that the powerful manipulator of Nevada politics, George Wingfield, was opposed to Stewart's policies.

Others urged that Reno's commercial progress demanded the abolishment of the redlight district—that its closure was prompted by far more practical reasons than a revival of reform. The city council and mayor concurred that there would ultimately be more profit for a clean and beautiful city than for a dirty one. Mayor Stewart's election ads argued that as Reno had grown into a "new and real progressive" town, it began to look around and when "eyes fell on this dirty spot," it said to itself: "Here is something that every other community in this fair country of ours has abolished, and yet, in our beauty and attractiveness and health and newfound progressiveness, we allow it to go on." He called it "Something sordid" and pledged, if reelected mayor, to oppose "in every way that rests within my power the restoration of the so-called restricted district to existence." He termed this the main issue of the campaign that had been spreading mainly by word-of-mouth and reminded voters that "a town run by a tenderloin district is no good." Opposition ads branded Stewart a "reformer" and spoke of Reno as a town with a live-and-let-live attitude "until the professional reformer came to stir up discontent and turmoil in our midst."

The race for mayor was a three-way contest. Candidate Frank Byington had views similar to those of Stewart, but the third candidate, E. E. Roberts, dropped strong hints that he held nothing but contempt for the city's efforts to enforce morality. The *Nevada State Journal* said Roberts, a divorce lawyer, had a reputation for frontier ethics that the *Journal* said was out of step with progressive reform. It believed Roberts misgauged public opinion when he proposed to remake Reno into a wide-open mining camp. But Roberts openly declared in his campaign:

> I don't believe in prohibition or any kind of reform that takes from any man or woman their right to find happiness in their own way. I would repeal all blue laws. I would make Reno the playground of the world.[6]

By election day, May 8, 1923, the *Journal*, which had backed Stewart, admitted that hopes for its candidate were doubtful. It admitted that the "open or closed" issue had surpassed in importance the "city beautiful" plea of Stewart. The reform element cried that an "open city" would mean ruin for Reno, and the "unreformed" retorted that Reno would be damned if it were not opened up. "Redlights and prosperity," said the paper, was the slogan heard around many business corners, whereas reform groups such as the Monday Club, Reno League of Women Voters, Reno Women's Christian Temperance Union, the Parent–Teacher Association, the Women's Faculty Club, the Reno Lions Club, and various church groups believed in the slogan "redlights and ruin" for the town.

The ballot count brought a stunning defeat for Stewart and Byington. Reno had made a crucial decision at this important crossroads in its history. It had opted for the wide-open city, the frontier ethics of Roberts, the grab-the-profits attitude of Wingfield and had rejected the planned, regulated society of the Newlands progressive tradition. The vote was totally lopsided in favor of the Roberts position: Roberts, 2,928; Byington, 970; Stewart, 737. In some disbelief at the election results, the *Journal* returned to its theme that it had believed Roberts too handicapped with his frontier ethics to win in a town that went to church as much as Reno did. The election pointed out the inaccuracy of this guess and illustrated an old political adage that the people usually did not vote the way they worshiped.

Who was Mayor E. E. Roberts? He would be Reno's popular and colorful mayor for the next ten years, until his death in 1933. As Nevada's congressman from 1911 to 1919, Roberts played the role of political maverick with a Republican label. He opposed President Wilson and his own party's leadership when he voted against U.S. entrance into World War I in 1917. He remained unmoved by the president's call upon the nation to make sacrifices to save the world for democracy and join the European war. He also shunned the enthusiasm for domestic reform in the Progressive Era. Now he stepped forward to rescue Reno from the clutches of the reformers.

During his two and a half terms as mayor, Reno assumed the character of a wide-open town offering drink, gambling, prostitution, quickie divorces, and instant marriages. The powerful Wingfield machine openly supported Roberts's reelection in 1927, as Roberts began acquiring the reputation of being the permissive mayor of one of America's sauciest towns. Roberts made no secret of his contempt for Prohibition and winked at its lax enforcement in Reno. When he ran for his third term in 1931, the minister of the First Methodist Church invited him to speak from the pulpit. In that famous speech he advocated placing open barrels of whiskey on every street corner with ladles for all. The Methodists, who were among the leading supporters of Prohibition, stood aghast. Shortly afterwards the Methodist bishop transferred the minister from the Reno church.

By the end of the 1920s, events relating to matrimony played an increasing role in Reno's economy. Local papers regularly carried news of divorce trials that might involve misconduct or large settlements. In 1931 Reno divorce-court Judge George A. Bartlett's philosophic study of marriage and divorce appeared in Reno bookstores as well as throughout the nation. Entitled *Men, Women and Conflict: An Intimate Study of Love, Marriage and Divorce,* the book drew upon his many years of experience hearing divorce cases in Reno courts. It included advice to young brides and husbands and comments on birth control, adultery, children, and divorce law. The Nevada legislature in 1927 reduced the divorce residency requirement in Nevada from six months to three months. In 1931 the legislature made the residency period a mere six weeks to keep Nevada competitive with some other states that were on the verge of tapping into the divorce business. None, however, dared to match Nevada's scandalous six-week law.

Another development relating to matrimony in Reno was the passage by the California legislature of the "three-day gin marriage law" in 1927. Californians believed that a waiting period before marriage helped prevent bad marriages. The lack of similar restrictions in Nevada spurred a Reno marriage boom that offered good business to those who would later be called "marryin' Sams," who flocked to Reno to set up business. Opening of the new Victory Highway in 1925, over the Sierra and directly through the Truckee Canyon, brought Reno divorce and marriage much closer to California. By 1933 the annual number of marriages in Reno was nearly 2,000 more than the number of divorces. The usual number of divorces a year in the late 1920s and early 1930s was 2,500, but after the passage of the six-week law in 1931, there were 4,250—more than double the number in 1930. The shorter divorce period brought a Reno divorce within the financial reach of more people and helped to democratize a process that was once reserved for the famous and the rich.

As the 1920s began, many of the famous and rich came for Reno divorces from the new movie industry in Hollywood. Mary Pickford, star of the silent screen, showed up in Minden, Nevada, in 1920 with Reno lawyer Pat McCarran to start proceedings on her divorce from husband Owen Moore before she could marry Douglas Fairbanks. The divorce was widely publicized and McCarran was reputed to have received a $20,000 fee plus the gift of a home in Reno worth another $20,000 for his services. The attraction of popular movie stars to Reno added to the glamour of the Reno Divorce Colony. Movies were becoming one of America's most popular leisure pastimes and the movie houses in Reno—the Wigwam, the Granada, the Majestic, the Reno, and the Nevada theaters—brought to the public movies with such stars as Gloria Swanson, Sally O'Neil, and Ramon Navarro, as well as images of racy life-styles.

In addition to the move revolution in entertainment, the 1920s brought a revolution in personal transportation. The automobile touched almost every aspect of American life from the way people earned their livings to the way they spent their money. After the war a new federal highway across the state took a route along the Humboldt River to Reno and then through the Truckee Canyon to Sacramento. The new "Victory Highway" (U.S. 40) guaranteed that Reno would reap huge rewards from the advent of the automobile and new highways. The airplane offered another link to the outside world with the building of Reno's first airfield in 1919 and the beginning of regularly scheduled passenger flights in 1927. KOH, owned by Sacramento interests, became Reno's first commercial radio station in 1928. A more accessible Reno advertised a marriage trade, a divorce trade, and beckoned to the seekers of illicit pleasures in gambling, drinking, and whoring. Unquestionably, Mayor Roberts's many years in office helped to mark Reno as an easy place to obtain almost anything money could buy, without fear of the law.

Figures from the underworld of the Midwest and San Francisco looked upon Reno as a safe place to hide out and even a profitable place to live. The extensive power of George Wingfield, now the owner of the rebuilt Riverside Hotel, encouraged a permissiveness of law enforcement in areas of personal choice—drinking, gambling, prostitution, and divorce. Wingfield exerted tremendous political influence over the state from his office, known as "the Cave," on the second floor of the Reno National Bank. The law firm headed by William Woodburn and George Thatcher also operated from the Cave, helping to direct state politics through something called a "Bi-partisan Machine." Wingfield was a power in the Republican party and his lawyer-associates controlled the Democratic party. Not much escaped their attention in either Reno or Nevada politics. Their telephone number, 4111, became famous. It was a number that elected officials often called before making appointments or casting votes in the legislature or even Congress.

A cut below the Wingfield political machine were the operations of James McKay and William Graham in Reno. The two owned gambling dens and drinking parlors and were behind the redlight district. The stockade, or "crib" as it was called in the 1920s and 1930s, consisted of a series of small motel-like apartments east of Lake Street and near the river. From these rooms prostitutes worked their trade in eight-hour, around-the-clock shifts. Some said that profits from this enterprise reached into the highest rungs of Reno society. In 1934 *Fortune* magazine referred to the five who ruled Reno, namely, Wingfield, Woodburn, Thatcher, McKay, and Graham. McKay and Graham owned the Cal–Neva Lodge at north Lake Tahoe and the Willows Roadhouse west of Reno, and they had investments in many other establishments including the Reno Social Club in partnership with Wingfield. Their businesses involved the risks of running liquor from the Bay area across state lines. They occasionally harbored big-time criminals—Baby Face Nelson, Ma Barker, and perhaps Alvin Karpis—in their Reno dives and laundered money and securities received from outside connections.[7]

The FBI finally brought charges that took them to trial in 1934. One of the chief witnesses against them was Roy Frisch, cashier of the Wingfield-owned Riverside Bank in Reno. Before Frisch could testify, he disappeared while on his way to a movie in Reno from his Court Street home. It was rumored that he was "rubbed out" by Baby Face Nelson as a favor to Graham and McKay for their protection in Reno. Possibly Frisch's body was tossed down a mine shaft near Yerington or sent to the bottom of Lake Tahoe in a cement casket. The event is one of the unsolved mysteries that illustrate the sordid side of the fun and good times that Mayor Roberts helped bring to Reno.

The fall of the stock market in 1929 signaled the end of the "roaring twenties" for Reno and the nation. A drought in 1930–31 dealt a crippling blow to the stock and feed crop industries in the state. This meant a constantly higher debt structure for the state's ranchers and greater risk for the financial institutions that backed them. One of these financial institutions was the chain of twelve banks owned by Wingfield. By the summer of 1932 the banks, including Reno's Riverside Bank, were closed under a general statewide bank holiday. But the Wingfield banks would never reopen and were ordered into receivership in late 1933. The party was over for the Wingfield financial and political machine in the state.

Before the disastrous failure of the Wingfield banks, Nevada in 1931 startled the nation by relegalizing gambling. In the same year the legislature passed the six-week divorce residency law as Reno businessmen cheered it on. Governor Fred Balzar signed the gambling and divorce bills on the same day, March 19, 1931. In the wake of these events the city's life quickened as it staged one of its famous Fourth of July boxing matches that captured national attention. The match featured Max Baer and Paulino Uzcudun, "the bouncing Basque," who surprisingly defeated the future heavyweight champion. But despite the heady celebrations over legislation that made Reno wider open than ever, the decade began a serious time for Renoites. Easy divorce and marriage, legal gambling, and legal prostitution, as well as the availability of drink, made Reno the target of national criticisms.

A series of articles by Paul Hutchinson in *The Christian Century* magazine, entitled "Nevada—A Prostitute State," "Reno—A Wide-Open Town," "Reno's Divorce Mill," and "Can Reno Be Cured?" portrayed Reno as the leading culprit in a statewide conspiracy to make money from sin. The author warned that Nevada and Reno would ultimately reap the whirlwind with a disorganized and crime-ridden society shot through with the social problems of venereal disease, alcoholism, suicide, and juvenile delinquency. The International Society of Christian Endeavor (Protestant youth) asserted that, "Reno is a blot on civilization, a menace to the American home and national prestige." This was not the Reno or the Nevada that Progressives envisioned earlier in the century.[8]

Reno had more to worry about than the consequences of sin, which it had already accepted as a fact of everyday life by 1931. The new legal gambling had little impact on the Depression-struck economy. After legalization, flashy gambling palaces did not suddenly spring up along Virginia Street. Gambling houses still retained a secretive air, preferring to remain in the back alleys, especially Douglas Alley, where the Bank Club, the Rex Club, and the Wine House Club did business. The typical atmosphere inside these clubs was dark and dingy. Aging men with green visors usually presided dourly at smoke-engulfed gaming tables. There were no glamorous floor shows or short-skirted cocktail waitresses. The gambling dens served a cheerless male gambling clientele. Legalized gambling assumed a low profile that reflected a fear that if it drew too much attention to itself the anti-gambling forces would once again vote gambling from the state. Graham and McKay's gambling enterprises were now legal, but Graham drew increased notoriety to himself when he shot a man in Douglas Alley. A grand jury quickly dismissed murder charges, accepting a plea of self-defense. Eventually federal authorities succeeded in jailing these two shady Reno figures.

As the stillness of the Depression settled on Reno, hope faded that gambling and divorce would render the city Depression-proof. With the failure of the Wingfield banks, the political powers that had held sway in Nevada for nearly two decades also toppled. The new political currents swept a Renoite into the U.S. Senate: Pat McCarran, the longtime enemy of Wingfield. The Democratic party captured offices in the state and brought Franklin D. Roosevelt to the presidency in the fall elections of 1932. When he took office in March 1933, Roosevelt declared that he offered America a New Deal, a multifaceted program designed to put the nation back to work. He announced massive programs in industry, agriculture, and national relief work employment to put the nation on the road to recovery. Those programs had a tremendous impact upon the local scenes throughout America, and Reno was no exception.

As the old Wingfield bipartisan machine crumbled, it was replaced by New Deal politicians and their local captains in the Democratic party who controlled the distribution of relief work employment. Unlike many industrial cities Reno did not face immediate, devastating unemployment from the Depression. While the economy was slow, many joined in the make-work and community improvement programs that provided jobs. An important service that the programs performed for the city was relief for hundreds of transients that streamed in and out of town from the more depressed areas of the country. Many were on their way to California or coming back disappointed. The Transient Service established camps to house people in hastily built quarters, encouraged garden planting, brought logs into woodlots so the unfortunates could cut their own fuel.

While Reno took as much New Deal aid as was offered, it did not feel overly indebted to the generosity of federal programs. It enjoyed gambling license fees and tax revenues that at the time went to county and city governments. Although few would admit it, Reno had already made its choice for profits and legalized vice. It seemed fairly self-satisfied even in the midst of the national Depression that still gripped the country in 1939. This aspect of self-content helps explain why the outlook of the New Deal never took firm root in the free private-enterprise soil of Reno. While other states launched their own "little New Deals," offering increased public services and consequently heavier taxation, Nevada shunned such programs.

Under the prompting of northern Nevadan Norman Biltz, who advocated the economics of "One Sound State," Nevada emerged from the Depression a lightly taxed state. Biltz, a real estate promoter at Tahoe and of Nevada ranch lands, in the depths of the Depression determined to sell Nevada land on the basis of a favorable tax structure for the wealthy. When other states moved to expand their governmental services in the spirit of the New Deal and sought new sources of wealth to tax, Biltz worked for limitations on taxes in Nevada, arguing that the wealthy could be convinced to invest in a Nevada with a tax structure that favored their interests. Constitutional prohibitions on inheritance and estate taxes and a limitation on state property tax rates were all in effect by 1942. This made Nevada and Reno attractive to the rich as they fled "soak the rich" taxes in other states. Biltz, soon to be known as the "Duke of Nevada," quickly impressed upon his clients the wisdom of buying large tracts of Nevada real estate to legitimatize their residency. For Nevada's less well-to-do, the "One Sound State" might also mean lower taxes, but it offered slim budgets for education, health care, recreation, and aid to the indigent.

While Reno continued to welcome the divorce crowd and the wealthy who sought refuge from higher tax rates in other states, it also attracted a new class of gambling entrepreneur. These new gamblers ultimately transformed Reno gambling houses, removing them from the alleys along Commercial Row, and placing them under bright lights in prominent locations on Virginia Street. Harold Smith arrived in 1936, followed soon afterwards by his father Raymond I. "Pappy" Smith and his brother Raymond. They established a small gambling club on Virginia Street. One of the early attractions of Harolds Club was a roulette game played with white mice. William Harrah, after earlier unsuccessful attempts beginning in 1937, opened the Tango Club in Douglas Alley in 1939 and eventually expanded to Virginia Street. Both of these clubs ultimately revolutionized Reno gambling by removing it from the back alleys and giving it an air of respectability. The upheaval in American life occasioned by World War II also promoted a permissiveness in American social attitudes toward gambling as a respectable leisure-time pursuit. Cloaked with a new-found social acceptance, Reno needed only the end of the Depression and subsequent wartime crisis to move to a future dominated by an industry traditionally viewed as naughty and vice related.

The glamour of gambling would far surpass the other institutionalized vices that Reno experimented with in the interwar years in the name of making a decent living. While gambling brought growth and prosperity, the heritage of the One Sound State made difficult the generous funding of social and educational services in the state. Nevada society in the second half of the twentieth century, with its lavish displays of private wealth and parsimonious public services, has been a far cry from the kind of society that the Progressives had envisioned at the beginning of the century when they set about with high hopes to build a "model Commonwealth" in the desert. Their efforts ultimately fell on barren ground with Reno sewing salt in the furrows. Many (perhaps most) will say happily so, because the defeat of the progressive society opened the doors for the economic growth of the new Nevada that emerged by century's end.

NOTES

1. Jeanne Elizabeth Wier, "The Mission of the State Historical Society," from an address to the Nevada Academy of Sciences in 1905, *First Biennial Report of the Nevada Historical Society* (1907–1908): 66.

2. Francis G. Newlands to H. F. Bartine, March 21, 1905, and Newlands to E. L. Bingham, January 23, 1905, Francis G. Newlands Papers, Sterling Library, Yale University.

3. Wier, "The Work of the Western State Historical Society as Illustrated by Nevada," *Second Biennial Report of the Nevada Historical Society* (1909–1910):68.

4. Wier, "Mission of the State Historical Society," 68; Newlands to T. Roosevelt, March 9, 1911, Theodore Roosevelt Papers, Presidential Papers Microfilm Project.

5. Anne Martin, "Nevada: Beautiful Desert of Buried Hopes," *Nation* 115, July 26, 1922, 89; Wier, "The Mystery of Nevada," *Rocky Mountain Politics*, ed. Thomas C. Donnelly (Albuquerque: University of New Mexico Press, 1940), 114.

6. *Nevada State Journal* (Reno), May 7, 1923.

7. "Passion in the Desert," *Fortune* 9, April 1934, 100–107.

8. Paul Hutchinson, "Nevada — A Prostitute State," *The Christian Century* 48, December 2, 1931, 1519–20; "Reno's Divorce Mill," *The Christian Century* 48, December 9, 1931, 1557–59; "Can Reno Be Cured?" *The Christian Century*, 48, December 16, 1931, 1592–94.

Reno   Myth, Mystique,   Ann
or Madness?   Ronald

Walter Van Tilburg Clark, Nevada's best-known novelist, opens his *City of Trembling Leaves* with an evocation of the Reno he loved, the small, but special Nevada community of the 1920s. First he describes it by orchestrating a symphony of its trees—"an air of antique melancholy," then "a brightening sound" of new growth, "the marching files of poplars," and finally "the twinkling aspen with their whispering and rushing leaves." He continues with a characterization of the city's sentinel mountains—Rose, "the white, exalted patron angel," and Peavine, "the great, humped child of the desert." For Clark, the essential Reno blends inseparably with its natural surroundings; what he calls the "moribund Reno," the treeless Reno, doesn't count. He dismisses the region behind the arch—"The Biggest Little City In The World"—as "the ersatz jungle, where the human animals, uneasy in the light, dart from cave to cave under steel and neon branches, where the voice of the croupier halloos in the secret glades, and high and far, like light among the top leaves, gleam the names of lawyers and hairdressers on upstairs windows."[1] His characters live and love in the other Reno, "the city of trembling leaves." Yet for most readers of fiction and for many non-Nevadans, Clark's Reno is the one that doesn't exist. Instead, it is "the biggest little city in the world" that is real, the one that counts. Why? Because rumor, myth, and the power of the press have combined to create a sense of place unique in this country. For reasons simple and complex, writers have sold the public a Reno that, while it may dismay Renoites like Clark, fascinates most twentieth-century Americans.

A surprising amount of fiction—and I use that word in both a conventional and an ironic sense—has been written about "the biggest little city." Most of it was published in the days of Reno's fame as a haven for divorcées; little of it emphasizes gambling.[2] All the fiction apparently depicts individual authors' notions of the "real" Reno, notions as diverse as the books themselves. Certain common strains, however, do recur. Stock characters appear and reappear, as do stock situations and actions. A similarity in tone exists; even individual phrases and figures of speech are repeated. Some changes of scene can be found—Virginia City, Tahoe, Pyramid Lake, for example—but the stories always return to the banks of the Truckee River. Because downtown Reno most interests both authors and readers, we inevitably find the focus of the action there. The reasons for Reno's attraction are various, but I suggest they stem from people's ambivalent feelings about divorce. Certainly individual attitudes toward Reno's best-known business, and most of the novels themselves, tend to conclude in a wash of ambiguities. Yet I find it possible to make sense out of the apparent contradictory attitudes and interpretations. To understand the paradox that is Reno, we need initially to look at ways the city has been characterized, next at unwritten truths underlying its descriptions, and finally at discrepancies between the two. Only then will we be able to explain the magnetism of "the biggest little city in the world."

Since similar elements found in the fiction keynote the city's portrayal, we should examine these commonalities first. So repetitive are they, that nine times out of ten the main character is the same—a potential divorcée who has come to Reno to complete her residency requirement. She generally arrives by train and is taken to the Riverside Hotel. There she will remain, permanently (that is, for approximately six weeks), or she will relocate to a guest ranch or boardinghouse. She never lives alone, because the author must create interaction between the heroine, other would-be divorcées, and various local citizens. Occasionally the protagonist is a man, sometimes a Renoite, but most often the central figure is a young, attractive, introspective, misunderstood, Eastern woman who has come west to end her marriage.

Her first few days in Reno are lonely. Initially she meets only women—dowdy, middle-aged matrons whose husbands have "sent them packing"; suave, sophisticated socialites trailed by unending strings of gigolos; broken-hearted, often suicidal housewives from American suburbia. Few Nevada women cross her path—only an occasional rancher's wife or housekeeper. However, she gradually is allowed, then encouraged, to meet Nevada men. Some are poor specimens—party-boys, gamblers, seducers. Others include fatherly and understanding attorneys. But at least one man per novel is handsome and competent, an outdoorsman with obvious duties to perform. He shows off the Nevada scenery, teaches "the Western way of life," educates the heroine in an appreciation of "true love." Sometimes an author allows an Easterner to fulfill this function, but more often the privilege goes to a Nevada native.

Not only the characters but also the activities are repeated from book to book. For example, we find a requisite number of auto trips to mountains, lakes, and desert; we are taken on at least one horseback ride and are offered at least one sunrise or sunset. We usually are titillated, too, by the intimation of one afternoon of sex in the great outdoors. Even more suggestive are the indoor and evening pastimes. An almost unbelievable amount of liquor is consumed, partying frequently lasts until dawn, and roadhouses are the loci for much activity. What I characterize as "flapperish" behavior continues for decades beyond the conventional 1920s' boundaries. The decadence of such action is emphasized by its juxtaposition against desert scenery, clean mountain air, and pure outdoor life. A majority of the protagonists, although first seduced by so-called "Eastern" mores, eventually learn "Western" ways—clean out their lungs, as it were—and then are allowed to live happily ever after. "Happily ever after," however, may be achieved in a variety of ways—the heroine may be reunited with her husband, marry another divorcé, wed a cowboy, or simply arrive at some kind of self-realized maturity. No matter which course the action takes, the reader feels satisfied that the character's future success is assured.

In many ways this over-used plot recapitulates thousands of works written in America between the two world wars. For example, Zane Grey made a fortune from just such a formula of adversity and despair crowned with success and daydreams that come true. Grey's novels and others under consideration here, all published in the East, were directed toward Eastern readers who, presumably, read them for vicarious pleasure and not for veracity. Furthermore, many Reno novels were written by individuals, like Cornelius Vanderbilt, Jr., who had come west for divorces of their own. Such writers, we must suppose, were inspired by a need for personal catharsis that inherently led to idealistic story lines. Some writers insisted that they portrayed reality, but most assuredly only Walter Clark among Nevada novelists remained uncaptivated by Virginia Street, the Riverside, the clubs, and the divorce colony—in short, by the sensational side of Reno.

One cannot fault these other writers, however, since for the most part their experiences isolated them from "the city of trembling leaves."

Their exaggerated perceptions of Reno are hardly surprising since even the local advertisements encouraged puffery. My favorite is a 1932 Chamber of Commerce brochure touting Reno as "A Land of Charm." The pamphleteer brags that

> the City—every foot of the way—looks the part! Finely paved streets and sidewalks, imposing business structures; most modern stores; substantial and attractive and, in many instances, imposing residences; a state university, comparing favorably with any like institution of its kind in the United States; a public school system that can probably be rated second to none, for its size, in the land; and progressive city, county, and state governments thoroughly appreciative of the value of leading the way with public improvements. Epitomized, that is the story of the city!

The brochure then describes surrounding scenic wonders and convenient modes of transportation. Finally, just after "excellent hotels, with accommodations to meet every taste," are praised, the writer asserts that "Nevada has done much for the race, and her work has just begun."[3] So although divorce, per se, is not mentioned, the not-so-subtle attempt to justify its value indicates the intent of an apparently massive advertising campaign. *Reno, Land of Charm* is only one of the many pamphlets published in reply to a flood of inquiries from the East.

Much less restrained were the privately printed responses:

> Reno . . . where the East and West meet, and greet, and kiss, and make up! Reno!—the ever boiling, seething, melting pot of grim Reality and alluring Illusion; where the multitude of Mistake Makers stage the mammoth battle of the world—The Battle of Human Hearts; where some win and some lose in their innermost struggle to become victors of the greatest asset to man— PEACE OF MIND![4]

And sometimes promoters even overrode the bounds of good taste.

> Reno is situated on an island in the Sea of Matrimony. It is parted in the middle by the Truckee River, which flows from the Reef of

Many Causes to the Harbor of Renewed Hope and More Trouble. The tide comes in regularly by the Southern Pacific and the untied depart the same way.[5]

I quote all these ostensibly nonfictional pieces because they demonstrate the kind of "truths" that people heard about Reno. In fact, from its earliest days Reno invited a reputation for fast living and greedy indifference. "There is no such thing as rest in Reno. People rush in Reno. The tavern keepers are bent on business, provide no rest and Reno cares nothing," wrote one journalist in 1868. "Busy Reno . . . is bent on making her pile with what speed she can command."[6] As Reno moved into the twentieth century, her fame grew as a haven for loose morals, and a mecca for divorcées. Increasingly, writers chose to capitalize on this side of the biggest little city. For example, one lurid exposé, published in *Real Detective* and entitled "The City that Sex Built," opens with a step-by-step description of a girl disrobing in a downtown crib, then slickly continues with a discussion of divorce and current lax laws. The author concludes, "Reno's motto is: 'You can't do anything wrong—we'll legalize it!'"[7] Another magazine devotes itself solely to *The Reno Divorce Racket,* while contrasting "our mad race for sex freedom and return to paganism" with the "stabilizing force of a great church."[8] Yet the bulk of this 1931 issue is pure sensationalism, filled with pictures of celebrities in Reno and captioned with detailed explanations of divorce procedures. In short, it is a "how-to-do-it" handbook designed to attract, rather than repel, readers. One more journalist summarizes the prevailing tone of the sensationalists: "Curious little Reno! So pretty, so uneventful, so isolated—so very 'small town'—yet so manifestly linked to a brilliant and lawless past; bearing for all eyes in the broad light of day the light flotsam of divorcées, the heavy jetsam of shifty, broken men."[9]

These comments also suggest the general tenor of a small group of somewhat "sick" novels that stress the "flotsam and jetsam" of humanity, emphasizing morbid relationships with gruesome details. Of these, Latifa Johnson's *Sheila Goes to Reno* is perhaps the best known.[10] *Sheila*'s plot is characteristic—she marries, has an abortion and thus alienates her husband, heads to Reno for a divorce, next marries a Nevada rancher, steps out on him, returns to New York, sleeps around, and finally loses her mind. The grotesque melodrama is a parody of any reasonable plot, but the physical setting is skillfully drawn. An undiscriminating reader, I suspect, might misinterpret

Johnson's effort and believe such actions possible or even probable in the Western locale, although actually the story is too absurd to happen anywhere.

Reno's seamy reputation has attracted another kind of novelist, too, the detective story writer.[11] Several murder mysteries are set along the banks of the Truckee River. While some are better written than others, all feature divorcées, racketeering, and booze. Even the famous Charlie Chan comes to Tahoe and Reno, while the infamous Matt Helm also appears to aid his ex-wife, break up a drug ring, and kill a number of traitorous enemies in various unsightly ways.

No one who knows Reno could mistake the portrayals in these books for reality. Less clear-cut, however, are the interpretations found in better writing, even though some readers were appalled by fictional descriptions of "their" city. Two authors in particular infuriated the natives. Cornelius Vanderbilt, Jr.'s, *Reno,* published in 1929, sparked a heated protest from both the local Chamber of Commerce and the Reno 20–30 Club. The Chamber fired off a telegram to the author: "The exaggerated picture that you have drawn . . . could only have been seen, with all its uncleanliness, through glasses that were colored elsewhere or with eyes unfitted to the better things of life. . . . We must express our contempt for this departure in the realm of fiction."[12] The 20–30 Club echoed the Chamber's outrage: "His portrayal of the citizenry of the community is a contemptible lie. . . . We believe the filthy situations pictured in Vanderbilt's book could be written by no one except one whose mind is filled with such degrading thoughts. Through his book defaming the name of this city Vanderbilt has shown Reno as a city of depravity, when as a matter of fact this is not true."[13] Finally, the Club insinuated they would like to run him out of town because "his presence in our community is distasteful."

Ironically, Vanderbilt's *Reno* seems mild compared to some of the lurid journalism available. Certainly the novel contains a fair amount of drinking, partying, and "flapperish" activities, but this outlay of decadence is carefully contrasted with the pure mountain air and vivid desert colors. Indeed, his characters are among those who "clean out their lungs" and adopt Western ways. Furthermore, in the midst of his book Vanderbilt heartily endorses the locale:

> Reno isn't any worse than any other city. All the outside world sees is the sensational side of Reno, the mad antics of a small group of its divorce colony. It doesn't realize that what it sees is

but a coarse, unnatural growth. The real city—the good, energetic, constructive city—lies beneath it, paying about as much attention to it as a cow does to a fly on her back. There's a world of
honest goodness and beauty in that little city, and it's easy to see, if
you're looking for the cleaner side of life.[14]

Apparently local businessmen lacked appreciation for his enthusiasm.

Two years later John Hamlin, author of *Whirlpool of Reno,* also came
in for severe criticism. Less enamored of Nevada natives than Vanderbilt, Hamlin turned on them in an open letter to the editor of the University of Nevada *Sagebrush.* "Reno warrant[s] every line of notoriety
circulated about it," he wrote. "This town is reaping precisely what it is
sowing, and has no grounds to howl because others turn back upon it
the fruits of its own planting." Hamlin argued that

when your governor and your mayor broadcast invitations to the
world to come to Nevada and Reno where there are so few laws to
be broken, when the newspapers are filled with glaring headlines
and feature stores about the gambling dives, the deluxe roadhouses, the weekly washday when the decrees are ground out by
the scores, why shouldn't the world be curious to read about the
"Biggest Little City in the World"?[15]

And so he "accepted the invitation and wrote *Whirlpool of Reno,*" a
novel which anticipates the point of view stated in his letter. Its heroine, in particular, speaks for its author when she shouts at her aunt, a
longtime Reno resident:

"Listen, Aunt! If you and your pious friends are so terribly
shocked by these loose divorcees, why blame us? You've made it
perfectly legal for us to come here, haven't you? You shortened
the time from six months to three, and not satisfied with the results, you even cut that period in half as an added lure to unhap-
pily married folk. And how about your wide open gambling, your
glamorous roadhouses, swagger apartments and shops—the
stand your mayor takes—broadcasting an invitation to the World
and his wife to come to Reno where there are few laws to break!
Your respectable voters and lawmakers are the ones to be condemned, not the divorce colony. You offer us every inducement
to come here, then damn us because we do. Go after us hand over
fist for all the money you can squeeze from us, then set up a howl

of indignation because Reno is known far and wide for its divorce colony, its blatantly licensed gambling, and nothing else." [16]

John Hamlin knew that by expressing such sentiments he would be touching raw nerves of respectable Renoites, but he couldn't resist voicing his analysis of the ambiguous stance taken by the local citizenry.

Perhaps Hamlin intended to stir controversy, but Vanderbilt insisted he didn't mean to alienate his Reno readers. Vanderbilt dedicated his book to the Westerners he had met and appreciated. From the Sagebrush Ranch he penned the words that appear on his title page:

> To my friends in Reno, who keep the hearthfires of gentleness, peace and beauty burning in the midst of the ugly wreckage that surrounds them; who take into their hearts and homes those world-weary pilgrims who are both heart-sick and homeless; to them—who have taught me to love the real Reno—I dedicate this, my first novel. [17]

Vanderbilt erred, I think, in trying to render verbatim the city around him, in attempting to copy exactly what he saw and in insisting that it was the truth. Those novelists who instead used Reno more creatively—as a jumping-off point, an inspiration, a metaphor, or symbol for something they needed to say—more successfully and more meaningfully depicted "the biggest little city in the world," and, by the way, caused much less controversy. Jill Stern, author of *Not In Our Stars*, realized that Reno should be treated as more than just another Western community when she wrote, "Reno isn't a place [at all], it isn't real, it's just a symbol to America and the rest of the world, a symbol." [18] Instead, she defines Reno as "a state of mind, a general state of the collective American mind." [19]

I quite agree with Stern, but I further suggest that Reno represents a complicated web of contemporary concerns, some great and some small, but all indicative of what troubles twentieth-century Americans. Dorothy Carman, writing in the 1930s, jumbles her metaphors while managing to convey the multiplicity of meanings carried by the city behind the arch. First she establishes its universality, generalizing that every family has somebody in Reno and affirming that "it's a cross section of our country." [20] Then Carman downgrades the seamier side of life in Reno, calling the city "a prostitute" while suggesting it is "losing its old identity but . . . making money."[21] Finally Carman reverses her point of view to one of optimistic idealism, comparing Reno to Oz, "set apart from the world,"[22] a land of enchantment where one takes "a vacation from life."[23] Assuming that Reno is indeed a universal symbol, and further, that its symbolism includes contradictory interpretations of the lax divorce and gaming laws, then Carman's other two observations generate some new perspectives. Divorce can be good or bad, gambling lucky or unlucky; Reno can symbolize either or both sides of life. The city can mean blight or blessing, last chance or first, nightmare or dream; that is, Reno can stand for what is wrong with America or for what is right. Most Reno authors agree that Reno is a paradox. Positive and negative depictions and interpretations alike can be found in their novels. Their opinions, advanced by the same stock characters and conventional plots already isolated, are then emphasized by some revealing figurative language.

Not In Our Stars serves as the best example. Stern's heroine, Sara Winston, joins a number of people at the Jolly-R Guest Ranch where each awaits a divorce. Their characters are all flawed—Sara's roommate Maggie is an alcoholic, as is her husband, who follows her to Reno; Belle is an overweight, discarded Jewish mother; Lou, a homosexual designer who thought marriage would set him straight; Van, Sara's lover, is attractive, compelling, but, in the long run, weak. Sara, as insecure and maladjusted as the rest, initially finds Reno reflective of these diverse problems. Standing in Harolds Club, she muses:

> the last frontier, where everything goes. . . . Oh, America, erstwhile land of the free, what has become of thee? What have they done to thee, my beloved? The profound dream . . . land of the mighty . . . refuge, once, of the persecuted, where each might have his chance at life, liberty, and the pursuit of happiness. But what *was* happiness and *where* could you find it? Was this, in fact, America? Did all roads lead to Reno?[24]

Actually, Sara is questioning what has become of *her* and asking where *she* can find happiness. But like so many characters in these novels, she converts her own inadequacies into statements about the city. A man from the same book reveals even more about himself when he calls Reno "the boil on the cover-girl face of our decadent western culture, . . . the ulcer in the soft underbelly of our shining civilization, produced by our collective tension and greed and fear."[25] For this disagreeable character, Reno becomes emblematic of his own failure. In fact, those characters who see Reno as a "blight"[26] tend to be the malcontents, second-rate, the so-called "flotsam and jetsam," or, "The Women," as Clare Boothe called them collectively and ironically in her 1937 Broadway play by that name. To these outcasts, Reno symbolizes what's wrong with the nation and, more subtly, with themselves. "It isn't only Reno. Standards all over aren't as high as they were,"[27] laments one poor soul who is troubled by "the modern pace." Conservative readers, finding their own beliefs confirmed, would agree. By using the breakup of the family unit as the cornerstone of their plots, exploitative authors have been able to turn Reno into a symbol of national decay, a "last frontier," as Stern writes in *Not In Our Stars*, of fast living and wasted lives.

However, those characters who succeed, and who achieve self-knowledge, view Reno quite differently by the time their stories end. Sara Winston, when she finally realizes that people's flaws arise "not in our stars" but in ourselves, is well on her way to maturity. No longer dismayed by Reno, "this tiny, tinseley, neon-lit metropolis, half circus, half resort,"[28] Sara sees the biggest little city in a different light. Stern explains the possibilities:

> a symbol of failure to some, of release to others, of despair to the unloved, of the promised land to the domestically trapped. It mean[s] quick marriage to impatient lovers, quick divorce to those who [have] found more desirable mates, the possibility of a quick killing for those with a lust for the wheel and the dice and the cards. *Could be, might be, maybe this time, maybe next time.* . . . Yes, Reno was a symbol of the second chance and the chance after that which every man always believed awaited him. . . . In America, everybody had a chance—and if they muffed it there was always the second chance. Reno . . . would give a second chance.[29]

So for people like Sara, Reno represents not the last frontier but a new one. Accordingly, Reno can be interpreted as a positive symbol of beginnings and possibilities, with the magic of Oz. Stern's characters acknowledge that "actually, all this is very peaceful. [They are] beginning to feel better already [after settling on the guest ranch]. Beginning to be able to face the future."[30] Faith Baldwin's collection of short stores, *Temporary Address: Reno,* stresses the same positive outlook, interpreting "Reno as a beginning and not an end,"[31] advocating ultimately successful adjustments and insisting upon using the word "beginning." Even a book which opens with a group of "misfits,"

Arthur Miller's screenplay by that title, turns the action around so that Reno becomes the jumping-off point for a meaningful relationship between the two main characters.

I already have indicated that most of the books under consideration here include both interpretations of Reno—blight and blessing, last frontier and first. *The Misfits* demonstrates exactly how that ambivalence works. The minor characters remain misfits; they succumb to the metaphorical "boil on the cover-girl face" of the nation. In contrast, the protagonists succeed, and, subsequently, view Reno in a different light. Able to take advantage of the opportunities offered by the new frontier, they reorient their attitudes and their lives in more positive directions. This pattern, which informs *The Misfits*, also recurs in *Not In Our Stars, Reno Fever, Reunion in Reno,* the stories in *Temporary Address: Reno,* even in Vanderbilt's *Reno* and Hamlin's *Whirlpool.* Apparently this mode of dual resolution—failure for secondary characters, success for major—is a convenient way of handling the paradox that is Reno. Each author can treat both sides of the city and include both philosophies at once, can create happy endings while describing depressing details, can project idealism while acknowledging decay. In effect, each author may have the reader eating spinach and dessert simultaneously, a feat which obviously attracts more patrons.

The audience must have been captivated, too, by a double set of extended metaphors used by most of these writers. Perhaps not surprisingly, the figures of speech grew from jargon used in the city by natives and divorcées alike. These metaphors are institutional in nature—that is, they universalize the city by tying it to familiar institutions, one medical, one educational. Thus both enable speakers to make abstractions concrete.

The first spreads from the notion of Reno as a malignancy, a symbol of decadent contemporary life. As one of Jill Stern's characters—the same man who earlier speaks of "cover-girl boils" and "ulcerated underbellies"—succinctly comments, "We're all marking time in our own self-created death house, we're all slowly dying of the same disease."[32] The disease? Loneliness, or, as one novelist called her book, *Reno Fever.* Paradoxically, marriage led to the loneliness of many would-be divorcées, so they headed to Reno to be cured. Indeed, in Reno of the '20s, '30s, and '40s, the euphemism for divorce was "the cure." Furthermore, Reno was known as "the clinic," or, "the national clinic for wrecked domestic nerves,"[33] as Max Miller describes it in his narrative. Stern attempts a comparison analogous to Miller's when she suggests similarities between the Jolly-R Guest Ranch and the sanitarium in Thomas Mann's *Magic Mountain.* Characters in both novels seek physical health, as well as emotional, spiritual, and intellectual well-being, by retiring to a self-contained retreat where their ills may be cured. Although I only with difficulty equate Sara Winston's stay with Hans Castorp's, the attempt remains interesting. Writers like Stern unknowingly show the pervasiveness in Nevada thinking of the metaphor of disease and the subsequent clinic and cure.

A somewhat different extended figure of speech was used to characterize Reno as an educational institution, where the interaction between would-be divorcées recaptures the atmosphere of college days. In *Reno Fever,* for example, four women take adjoining rooms at the Riverside and live like sorority sisters—flitting from room to room, forming intense friendships, swapping boyfriends, and somehow managing to grow up. The title of Mary Warren's *Reunion in Reno* suggests a school theme, too, with old friends getting together again—and, in this instance, remarrying. However, the significant thrust of the metaphor comes with its conventional expression on the streets of Reno. The day one received a divorce was known as "graduation day"; a divorce decree, "the diploma"; the subsequent celebration, "a graduation party." Such language, reiterating the belief that Reno prepared people for the future and offered them a second chance, supplies another restatement of the frontier theme.

One could, of course, jumble both sets of institutional metaphors, and people often did, to express a continuous operation—illness, clinic, cure, graduation, diploma—so that all interpretations lead to a positive outcome. Certainly this would cohere with the "jackpot" mentality that has pervaded Reno's life from its earliest post-Comstock days to its latest twentieth-century casino boom. Despite Reno's tarnished reputation and the sensationalism foisted upon it by the press, the city, in the minds of most people, finally spells success—or at least it spells possibilities. The prevailing figurative language advances that optimistic point of view.

This is true, in part, because Reno tends to loom larger than life. And Reno's reputation has been magnified because fiction and nonfiction alike have chosen to exaggerate it. For example, nearly every book or article mentions Reno's most famous myth—that each new divorcée, upon leaving the judge's chambers, first kisses the pillar on the courthouse porch and then tosses her old wedding ring into the Truckee River. Perpetrated by mocked-up photographs in slick magazines, this action took place mainly in the imagination. Yet advertising men favored the story in pamphlets, and fictional characters love to mention the supposed ceremony because it provides a moment of vicarious pleasure to the contemplator and to the reader: "Wouldn't it be fun to . . . ?" Even realizing that Reno novels exaggerate, the public reads them anyway because, quite simply, they stimulate the imagination. And by translating the city's symbolic potential into accessible terms, they also reinterpret contemporary life with its modern problems. So readers seeking escape and readers looking for answers can find what they want in novels written about Reno. In short, it's the old spinach/dessert conflation all over again.

For everybody, then, the city behind the arch serves a purpose. It emanates different ideas to diverse people, or, as one writer explains, "the theme of Reno is bigger than the little town itself."[34] That theme, I argue, is the theme of modern America, the curious paradox of the "decadent modern pace" juxtaposed against the perennial "pot of gold" mentality. The duality that is Reno thus is a projection of the ambivalent attitudes that make up the average twentieth-century mind. Hamlin said as much in *Whirlpool of Reno* when he portrayed the hypocrisy of the natives and the indolence of the divorcées as a microcosm of the country. Surely that contradicts Walter Clark's representation of the two "colonies" living separately, one in "the city of trembling leaves," the other in "the biggest little city in the world," but obviously Hamlin's portrayal is more attuned to that of the majority of Reno novelists. Symbolically, for the writers and for their readers, Reno reflects reality, ambiguous reality, and Reno *is* a big little city— indeed, "the biggest little city in the world."

NOTES

1. All quotations in the first paragraph are from the "Prelude," Walter Van Tilburg Clark, *The City of Trembling Leaves* (New York: Popular Library, 1945), 5–13.

2. For casino novels, one must turn to the plethora of books set in Las Vegas.

3. Reno Chamber of Commerce, *Reno, Land of Charm* (Reno: A. Carlisle and Co., [1932]), [1–2].

4. Tom Gilbert, *Reno! "It Won't Be Long Now"* (Reno: Gilbert & Shapro, 1927), 25.

5. Leslie Curtis, *Reno Reveries* (Reno: Armanko Stationery Co., 1924), 42.

6. Annie Estelle Prouty, "The Development of Reno in Relation to its Topography," *Nevada Historical Society Papers,* 4 (1923–24), 101, quotes a San Francisco *Times* correspondent writing in the August 27, 1868, Carson *Daily Appeal.*

7. Con Ryan, "The City that Sex Built," *Real Detective,* 39 (1936), 15.

8. *The Reno Divorce Racket* (Minneapolis: Graphic Arts Corp., 1931), 3; significantly, this pamphlet was published in the same year that the Nevada State Legislature had enacted a six-week divorce law and had legalized open gambling.

9. Mrs. Katharine Fullerton Gerould, *The Aristocratic West* (New York: Harper & Brothers, 1925), 182.

10. Others include James Gunn's *Deadlier than the Male* and Gloria Hope's *Inside Reno*—actually a collection of repulsive little short stories.

11. See, for example, Helen Arre's *The Corpse by the River,* Dean Evans's *No Slightest Whisper,* and Gay Greer's *The Case of the Well-Dressed Corpse.*

12. "Chamber Raps Novel On Reno," *Nevada State Journal,* March 6, 1929, p. 8, col. 8.

13. "Vanderbilt Told in Wire That He Disclosed Ingratitude," *Reno Evening Gazette,* March 5, 1929, p. 12, cols. 2–4.

14. Cornelius Vanderbilt, Jr., *Reno* (New York: Macaulay, 1929), 228.

15. "Letter to the Editor," *Sagebrush,* October 9, 1931, p. 4, cols. 3–6.

16. John Hamlin, *Whirlpool of Reno* (New York: The Dial Press, 1931), 164; again, the year of publication, 1931, is significant.

17. Vanderbilt, [3].

18. Jill Stern, *Not In Our Stars* (New York: David McKay Co., 1957), 28.

19. Ibid., 257.

20. Dorothy Wadsworth Carman, *Reno Fever* (New York: Ray Long & Richard R. Smith, Inc., 1932), 9.

21. Ibid., 37.

22. Ibid., 58.

23. Ibid., 208.

24. Stern, 64–65.

25. Ibid., 148.

26. Earl Derr Biggers, *Keeper of the Keys* (Indianapolis: Bobbs-Merrill Co., 1932), 51.

27. Carman, 21.

28. Stern, 28.

29. Ibid., 256.

30. Ibid., 81.

31. Faith Baldwin, *Temporary Address: Reno* (New York: Farrar & Rinehart, Inc., 1941), 333.

32. Stern, 148.

33. Max Miller, *Reno* (New York: Dodd, Mead & Co., 1941), 1.

34. Ibid., ix.

Suburban Resorts and the Triumph of Las Vegas

Eugene P. Moehring

Today Las Vegas enjoys an enviable reputation as one of the world's great resort cities.[1] Yet less than five decades ago this fate hardly seemed assured. With a population of 8,000 and no major industries other than railroading, the town seemed destined for little more than whistlestop status. This was particularly frustrating to longtime Las Vegans who, from the beginning, had dreamed of transforming their little community into a booming metropolis. Like the pioneers of other towns across the nation, they exuded an unrestrained optimism about the future. In a 1905 statement, booster newspaperman Charles "Pop" Squires characterized newly born Las Vegas as a "magic city." In convincing fashion, he argued that "nature intended a city here," because Las Vegas Valley possessed "every element necessary to our development," including "rich and productive" soil, the "purest water," and a climate "not excelled by any locality in the United States."[2]

For three decades, Squires and other boosters struggled to ease the unwanted dependency upon the railroad by diversifying the town's economy. Agriculture held the most promise. Sandwiched between southern California and Utah, two spectacular examples of modern man's ability to "make the desert bloom," Las Vegans were determined to fulfill the prediction of one Salt Lake reporter who in 1905 had asserted that the valley would "one day be the center of an agricultural region of wondrous wealth." Since the Mormons' initial settlement in 1855, the valley had witnessed periodic efforts to grow fruits and vegetables for travelers plying the trails between Utah and Los Angeles.[3] The opening of Clark's Las Vegas Townsite in 1905 encouraged the planting of even more farms in the valley. Moreover, the formation of the "Vegas Artesian Water Syndicate" by several local businessmen in November 1905 and the successful drilling of artesian wells a few years later encouraged experiments to develop a cash-crop economy. The search for a staple crop prompted experiments with corn, alfalfa, cantaloupes, cotton, and virtually every other fruit, vegetable, and cereal imaginable, but, in the end, the local soil's alkalinity defeated all efforts to develop large-scale, commercial agriculture in the Las Vegas Valley.[4]

A similar fate befell the campaign to provide Las Vegas with a vibrant mineral processing industry. As early as 1905 Senator William Clark laid the foundation for centralizing southern Nevada smelting operations in Las Vegas when he began construction of a railroad northwest from the city to tap the rich mineral deposits of the Bullfrog Mining District. By 1907 track-laying crews had reached Goldfield and Rhyolite. It was the junction of Clark's Salt Lake and Tonopah lines at Las Vegas that eventually brought the locomotive repair shops in 1909. Completed in 1911, they immediately added 175 jobs to the local payroll and encouraged the platting of new residential subdivisions along the edges of the business district. Las Vegas's strategic location at the heart of a railroad system whose fingers touched many of southern Nevada's copper, silver, and gold mining districts inspired Clark to suggest the construction of a great smelting complex in the city to process ore from Bullfrog, Pioche–Delamar, and other mining centers. Local newspapers applauded Clark's foresight, but the celebration was premature.[5] A diminishing supply of high-grade ore combined with sluggish prices to short-circuit the booms in many areas even before World War I. The final blow came on October 31, 1918, when Clark suspended all service on his Tonopah line. The impending construction of Boulder Dam triggered new rounds of optimism in the 1920s and '30s, but, following the project's completion in 1936, no major chemical companies came to exploit this new cheap source of electricity. Wide-open gambling and the multimillion-dollar cost of a 20-mile water line to Lake Mead were the obvious culprits. Even though the federal government came to the rescue briefly during World War II with the Basic Magnesium Complex, postwar employment at the chemical plant (2,000 in 1980) never again approached wartime levels (13,000 in 1942).[6]

So, as late as 1940 Las Vegas still lacked the key to achieving the kind of growth which could propel the little city to metropolitan size, much less world fame. And yet, while few people realized it, the long-awaited breakthrough was at hand. Surprisingly, the key industry was not railroading, agriculture, or mining, but a less obvious candidate, tourism. Of course, visitor trade had long been a staple of the local economy. For seventy years the desert oasis had supplied the needs of nineteenth-century travelers. Then, following the town's formal settlement in 1905, Las Vegas began promoting itself as a regional center. The city's role as a railroad hub had confirmed it already as the business and trade capital of southern Nevada. As host of the county's only high school, it soon became the educational center, and as county seat, it monopolized most legal and administrative functions. Gradually, Las Vegas became the region's social center as well, especially after the new Clark County Fairgrounds opened (on a site just west of City Hall) in October 1923. Thousands flocked to Las Vegas for the Indian exhibits, horticultural displays, races, baseball games, and "academic contests" between southern Nevada's students. By 1925 Las Vegas had parlayed the newly created "Southern Nevada Fair" into a major venue for showcasing "agricultural exhibits" from Moapa, Virgin Valley, and other Clark County areas. The goal was to stimulate the interest of farmers as well as out-of-state investors. At the same time, Las Vegas continued to use its railroad connections to boost its annual Labor Day festival and other events which drew even more revelers from communities along the line.

Aside from these holiday celebrations, the small railroad town with its substantial hotels, gambling parlors, and speakeasies had long provided a comfortable setting for regional business meetings and small conventions. By the early 1920s the chamber of commerce had begun to extend its marketing borders beyond southern Nevada and compete for intrastate convention business with Reno. In 1922, for instance, Las Vegas undertook a spirited campaign to lure the American Legion's state convention. Reno prevailed, however, after delegates from Winnemucca, Carson City, and Fallon objected to paying the substantial railroad fares for the trip to Clark County. While Las Vegans lobbied the railroad in vain for lower excursion rates and even promised to meet their northern counterparts in Tonopah and drive them to the meeting, they realized that if their town were to attract substantial conventions in the future it would have to form stronger alliances with Pioche, Caliente, Searchlight, Goodsprings, and other communities in southern Nevada.[7]

Las Vegas was an ideal location for conventions and meetings because, in its role as a railroad center, it had operated restaurants, bars, and hotels on a 24-hour basis since its founding in 1905. When the railroad first advertised lots for sale in Clark's Las Vegas Townsite, it carefully reserved Blocks 16 and 17 (bordered by Fremont, Second, Third, and Stewart) for the sale of intoxicating liquors. Almost immediately, a jungle of tent bars sprang up in the zone. The Star, Gem, Red Onion, Arcade, and a host of other dives thrived, catering to travelers and locals anxious to quench their thirst, gamble, and carouse with the legions of "ill-famed women" who plied their trade in the infamous cribs to the rear. Most popular of all was the Arizona Club, built in 1905 by its flamboyant proprietor James O. McIntosh. Within two years, bar profits financed a pretentious new building, featuring solid oak doors, beveled glass windows, and fine imported whiskey.

While the city's fortunes ebbed and flowed with the national economy, local clubs continued to thrive. Gambling also prospered on a limited basis, surviving both state and local efforts to ban or restrict it. Following the state legislature's epic decision to relegalize wide-open gambling in 1931, a modest number of establishments (mostly existing bars and hotels) were licensed in the city and along the new Boulder Highway toward the damsite. Yet gambling, while helpful, was hardly the road to metropolitan status—a fact made evident in 1936 when the dam's completion and the resulting outflux of workers triggered a round of casino bankruptcies which included the swank Meadows Club. Even in the 1940s, the construction of Basic Magnesium and the activation of the Air Gunnery School (today Nellis Air Force Base) multiplied the number of downtown clubs but did not transform Las Vegas into a world resort. The key to fulfilling the "magic city's" destiny still proved elusive.[8]

To a large extent, the barrier blocking Las Vegas's development as a major city was spatial. Prior to 1940, all local schemes for economic growth were city-oriented, revolving around the railroad station at Fremont Street. Yet, as was the case in most American cities, downtown lots were too confining for most industries. With the exception of commercial office buildings, Las Vegas's restrictive system of narrow blocks and lots could not have accommodated the smelters, mills, silos, and other industrial structures envisioned by promoters. The same was also true for gaming. When Nevada legalized casino gambling again in 1931, the small-time clubs and hotel barrooms lining Fremont and Ogden streets recreated the smoky, green-felt atmosphere of bygone days for a small, but steady clientele. Yet even with the arrival of Guy McAfee and other Los Angeles gamblers in the later 1930s, Las Vegas remained a small city. Like hundreds of its counterparts across the west, Las Vegas retained the characteristic appearance of a railroad town. Clubs and hotels dotted the first few streets immediately east of the station, intermingling with small office buildings housing the supply firms, shipping merchants, and other mainstays of the town's transportation economy. At the same time, real estate agents, attorneys, bailbondsmen, and other court-related officials dominated the main and backwater thoroughfares of the county seat.[9]

Despite its newfound status as the "gateway to Boulder Dam," prewar Las Vegas, like Reno, was hardly destined to become a world resort. To some extent, the patterns of development in both cities were similar. Like Fremont Street, Reno's Virginia Street snared most of the major casinos in town, including Harolds Club and Harrah's. As northern California's population mushroomed after 1930, Reno saw its tourism expand somewhat proportionately. To handle the influx, Reno multiplied the number of hotels and casinos near the railroad station. By the 1970s, the casino district stretched along South Virginia Street from the courthouse north across the Truckee and beyond the railroad tracks as well as east and west along Center, Sierra, and other side streets. Yet, in spite of its well-earned reputation as a gaming mecca, modern Reno never really matched the popularity of Las Vegas.

One crucial event triggered the process that eventually vaulted Las Vegas ahead of its northern counterpart. In 1940 Thomas Hull, a California hotelman, came to Las Vegas and decided to build a ranch-like resort similar to his others in the golden state. To everyone's amazement, he chose a site not in Las Vegas proper but across the city line on the southwest corner of Highway 91 (the Los Angeles Highway) and San Francisco Street (today Sahara Avenue and the Strip). By the simple act of erecting his hotel beyond the municipal limits, Thomas Hull planted a seed which eventually blossomed into the famed "Las Vegas Strip."

The advantages of a county location were obvious. First, taxes were lower. Since few people lived in the area, there were no special levies for police or fire protection. Moreover, water and waste removal were easily handled by the hotel's well and cesspool system. Although Las Vegas and Clark County both assessed table taxes, Hull's El Rancho (like the few small clubs beyond the city limits) escaped the municipal levy as well as its special tax on slot machines. As was the case in other cities, less restrictive fire and building codes were also an incentive, reducing the costs of original construction as well as future expansions.

Hull's suburban location also placed his operation safely beyond the control of the city's powerful casino interests led by Las Vegas Club owner J. Kell Houssels. Throughout the 1940s the powerful Houssels wielded substantial influence over the policies of Mayor Ernie Cragin as well as city commissioners Pat Clark, Bob Baskin, and others. Any large new competitor who built within the city limits could have been a target for liquor, business, and gaming license revocation, as well as "red line ordinances" leaving his property outside the approved casino district. The city commission was not above using its licensing powers to zone out certain businessmen. Witness the case of black businessmen in the 1940s, who were forced out of downtown and across the tracks to the emerging Westside ghetto. Even many white tavern and lodging house operators were victimized by sudden nonrenewals. As a result, Hull, like succeeding hotel owners on the Strip, was careful to remain outside the city's jurisdiction.[10]

While significant, all of these factors were dwarfed by one additional concern, space. Hull's move to the suburbs immediately released the brake on Las Vegas's growth by opening a new frontier for resort development. The Californian exploited his spacious lot to the fullest, covering it with a sprawling, ranchlike hotel built in Spanish mission style. Boasting a rustic interior, El Rancho's main building housed a casino, a restaurant, a showroom, and several shops. Low-rise bungalow and cottage buildings radiated outward from the main structure. From opening day, the El Rancho was a sensation, luring thousands of tourists from southern California. By demonstrating the value of a location near the highway as opposed to the railroad station, Hull revolutionized Las Vegas's development. Within a year, he was joined by theatre magnate R. E. Griffith, who built his pretentious Last Frontier Hotel about a mile farther south on the Los Angeles Highway. Adopting the El Rancho's western motif, Griffith's resort epitomized the ultimate in frontier style. Wagonwheel lights, expensive flagstones, western murals, stuffed animal displays, and other extravagances provided the Last Frontier with instant notoriety. Complementing the western atmosphere was a touch of Palm Springs: spacious lawns, willow trees, a sundeck, and a large pool (everything was larger than at the El Rancho) fronted the resort's entrance to attract passing motorists. In addition, the hotel provided guests with horseback and stagecoach rides, pack trips, a showroom seating 600, and, most important, parking for 400 cars.

While elegant in a western sense, the El Rancho and Last Frontier were still little more than opulent dude ranches. It was Bugsy Siegel's Flamingo Hotel that transformed Las Vegas from a recreation town to a full-fledged resort city. The Flamingo was the real turning point because it combined the sophisticated ambience of a Monte Carlo casino with the exotic luxury of a Miami Beach-Caribbean resort. The Flamingo liberated Las Vegas from the confines of its western heritage and established the pattern for a new "diversity of images" embodied in future Strip resorts like the Desert Inn, Thunderbird, Dunes, Tropicana, and Stardust. When it finally opened in March 1947, the Flamingo was undeniably the most glamorous hotel in Las Vegas, featuring 105 lavishly appointed rooms, a health club, gym, steam rooms, tennis courts, and facilities for squash, handball, and badminton. In addition, there were stables for forty horses, a trap-shooting range, a swimming pool, a nine-hole golf course, and assorted shops. Surrounding the magnificent three-story waterfall in front were acres of beautifully landscaped grounds containing Oriental date palms, rare Spanish cork trees, and gardens of exotic plants. In just seven years the Las Vegas area experienced a dramatic revolution based on space.[11]

Of course, all these events were part of a larger movement sweeping the nation. Hull, Griffith, and Siegel symbolized a suburban trend which began in the nineteenth century and intensified after 1910. Thanks to technological advances, American industry had begun shifting away from its traditional downtown location and toward the retreating edges of the urban periphery. In the early nineteenth century, reliance upon steam power had forced companies to locate in central cities where aqueducts fed vitally needed water into convenient street networks. By 1890, however, electricity had broken the casements imposed by steam and permitted growth farther out from the urban core. Industrial cities like Pittsburgh and Birmingham saw their steel mills, coal plants, wire and cable factories move outward to suburban locations. Farther west in Chicago, hundreds of old and new companies settled in a growing belt of industrial districts stretching down the Calumet from South Chicago eastward along the lakefront to Gary, Indiana. During this same period, New York lost much of its heavy industry to surrounding areas in Long Island, New Jersey, and Connecticut, while San Francisco's crossed the great bay to Oak-

land, Alameda, and Richmond or veered southward down the pen-
insula to Burlingame, South San Francisco, and even San Jose. Los
Angeles also witnessed a rapid decentralization of its old and new industry in the 1920s and '30s as companies fanned out in all directions
along a spindle of newly constructed boulevards and freeways. The
film industry settled in Hollywood, aerospace in El Segundo, and
chemical plants in Long Beach. Across the Sierra, Reno also experienced the so-called suburban trend, as its railroad freight and repair
facilities nursed the emerging suburb of Sparks.[12]

Yet in Las Vegas, gaming remained strangely unaffected—until
Thomas Hull came to town. A shrewd businessman, Hull recognized
how California's burgeoning power network had teamed with the
growing popularity of cars and trucks to decentralize industry and
residence. At the same time, roads not only knitted the metropolis
closer together but also made Las Vegas more accessible. Indeed, by
1940 the Los Angeles Highway had convinced thousands of Californians that the once-formidable Mojave Desert could now be comfort-
ably traversed in seven hours—a fact which forever abolished Nevada's remoteness.

While cars brought the casino city strategically closer to California
tourists, trucks promoted the suburbanization of gambling in Las
Vegas. After 1940 they gradually eclipsed the railroad's commercial
importance and, in the process, rendered Fremont Street's small club
structure increasingly obsolete. Like hundreds of roadhouse and tavern operators across the nation, Hull, Griffith, and Siegel recognized
that bars and even hotels were no longer dependent upon downtown,
railroad-oriented locations to receive their supplies. Trucks could
haul beer, liquor, soda, food, furniture, bedding, and even building
supplies to any point in the metropolitan zone. So, thanks to Hull and
his successors on the Strip, Las Vegas followed the example of Los
Angeles, Pittsburgh, New York, and other cities by spawning its own
"industrial suburb."[13]

Infrastructure, especially the Los Angeles Highway, played a crucial role in shaping these events. After World War II the development
of the Strip along the Los Angeles side of town helped shift the tourist
zone to the south. The new airport was one of the first physical mani-
festations of this trend. In 1947 Clark County commissioners decided
to reserve the old airport-gunnery school zone on the north side of
Las Vegas for the military and build a modern airport on the Los An-

geles Highway two miles south of today's Tropicana Hotel. Finished in 1948, the new terminal confirmed the growing importance of the emerging Strip.

Lying between the new airport and the Las Vegas city line, the Strip hotels utilized their spacious tracts to build a substantial tourist infrastructure of their own in the years after World War II. Replicating an effort already under way in Miami Beach, Honolulu, and Scottsdale, the hotels laid out tennis courts, riding trails, and nine-hole golf courses in a bid to lure more tourists. Even though the Strip properties were denied access to the city's water system in 1947, resort executives pushed ahead with their building plans. The initial attempt to maintain lawns and fairways relied upon the use of wells, but following creation of the Las Vegas Valley Water District in 1948, it was apparent that Hoover Dam would eventually come to the rescue. In 1955 the Strip and city finally received their first drops of Lake Mead water. And while the supply was not enough to meet the area's long-term needs, Strip executives were confident about Hoover Dam's ability to support a substantially larger tourist infrastructure. Accordingly, the Desert Inn, Tropicana, Dunes, and Stardust all made plans to build eighteen-hole golf courses.

To be sure, the dam was crucial to the Strip's success. Aside from the water it provided, dam power was also vital. Prior to 1936 most casinos were dependent upon a downtown location near the city's electrical generators. Of course, the small town's power capacity was limited and could never have supplied the air conditioning and lighting needs of later Strip resorts. But by 1937 Hoover Dam had solved that problem, providing Las Vegas with enough kilowatts to satisfy the neon industry's voracious appetite for power. Just like cars and trucks, the dam promoted the decentralization of gaming because electricity could be transmitted anywhere in the metropolitan area.

Besides expanding the valley's power and water supplies, Hoover Dam also promoted casino play downtown by luring motorists to southern Nevada. By 1937 over 300,000 dam visitors annually patronized the cluster of clubs on Fremont Street. This trend continued until 1941 when Thomas Hull attempted to alter the pattern by building his resort hotel apart from the club center. After World War II the clustering of resorts along the Strip diverted thousands more dam tourists away from the clubs downtown. At a time when space-consuming businesses like factories and warehouses were flocking to

America's suburbs in search of cheaper land, Hull did the same in an effort to lure guests with more spacious facilities than Fremont Street offered.[14]

His appeal to southern Californians was particularly clever. As early as 1930 Los Angeles claimed the highest percentage of single-family dwellings (94 percent) in urban America. So, even before 1940, Angelenos were in the process of building a new, decentralized, low-density megalopolis composed largely of homes with the most per capita living space in history. Not surprisingly, these tourists preferred Hull's low-rise, ranchlike hotel with its many individual bungalows over the traditional "hotel rooms" downtown. While the motor courts bordering the casino center were admittedly popular, the El Rancho's location in the less congested suburbs appealed even more to the freeway-loving Angelenos who disliked the downtown orientation of San Francisco, New York, and other cities.[15]

Like the tourists, Las Vegans also embraced the suburban trend. Indeed, the emerging Strip mirrored the growing national tendency toward decentralized employment. In a city where car ownership was high, many casino employees living south of Fremont Street undoubtedly preferred driving to work in the suburbs where parking was convenient. Gradually, they moved out of town altogether, as the Flamingo, Dunes, and Tropicana extended the hotel zone farther south. With the proliferation of resorts after 1947, the Strip resort industry eventually created a demand for its own residential suburb in Paradise Valley. Although postwar Las Vegas, like other core cities, continued as the center of railroad transportation, credit, labor, and administration for southern Nevada, the nascent Strip suburbs of Paradise and Winchester slowly decentralized the metropolitan area's residential, shopping, and educational patterns. By 1955 the growing number of Strip hotels had created a huge suburban job zone, which, in turn, supported miles of low-rise subdivisions. In time, the futuristic Strip "Los Angelized" the metropolitan area.

By the 1960s a bustling new city of office parks, shopping centers, restaurants, homes, and condominiums boasting the latest in Spanish Mission elegance increasingly graced the roads branching off Desert Inn, Flamingo, Sahara, Tropicana, and other Strip arteries. Buttressed by a soaring population of upwardly mobile casino workers, these suburbs soon challenged the city's economic and demographic hegemony. In 1960 the Strip suburbs counted only 27,000 residents compared to the city's 64,000. By 1970, thanks to the Strip's multiplier effect upon the metropolitan economy as a whole, the Strip suburbs edged up to 89,000, while the city's figure jumped to 125,000. Then in 1980 Paradise and Winchester finally triumphed by a count of 220,000 to 164,000! Space, low taxes, and permissive county government had won their inevitable victory over Las Vegas just as they had in cities across the nation. The key factor was the shift of employment to the suburbs. By 1970, in nine of fifteen of America's largest metropolitan areas, including New York and Los Angeles, the suburbs counted more jobs than their central cities.[16]

When Thomas Hull, R. E. Griffith, and Bugsy Siegel opted to stretch the town's casino industry beyond the city limits, they assured Las Vegas's future by placing it in the mainstream of American metropolitan development. But unlike the rest of urban America, Las Vegas pioneered a unique suburban industry, casino gambling. While the nation already possessed a number of "resort suburbs" like Scottsdale and Miami Beach, Las Vegas claimed the first "casino suburb" and certainly the first suburb whose industry competed with and eventually transformed the main industry of its own central city! The farsighted hotelmen along the Strip understood the spatial demands of this new leisure business. Broadway stars, Hollywood celebrities, and nightclub performers from all the big cities converged upon the Strip's spacious showrooms, competing for the attention of hotel guests. In time, this glittering new suburb remade its central city over in its own likeness. Indeed, by the late 1950s downtown casinos were building substantial hotels with showrooms and expanding their barrooms into spacious lounges for smaller acts. Pools, health clubs, and gourmet restaurants had all appeared by 1960, as the Golden Nugget, Pioneer Club, and other landmarks vied for Strip customers.[17]

While the Flamingo, Desert Inn, and other famous hotels clearly overshadowed the city, their contribution to Las Vegas cannot be denied. Had it not been for the Strip's success, Las Vegas as a whole would never have realized the enormous potential of the California gaming market. The suburban resorts, with their posh suites, gardens, pools, sports facilities, and parking lots, provided tourists and celebrities alike with a full-fledged resort destination. As Bugsy Siegel demonstrated, the mere act of luring Hollywood stars instantly glamorized Las Vegas, which, in turn, expanded its tourist market to national and even international dimensions. Once again, technology aided the cause, bringing Las Vegas to an ever-expanding audience. In the 1950s and '60s television and movie publicity only catalyzed the marketing effort, while air-conditioned cars, buses, and jet planes combined to smash the distance barrier once and for all.

Given the casino city's relative failure to compete with Phoenix, Tucson, and southern California in the struggle for mills and factories, the Strip hotels literally rescued Las Vegas from a whistlestop fate. In just twenty years, the great resorts transformed Las Vegas from a desert town to a "magic city," fulfilling the dream of local pioneers. The key to this triumph lay in Thomas Hull's ingenious move to place gambling in a resort setting that only the suburbs could provide.

NOTES

1. For excellent coverage of the city's growing popularity, see John Findlay, *People of Chance: Gambling in American Society from Jamestown to Las Vegas* (New York: Oxford University Press, 1986), *passim*.

2. *Las Vegas Age*, July 29, 1911, 1.

3. Florence Lee Jones, "Golden Anniversary Edition," *Las Vegas Review-Journal*, February 28, 1955, 11; *Clark County Review*, February 21, 1914, 1−2.

4. *Las Vegas Review*, February 25, 1911, 1; *Las Vegas Age*, July 19, 1919, 1; *Las Vegas Review*, June 2, 1922, 1.

5. *Las Vegas Age*, July 24, 1909, 1, 8; *Las Vegas Review*, June 9, 1922, 1.

6. *Las Vegas Times*, September 23, 1905, 8, 1; December 2, 1905, 8, 3; March 24, 1906 1, 3; Michael Green, "Boosting Beginnings: The *Las Vegas Times*, 1905−1906," (unpublished paper), 6−7. For oil drilling at Goldfield, see *Las Vegas Age*, January 9, 1909, 1.

7. Jones, "Construction Section," 4, 8.

8. *Las Vegas Review-Journal*, June 10, 1979, 3J−5J; Russell Elliott, *History of Nevada* (Lincoln: University of Nebraska Press, 1973), 248, 278−79; and James Hulse, *The Nevada Adventure* (Reno: University of Nevada Press, 1978), 250−56.

9. *Insurance Maps of Las Vegas, Clark County, Nevada* (New York: Sanborn Map Company, 1928, 1961 updated), 6−7, 4−5, 8−9, 12−13. Also see *Directory of Las Vegas and Vicinity, 1943−44* (Las Vegas, 1944).

10. Perry B. Kaufman, "The Best City of Them All: A History of Las Vegas, 1930−1960" Ph.D. dissertation, University of California, Santa Barbara, 1974), 337−39.

11. For a good description of these three hotels, see *Las Vegas Sun Magazine*, April 1, 1979, 6−10; April 8, 1979, 6−11, and April 22, 1979, 6−11. For more on Siegel and the Flamingo, consult Ed Reid and Ovid Demaris, *The Green Felt Jungle* (New York: Pocket Books, 1964), 20−22, 27−38.

12. Two classic works on the suburbanization of early twentieth-century America are: Harlan P. Douglass, *The Suburban Trend* (New York: The Century Company, 1925) and Graham Taylor, *Satellite Cities: A Study of Industrial Suburbs* (New York: D. Appleton and Company, 1915). Richard C. Wade, *Chicago: Growth of a Metropolis* (Chicago: The University of Chicago Press, 1969), 188–250; for a brief discussion of New York, see Eugene P. Moehring, "Space, Economic Growth and the Public Works Revolution in New York," *Essays in Public Works History*, no. 14 (December 1985): 46–55. For Los Angeles, consult Mark S. Foster, "The Model T, the Hard Sell and Los Angeles Urban Growth: The Decentralization of Los Angeles During the 1920s," *Pacific Historical Review* (1975): 459–84; Kenneth T. Jackson, *Crabgrass Frontier: The Suburbanization of the United States* (New York: Oxford University Press, 1985), 178–79.

13. Jackson, op. cit., 183–84.

14. *Las Vegas Review-Journal*, April 22, 1974, 1; April 23, 1947, 18. For Hoover Dam's contribution to the growth of southern Nevada, see ibid., September 8, 1985, "Hoover Dam Workers Also Built a New West," 13L–15L.

15. Jackson, op. cit., 179.

16. Las Vegas Planning Department, *Population Profiles: Population, Income, Housing, Occupation, Education Analysis of the 1970 Census*, n.d., 3; Ward H. Gubler, "Las Vegas: An International Recreation Center" (master's thesis, University of Utah, 1967), 133. Nevada Development Authority, First Interstate Bank, *Las Vegas Review-Journal, Las Vegas Perspective* (Las Vegas, 1981 ed.), 19, 16.

17. See, for example, how the new Fremont Hotel downtown was laid out in 1956. *Las Vegas Review-Journal*, May 17, 1956, 32; May 18, 1956, 1; Kaufman, op. cit., 207–8; *Las Vegas Sun Magazine*, July 29, 1979, 6–11.

Las Vegas   West Egg?   John H. Irsfeld

There are probably only four good and influential imaginative utterances about Las Vegas. They are *Fear and Loathing in Las Vegas: A Savage Journey to the Heart of the American Dream* (1971), by Hunter S. Thompson; *Vegas: A Memoir of a Dark Season* (1974), by John Gregory Dunne; *Fools Die* (1978), by Mario Puzo; and *The Desert Rose* (1983), by Larry McMurtry.

By "imaginative utterances" I mean those written works that purport to be more re-creations of experience than vehicles for information. Let us say, with Valery, that an imaginative utterance is to dancing as an informational utterance is to walking to the store.

I say that these four books are "about Las Vegas," but I say it with reservations, since it may fairly be said that in the truest sense none of these really is about Las Vegas, but more about what Las Vegas symbolizes, or about that version of the reality of Las Vegas that each of these artists has experienced, has chosen as his truth for the nonce. These books can be examined as Las Vegas books and also simply as books, as artistic achievements, over and above what they are about. My primary interest, as a fiction writer who lives in Las Vegas, is in the experience of place that each reveals.

Fear and Loathing is fairly titled, and refers to the primary emotions that Las Vegas elicits from Raoule Duke, the persona who narrates the events of a few drug-crazed days in the city. He says early in the book that "Las Vegas is just up ahead," but in a sense he never reaches it at all. What he reaches instead is a gonzo journalist's account of his anger and resentment at all those straight, middle-class Americans for whom Las Vegas *is* a proper place to go to while away the time. Las Vegas becomes a whipping boy, a scapegoat upon which the sins of the great middle are laid. And Raoule Duke terrorizes both, beating them up much the way the police beat up the kids in the summer of '68. Fair is fair.

The book is a picaresque novel that moves in its series of slightly illegal adventures from L.A. to L.V., is unsuccessful when it tries to go back again to L.A., and moves finally east, back to Denver and then home to Aspen (which, like Las Vegas, is an easy target for fun, but one that I'll pass on for now).

As a book *qua* book, it is what they call in the trade a *tour de force*, a feat of strength, of skill, of ingenuity. It reads as easily and as quickly as its original two-part appearance in *Rolling Stone* magazine suggests it would. And still, for all that, it is not what one would safely call a work of the first intensity. The word "hopefully" is used in its colloquial misplacement; "or whatever" dangles uselessly, emptily, at the end of too many clauses. Works of the first intensity lack such rough edges.

Druggies are feared and hated by a straight, middle-class world that the druggies, in turn, hate and fear. On the face of it, the druggies are the crazies, not the straights. This book speaks for those for whom the truth is not that simple. For even as the perceptions of the one world are altered by chemicals, so the perceptions of the other are altered by the sometimes overwhelming pressures of the very process of living, by acculturation; by the demands of any society that the mass of its members get in the box, so to speak, if not for their own good, then at least for the good of the majority. It is, of course, the cry of any minority voice in the wilderness of democracy; only here the plea is marked by a tone of absolute certainty that it is right and the rest of us wrong. *Fear and Loathing* gets a B+ over an Unsatisfactory in behavior, for acting-out, as they used to say, during civics class. Such behavior may be disruptive, but for a democracy, at least, it is also vital.

Vegas: A Memoir of a Dark Season is another title that won't lead an uninformed reader astray. It *is* a memoir, which is to say that it is a narrative composed from personal experience, autobiography. As such, it is—like *Fear and Loathing*—more a map of its author's boundaries than it is a map of Las Vegas.

Still, it provides a more accurate re-creation of what it is like to live in Las Vegas than does the Thompson book. It limits itself, however, to certain deep holes along the edges of the fast water but is more like the fast water than the sleepy eddies along the banks where most of us citizens live.

Dunne comes to Las Vegas at a low point in his own life—the dark season of the title—almost as a soul comes into Purgatory to cleanse itself before going on to glory, which is L.A. He is prompted to make the visit when, in the depths of a great despair and an almost suffocating sense of his mortality, he sees a giant sign in L.A. that says, VISIT LAS VEGAS BEFORE YOUR NUMBERS [*sic*] UP." In this day we don't depend upon the turns that flying birds make, to serve as omens, or upon the pattern of the sediment in the bottom of a teacup. These methods are quaint and our responses to them as augurs of the future are self-conscious, and not vital, not real, not binding. They do not speak, even as astrologers do not speak, directly to our actions. Advertisements, on the other hand, do, even when the grammar or punctuation or syntax is less than we might wish.

Dunne's first stop in Las Vegas—as was Raoule Duke's—is the Mint Hotel. Later he finds a place to live on Desert Inn Road, a place called the Royal Polynesian. It is not down on any map. It is here, once settled, that the narrator tells what his purpose is. If Duke was in search of the American Dream, as he ostensibly was, Dunne is in search of release from the dream his own life had become:

> It seemed a perfect place to spend that summer, a paradigm of anti-life. I did not gamble, cared not at all about the Mob and even less about Howard Hughes. But there were other stories and other people, and there were days when I told myself that through the travail of others I might come to grips with myself, that I might, as it were, find absolution through voyeurism. Those were the good days.

While he writes of the lives of others than these, there are three main characters besides himself in Dunne's book. The first is Artha Ging, beautician school student by day, hooker by night. At first she recalls the ethnic—Polish—sexual curiosity of Dunne's upper-middle-class New England youth. Later, she is transmogrified into a sexual version of himself as journalist-prostitute. She uses Dunne to gain safe access to a variety of Las Vegas places and functions without the fear of being hassled by police. He uses her as an object of his method of absolution. The second character is Buster Mano, a private detective whose jobs in life are to overcome his chronic constipation and to solve, for money, problems caused by other people's misbehavior. He represents a version of Dunne, too, the reporter as researcher, as digger-after-sordid-details. The third is Jackie Kasey, a stand-up comic who has opened for major acts in main showrooms—even for Elvis— and who is now trying to make it on his own in a lounge. While Artha Ging and Buster Mano barely scrape by financially, Jackie is pulling down $10,000 a week. And I suspect he represents for Dunne the easy money that he himself had made in ways that, given his Catholic up-bringing, he must, at some level, have disapproved of. Kasey uses Dunne as someone to talk to, to try out his version of things on, to see what works. Like many writers, Jackie doesn't know what he means until he sees what he says.

There are other characters in the book, such as Marvin Berlin, who owns a dealer's school, and Bill Parsons, the bail bondsman, but it is essentially the lives—the travails—of Artha, Buster, and Jackie of which Dunne writes:

> I liked to think, I told myself . . . , that I could learn something about myself from the people whose lives I intruded upon, in-deed that was the reason I had taken up residence in an apart-ment behind the Strip. Perhaps I even believed this. Perhaps it was even true.

In a larger sense, it can be said that to the extent that drugs consti-tute the context of *Fear and Loathing,* sex is that same context in *Vegas: A Memoir of a Dark Season,* for it dominates the behavior of everyone in the book.

But when all is said, the book—like *Fear and Loathing*—is more truly an account of its author, of its narrator, at any rate, than it is of Las Vegas, or even of Artha Ging, Buster Mano, and Jackie Kasey. Even though this book is laced with such lines as "Vegas has a way of coopt-ing burned-out cases; there is a sense that failed expectations are the mean, the norm," there is also the sense that it is more himself the narrator is speaking of than anyone else. For as he reminds us, "I loved confession, the sense of a burden removed when one said the magic formula. . . ."

Magic is at the heart of the third Las Vegas book, *Fools Die,* by Mario Puzo. It *is* a title which will lead readers astray, however, unlike the previous two. On top of that, it begins with an absolutely God-awful first chapter that took me three separate tries to get through. I kept thinking, rather ungenerously, that this book was simply bad; I thought I would not be able even to read it. Unlike the others, it is a giant work of 572 pages in hardback. That comes to something like 225,000 to 230,000 words. That's a lot; it's too much.

But the funny thing is, it is remarkably good at what it does. And another thing is, flawed though it is, it may be the best book of the bunch.

To the extent that this is a book about Las Vegas, its context is mostly gambling, a subject given only passing attention in the other books under consideration. And when Puzo writes about gambling, he's magnificent. Sex plays a large part in this book, also; drugs, only a tiny part.

The central character is a writer named John Merlyn, like the magician only with an older spelling. He thinks of himself as a magician most of the time, that is the writer-as-conjuror, and is OK when he does that. When he thinks of himself as an artist, which he does when he goes to Hollywood to work on the filmscript of his finally successful novel, he is not so OK. On the subject of writing, he is at his best when he says:

> The truth was that you were like a safecracker fiddling with the dial and listening to the tumblers click into place. And after a couple of years the door might swing open and you could start typing. And the hell of it was that what was in the safe was most times not all that valuable.

Thirty pages later he says it again: "I'm just a safecracker. I put my ear to the wall and wait to hear the tumblers fall in place." Anybody who realizes this central truth about the craft of writing has a claim on my attention, on my commitment to a tactful reading.

Gambling starts out as the context—or subtext, which may be a better word—in *Fools Die,* but it does not remain so, because a great amount of this giant work does not take place in Las Vegas. To the extent that the scenes shift to New York or to L.A., the other two main settings, the subtexts become power and sex. With all three, of course, money lies at the bottom, controls or is controlled by the gambling, the sex, and the power. To have it our own way is, as we all know, evidence of our worthiness. In the case of gambling, winning clearly proves that God loves us best, especially in those games which favor luck over skill. Still, as the wise and terrifying owner Gronevelt constantly reminds everyone, the percentages will do you in. As he is forced out of control of his hotel, the Xanadu, Gronevelt goes gambling with his #2 man, Cully "Countdown" Cross, a man he ultimately has to have disposed of. Gronevelt seems to be going against his creed of a lifetime. At first he wins, gambling with a million-dollar stake he has drawn from his holdings. But:

> By the middle of the second week Gronevelt, despite all his skill, was sliding downhill. The percentages were grinding him

into dust. And at the end of two weeks he had lost his million dollars. When he bet his last stack of chips and lost, Gronevelt turned to Cully and smiled. He seemed to be delighted, which struck Cully as ominous. "It's the only way to live," Gronevelt said. "You have to live going with the percentage. Otherwise life is not worthwhile. Always remember that," he told Cully. "Everything you do in life use percentage as your god."

Malomar, the Hollywood moviemaker with whom Merlyn makes a kind of peace, says of Merlyn's snotty attitude, "You came here for a few months and you pass judgment on everybody. You put us all down." In a sense—with the qualifiers I have added—this is true of the first two books I've written about here. It is not true of *Fools Die*. Puzo is far more generous about Las Vegas than is either Thompson or Dunne. But he is far more generous about everything else, as well. I think he has a larger heart. He doesn't find human beings any better overall than do Thompson or Dunne, but he is far more forgiving of that fact that they are. He seems to hate less, to love more. I suspect this generosity of spirit has cost him some of the critical acclaim he might otherwise have realized.

I hasten to add, however, that for all its virtues, *Fools Die* has its problems. I condemn, for example, the device of that first six-page chapter of the book which shows up again forty pages from the end as the first (and final) six pages of an unfinished work by one of Puzo's characters. This man, an Italian-American writer, as he is slyly referred to, appears to be a maniacal cross between Norman Mailer and Puzo himself. Merlyn constantly reassures us and himself that he is a far better writer than Osano, who is much heralded. Yet Puzo uses the pages of Osano's unfinished manuscript as the opening of his own book. I don't know if Merlyn is a better writer than Osano, but Puzo sure is, and his book would be the better without those six pages, either at the end—where an argument for retaining them could be made—or at the beginning—where they serve only as evidence that after *The Godfather*'s great success, Puzo could write whatever the hell he pleased. Where is Maxwell Perkins when we really need him?

I'm at a loss about the final work, Larry McMurtry's *The Desert Rose*. He has been more than generous in his reviews of my own books, and I owe him for that. (As I owe Puzo; the success of *The Godfather* allowed Putnam's the luxury of publishing my novels, knowing they would not make any money from them.) At the same time, McMurtry's new book throws me. I would love to praise it and move on, happy that I'd re-paid in part a debt I think I owe. But praise is not in order here as much as simple curiosity is.

The Desert Rose, like *Fools Die,* is a novel, an imaginative utterance that does not pretend to be an informational utterance in the same way as do the Thompson and Dunne books. The pictures it paints are mostly verifiable and accurate, the lapses few (one cannot buy fur-niture off the floor at Neiman's here, for example). But the narrative points of view that McMurtry chose to carry the story baffle me.

Here's the situation: The novel is divided into seven sections. Har-mony, the mother in the story and one of the two main characters, is at the center of sections I, III, V, and VII. Her daughter Pepper is at the center of sections II, IV, and VI. Harmony is a showgirl at the Stardust with over twenty years on the Strip. Her daughter, sym-bolically named, I suspect, though not so peppery perhaps as simply bratty, is just sixteen. She is offered the job as lead dancer in the same show Harmony has been a showgirl in for so long. In the meantime, Harmony has her thirty-ninth birthday and is fired from her job. The boss points out to her that it just wouldn't look right for a mother and a daughter to share the same stage.

The truth is, of course, and the *point* is, that the shows on the Strip, and by extension all that makes this town work, depend on youth, hard-bodies, and beauty. And that, even though Harmony has gained only a pound or so in over twenty years and is acknowledged by every-one as still beautiful, still, she is thirty-nine years old. Those older than that see the humor here, as well as the injustice, but when that's the way it is, that's the way it is.

There's no problem with this as a plot line for a novel, and God knows, McMurtry has enough going for him for me not to be too picky about it at that level. But for a reason I can't figure out, he has chosen to tell his story from a third-person point of view refracted through the marginal intelligences of these two women. Harmony is sweet enough, but even the other characters see how simple-minded she is. And Pepper may be full of vinegar, but contentiousness ain't *prima facie* evidence of good sense. They both think and speak a frozen-peas kind of Vegas Strip-show Valley-girl. So, even though the book is not written in the first-person point of view, alternating Harmony's sections with Pepper's—as I probably would have done it—that's what it amounts to. The level of language used is appropri-ate to Harmony and Pepper and not to some narrator who, presumably, knows more about what is going on than either of them. The book is, thus, heavily laden with "sort of," and "totally" (or, "sort of totally," which occurs at least twice), and "or something."

This kind of language does reveal the kinds of minds the two main characters have, but it does an injustice to the narrative. So I quarrel with this initial decision on McMurtry's part. The aesthetic problem here is the same one encountered, for example, by any writer who ever tried to convey in an interesting way the essence of a boring conversation.

And yet McMurtry knows the game and has the insights. With all my quibbles, the book is still worth the money for lines like this: "Jealousy doesn't preserve anything."

The contexts of this book, by the way, are youth worship, relationships, the lure of the surfaces of things, and the war against boredom that too many of us face every day.

All four of these writers, like the man in Robert Pirsig's book *Zen and the Art of Motorcycle Maintenance,* can be suspected by those of us who live here of having stopped the car on the highway, run out into the desert and picked up a handful of sand, and said, "Here is the world." It's an unfair accusation given their apparent intentions, and yet we are left after reading them with the nagging certainty that they have omitted something essential about us.

Still, there is hope. The definitive imaginative utterance "about Los Vegas" has not been written yet, or at least published. None of *these* is it, anyway. That means the gold ring is still there for the grabbing, a prospect which should give some hope to the dozens of writers in this town, many with talent, some with endurance and clear intention. The book on Vegas isn't closed yet.

For while this *is* a gambling town—with all that goes along with such a place—it isn't *just* a gambling town. But the part of it that is not is different in many ways from other places because of the gambling part. There is fast water here in the middle of the streambed, no question about it; but along the banks are quieter pools where the old-timers hang out. They've seen the fast-water fish come and go, and many of them have themselves darted into the fast water for adventure or for gain. But they know you cannot live there all the time; nobody can have fun twenty-four hours a day, even if it's there for the having. Those who try to do it burn out early, short-circuited by the overload.

The Las Vegas novel in my mind is a novel that includes both the fast water—for it must—and the pools along the sides, as well. It is a novel not just of gambling, but of all those other games we play to fill out our days and ways; not just of lust, but of love; not just of wealth and fame, but of that quest also that many of us engage in—even here—for those values we mean to live and die for. It is a novel, in other words, that brings *the news*—as the word *novel* used to mean—of life as it is, in fact, lived; not a caricature of life, not a distortion of the truth.

If Scott Fitzgerald were alive today, I have no doubt that he would choose Las Vegas as the setting of at least part of *The Great Gatsby*.

In that book, Nick refers to West Egg, the place where he lives out on Long Island, as "one of the strangest communities in North America." It is not fashionable as is its neighbor East Egg, just as Las Vegas is not fashionable. But, as is often the case, people like Gatsby live in West Egg; people like Tom Buchanan live in East Egg. Given the choice, I'd take Gatsby any day of the week. For even though Gatsby "represented everything for which I have unaffected scorn," as Nick puts it, still he "turned out all right at the end." He turned out all right because he had "an extraordinary gift for hope, a romantic readiness." Because of its youth, something like these qualities infects Las Vegas. And it is because this part of its personality has not yet been represented in the major fiction written about it that I contend that the book on Vegas has not been written yet; it remains, like the green light that Gatsby believed in, "the orgiastic future that year by year recedes before us. It eluded us then, but that's no matter—tomorrow we will run faster, stretch out our arms farther. . . . And one fine morning—"

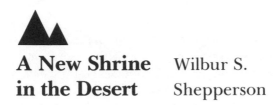

A New Shrine in the Desert

Wilbur S. Shepperson

In the 1980s Nevada hosted the largest conventions in the country, established new businesses at three times the national average, and entertained over twenty-seven million tourists per year. National trends, as well as internal state efforts, had prompted a half century of uninterrupted economic growth. A new Nevada image has slowly eclipsed the old—so long embossed with dust, sage, and untamable distance. A massive influx of construction money, an expanded wave of social democracy, a breakdown in the old codes of morality, an unprecedented mobility, and a revolution in consumer technology have revitalized the state. Rapid transport followed by air-conditioned luxury hotels and casinos became the cake; the technicolor fantasia of neon and pop art, complemented by major changes in entertainment patterns, has supplied the icing. Through a sophisticated use of technology, Nevada has triumphed as a master salesman, showman, and popular mythmaker. Slowly, residents have come to believe that the state's century-long, boom-and-bust cycle has been replaced with economic stability. The old Spanish adage, "There *will be* birds again this year in last year's nest," has meaning for a state that survived most of its history in the shadow of mining depressions.

With the changing American attitudes and social institutions, there has been a mellowing toward, and a greater public acceptance of, much of Nevada's "questionable" behavior. Earlier in this century divorce was not countenanced by any major religious group, patrons at nightclubs were declared unchaste and morally unwashed, and gambling was illegal everyplace in the country. Indeed, the evolution in attitude surrounding the current acceptance of gambling is in many ways similar to the provisional acceptance of privateering on the high seas some two centuries ago.

The illicit commerce that once helped to build prosperous seaports like Boston, New York, Charleston, and New Orleans is comparable to the economic importance of gambling for Nevada cities. Smugglers were among the first to become aware of the overall importance of commerce to the national economy, and several of them were to be involved in the founding of the Republic. Article I, Section 8, of the Constitution gave the young United States the authority to "grant Letters of Marque and Reprisal and make Rules concerning Captures on Land and Water." In the seventeenth and eighteenth centuries entrepreneurs invested in privateering in much the same manner as today's wealthy investors buy into corporate gambling. Just as piracy has been declared the oldest trade and prostitution the oldest profession, gambling and games of chance are as old as written records. Actually, there has often been little distinction between the freebooter and the trader, the prostitute and the entertainer, the gambler and the broker.

Governments and the populace were ambivalent in their attitudes toward illicit trade. Nevertheless, commerce built prosperous cities, introduced cosmopolitan goods and ideas, radically improved the lifestyle of most citizens, and profoundly changed the cultural and intellectual condition of society. It was difficult to manage the relationship between ethical demands, government revenues, and community prosperity in 1770, and it is equally difficult today.

Gambling, horse racing, cockfighting, gander pulling, lottery games, and similar sports arrived in America as both the product of British aristocracy and sportsmen and the rowdy contests of backwoodsmen. As civilization moved west, the games took on new forms and borrowed from both the French and the Spanish; they made the Mississippi riverboats and the southern plantations equally famous. Gambling flourished on the mining and cowboy frontier; at the same time, organized syndicates, along with the police, protected gambling parlors in most American cities. For a time gambling was legal in most western states, and although illegal in Nevada between 1910 and 1931, games of chance remained readily available. Soon after World War II, however, the Old West's legendary speculation and betting were tied into the New West's search for glamour and upward mobility. A new industry much like that of the pirate-traders was born. While exerting an independence and individualism worthy of the freebooters, the new entrepreneurs were soon cultivated, regulated, and taxed. And much like earlier traders, they provided for the economic flowering of colorful cities.

Nevada's buccaneer economy has been phenomenally successful. Because of a series of fortuitous circumstances, cities like Las Vegas have gained a flashcard recognition that rivals that of Disneyland or Hollywood. Millions of Americans and foreigners alike now recognize the city's late-twentieth-century trademark: spectacular entertainment. Most travelers relate to the emotional escapism that allows ageless children to live recklessly for forty-eight or seventy-two hours. Nevada provides an elaborate tableau that beckons these aging, youth-obsessed Americans to press their faces to the shop window and be titillated and fixated by a style and a wealth that is an end in itself.

For forty years Nevada has shown a superior sense of timing. The exuberant publicity, depicting a grainy, immediate, but highly sophisticated slice of life, has been uniquely successful. The visual fixation with repetition and glut and objects of desire stems from the very heart of the American consumer economy. But Nevada has gone much farther: there is the appeal and the power to dictate appetite. An artistic and social image of forensic brilliance has been created. The state's cities are much more than a catering service; their very rituals and openness have released powerful steroids into the stream of American desire. Las Vegas, in particular, is more than a place: it has become an idea, an object, an appellation, like the Cote d'Azur.

For thousands of years man has built a mystique around certain locations; he has changed nondescript areas into shrines, rugged mountain peaks into sacrificial altars. During the twentieth century the phenomenon has most often occurred simultaneously at the artistic, psychological, and commercial level. For example, over a few decades at the turn of the century, Cézanne, Picasso, Matisse, and a few others, because of their art and life-style, created an image for the Cote d'Azur. Slowly in the minds of European and American bourgeoisie the coast became much more than a pleasant beach: it became a prized symbol, a valued illusion, a source of inspiration and meaning. In only a slightly different sense and for a different segment of society, Coney Island, Niagara Falls, or the old Atlantic City were once goals to be sought or places embodying a dream. The name *Las Vegas* is now emotionally charged throughout most of the western world. Whether performing in a club in London or Paris or New York or even Hollywood, it is a mark of high showmanship for an entertainer to be advertised as "just in from Las Vegas." While the self-righteous might equate the name with unvarnished sin, social mores have so radically shifted during the past few decades that Billy Graham could be flattering when he held a crusade in the city. He likened Las Vegas to New York's Wall Street or London's Soho.

Nevada has reaped great profits from the liberalized moral and cultural outlook of late-twentieth-century America. Sociologist Joshua Meyrowitz in *No Sense of Place: The Impact of Electronic Media on Social Behavior* argues that the pervasiveness of television and modern electronics have eliminated many of the old distinctions between what is personal and private and what is publicly acceptable, between what may be seen and what should remain censored. Last century the pornographic murals of Pompeii were available only to a select group of judicious men, and the reading of novels was condemned from the pulpit; earlier, the Continental Congress banned plays because they were immoral and not compatible with republican virtues. As American attitudes on sex, nudity, Sunday recreation, and gambling changed, Nevada moved ahead of the mainstream and became a pacemaker in popular entertainment. Indeed, it was the rapid democratization of recreation, the sexual revolution, and the feminist revolt that allowed for the creation of contemporary Nevada. It was necessary for the old forms—like men gambling in the drab half-lit back room of a bar and racial exclusions—to be swept away so that the state could become the purveyor of the modern barrier-free amusements. As censorship by church, state, and other authorities has collapsed, women as well as men and minorities as well as the masses have been drawn to Nevada's shrines of pleasure and equality.

In the early sixties Tom Wolfe saw Las Vegas as a "profound symbol" and a "founding muse" of the new style of life then emerging in the United States. He christened the city "the Versailles of America." Of course, Las Vegas was being created by a different social class than Louis XIV's baroque Versailles. The Nevada city was designed by and for the proletarians. Petty-burghers, investors, and rogues, mainly from the West Coast, had grown rich during World War II. For the first time in history, uneducated, but shrewd men had accumulated enough wealth to finance a monument to themselves and to launch a profitable industry representing new forms and tastes. This social avant-garde was for a time ignored, except by the peddlers of sleaziness and those seeking cheap sensationalism. But the democratic masses responded, and the gaudy kingdom in the desert became part of the American fantasy.[1]

The man-made oasis quickly developed its own charms and with surprising speed came to be compared with the grand designs of American and European landscape artists. Imaginatively blending the past into the present, California's literary historian, Kevin Starr, has compared a Las Vegas golf course to a fine Italian garden. The engineering, the landscaping, the botanical skills, and the basic environmental necessities are clearly greater in Las Vegas than they were in Napoleon's gardens at Turin. Both were created for the pleasure of the upwardly mobile and the aspiring *nouveau riche*.

Nevada's emerging folklore and cultural imprint upon the desert has not been fully interpreted and is as yet without lengthy tradition. But while grounded in the past, culture, like science, perceives new horizons and designs the future; it is as Wallace Stegner has said, "a pyramid to which each of us brings a stone." The 440 episodes of the forever popular television series, "Bonanza," set on Nevada's Ponderosa Ranch between 1959 and 1973, were within fourteen years translated into a dozen languages and seen in eighty countries by 400 million people. We are told by psychiatrists that this type of televised drama "is a storehouse for the intra-psychic images of our time," and that it serves us "in the same way tragedy served 5th century Greeks." [2] In three decades "Bonanza" may have had a greater impact on American clothes, drama, finances, and even thought and culture than all of Jack London's books. Similarly, Caesar's Palace on the Las Vegas Strip may yet inspire as many articles and as much critical comment as England's historic and controversial Crystal Palace. It has already entertained more visitors from more countries. It does not devalue culture, history, or human reason to find form and direction evolving from economic expansion and mass social spontaneity. For example, historian Warren Susman has suggested that "Mickey Mouse may in fact be more important to an understanding of the 1930s than Franklin Roosevelt." [3]

While unwise to exaggerate the historic divergence between a "public" and a more sophisticated "elite" culture, the elite or high bourgeois always represented a culture of the minority. According to labor historian Eric J. Hobsbawm, the twentieth century has seen a conquest of the world by "industrialized entertainment," which he labels "the plebeian arts." Cinema, comic strips, television, and sights and sounds of Nevada's casinos have become the basis for man's new myths and fantasies. The emerging electronic motif is broad, democratic, and, above all, technological and for the masses. The plebeian machine-age arts helped to create contemporary Nevada, and Nevada has done much to popularize the ever-expanding plebeian culture. [4]

But despite achievements, Nevada's cultural successes have limitations. The Las Vegas Strip does not threaten Stratford-on-Avon or other hoary institutions; it has not stood the test for 400 years. Nor has it become the authority for an age or provided exacting standards and quiet urbanity. Nevada is only beginning to impart a belief in itself and in eternity; it still makes massive concessions to contemporary fads and follies. However, design and culture and human lore is where you find it, where man has the time and resources to point it up and give it meaning and place. T. S. Eliot explained that tradition is something you have to work at: "you create it as time passes."

It would be difficult to overemphasize the impact of science and technology on Nevada's present society. By a strange quirk of fate, America's march to the West and claims of manifest destiny relied heavily on the rapidly expanding industrial revolution. As the telegraph and the railways opened up the Great Basin, the major mining centers required sophisticated technical organization and advanced engineering skills. Water, food, lumber, and industrial power often had to be moved great distances. The West in general, and Nevada in particular, became, step by step, the product of scientific advances. And like America, twentieth-century Nevada has produced a version of civilization skewed toward the new technological breakthroughs. One of the results has been Las Vegas and the roadtown strip. This western phenomenon was made possible as more and more people undertook the relatively quick auto trek from Los Angeles. Today the success stories along Nevada's borders at Boomtown, Jackpot, Wendover, and Laughlin are the product of good highways and comfortable cars and buses. The architecturally controversial air terminal at Las Vegas further suggests the close relationship between Nevada's economic successes and the cutting edge in air transportation. The gargantuan consumption of electricity to light up the landscape with neon signs, to cool the windowless casinos, and to operate the computerized gambling devices suggest the total marriage between Nevada life and the electronics industry.

English historian Herbert Butterfield sums up the Nevada experience when he argues that the past is not a line of causation "bound to converge beautifully upon the present." Rather, contemporary "changes wrought by technology outshine other forces" and have literally reshaped the character of man, his mental functioning, his view of the world, and his social conduct.[5]

As more and more people freed themselves from the prewar depression mentality and from the constraints of life's traditional routines, they turned to the Sun Belt. Often inelegant and with neither sensitivity to nor affection for the new home, the masses began to arrive. The bold new West that Las Vegas epitomized and publicized, was recreationally motivated, multicultured, fast changing, informal, restless, and, above all, automobile oriented. As the student of gambling, John M. Findlay, has carefully explained, automobiles transformed a railroad town into a resort city. Physically and psychologically Nevada joined southern California in becoming the pacesetter for the nation. Nevada, and particularly Las Vegas, became an amusement park by emotionally and technically providing a sense of freedom, fantasy, luxury, and mobility for both the affluent and those seeking employment. As America's work habits became interspersed with play and vacations, as the eight-hour-day, blue-collar tradition disappeared, as more social security and pension checks were issued, Nevada became "the super-hyphen-version of a whole new way of life."[6]

For good or evil Nevada has come to embrace the new rules. Technology has been utilized to create a society. Rather than being out of step, Nevada has come to set the pace. Indeed, most states are now moving to espouse tourism, convention spectaculars, design centers, lotteries, off-track betting, prizefighting, and even casino gambling and easy divorce. As in the industrial revolution, the first exploiters of the innovations enjoyed many advantages and reaped significant financial rewards. For forty years Nevada has built upon easy riches. But rapidly expanding societies also face major human and cultural adjustments. They have difficulty in balancing the patterns of the past with the demands of a changing present. Nevada's new citizens have been a third more likely than in other states to be perennial transients—rootless and personally isolated. Nevada has not yet successfully reordered its priorities to deal humanely with the new age.

English novelist Graham Greene once journeyed to Haiti and quickly assessed the confusion as "Tragedy With a Banana Peel." Nevada has endured similar stings from itinerant scribblers since J. Ross Browne focused his humor on "A Peep at Washoe" in 1860. Over the decades, as a hundred mining camps were founded and quickly collapsed, local citizens and journalists refined the high art of criticism into satire that was often more indulgent than pleasant, more cruel than compassionate. The early twentieth century brought progressive reformers with their habit of questioning society. In public lectures, official reports, and popular journals, intellectuals, social critics, and feminists envisioned quiet rural homesteads, an educated citizenry, and a state sensitive to traditional moral values.

As Nevada's permissive institutions were legalized, a barrage of books and articles reported on the scandals, the gossip, and the tawdry tales of quick gain and ruinous losses: Nevada became "a canvas for the smudging." By mid-twentieth century, few isolated regions of America were as well known and yet so unknown, so fleetingly experienced and so often cheapened by clichés. The sardonic commentators became more sophisticated during the 1950s with reports from the Kefauver Crime Commission and exposés from *The Las Vegas Sun*. During the 1960s, books like *The Green Felt Jungle* (1963), *Nevada's Key Pittman* (1963), *Gambler's Money* (1965), and *Nevada: The Great Rotten Borough* (1966) set the semiprofessional, albeit highly critical tone. In recent years the moralistic and subtractive assessments have become less dramatic and anecdotal: criticism is more often directed toward ecological, artistic, or socioeconomic failures.

During the eighties the most provocative economic issue within the state has centered around diversification. Most planners and public officials argue that any one-crop economy, be it sophisticated or primitive, is a road to instability and eventual economic and social disruption. Whether it is sugar in the Mississippi Delta, wheat on the Great Plains, oil in West Texas, the one-factory town, or casinos in Nevada, a society is in jeopardy when it ties itself to one overriding source of income. For most of its history, and always in times of prosperity, Nevada has been the victim of the one-crop industry. Mining created the state in 1864, and with mining's collapse after 1880, the state suffered major decline. With the resurgence of mining after 1900, the state again enjoyed modest prosperity until the end of the First World War.

According to the theory, Nevada's extracting economy merely changed directions during the 1930s when the state stopped taking gold from the hills and began taking it from gambling tables and tourists. Critics like James Hulse expand the theory by suggesting that the casinos, the big hotels, the banks, and other power elites appropriated the lion's share of profits, victimized workers, and ignored educational and cultural institutions. Over recent years, however, the occasional attacks on gaming have fallen on deaf ears. Even utopian reformers have come to admit that support for the "peculiar" institution has conclusively overshadowed any opposition.

But Nevada has also enjoyed a modest economic diversification.

Greater use of the "free port" laws (nontaxing of goods in transit and storage) has assisted the warehouse industry in attracting major new foreign and domestic distributors. Indeed, merchandise can now be assembled, processed, relabeled, and repackaged without being subject to taxation, thus gaining new industries for Nevada. Although highly volatile, the electronics manufacturers of the state have generally prospered. And Nevada has again become a leading gold mining center with the state extracting 56 percent of the entire American domestic production in 1986 and 1987. The estimated production in 1988 of 5.8 million ounces, with Nevada contributing over half of the total, will achieve a billion-dollar mining industry for the state.

A student of gambling, Eugene Martin Christiansen, gives the "one-crop economy" theory a more personal and dramatic twist by declaring Nevada the only American state that is and always has been "a company town." Although the mineral discoveries of the Comstock produced great wealth, it was inevitably drawn off to larger financial centers. Hotels, railways, and other mine-supported industries failed to diversify the economy or save the hopelessly exploited society. According to Christiansen, the "die of Nevada's history was cast." The state would belong to "the concentrated interests of a single-source system." The West would grow and develop but Nevada was to remain dependent upon and at the mercy of outside capitalists.[7]

In 1931 the legislature set in motion the process whereby the company merely changed hands: Nevada became the property of and held the American monopoly for casino gambling. According to the dialogue, the state—like hundreds of desperate villages from Pakistan to the Basque country, from Bolivia to Mexico—survived on a system of legal, semilegal, and illegal trade, tourism, and vice. But in time, because of Nevada's unique location, technological timing, and America's wealth, the state's one industry became phenomenally successful. Theorists warn us, however, that the "company town" gambling mentality has robbed Nevada citizens of a realistic social order, a quiet diversity, and a moral heritage.

Yet another closely related theory suggests that Nevada has always been the product, or more precisely the by-product, of the federal government. The state was quickly branded the "beggar boy" and the "toy of Washington": a state created by President Lincoln out of political caprice to get senators for the Republican Party. Certainly at the beginning of the twentieth century Senator Francis G. Newlands reached out to Washington and "beckoned with an up-turned hand."

The state received the firstfruits of the federal reclamation program in the Lahonton flood-control and Fallon irrigation projects. It was followed by Hoover Dam and Lake Mead, by Rye Patch Dam and miles of alfalfa fields around Lovelock, and by other smaller projects. The state also absorbed the huge ammunition storage facility at Hawthorne and, starting with World War II, several air bases. After the war came the atomic test site at Yucca Flat and the nuclear waste dump at Beatty. In the late seventies Nevada citizens for the first time opposed a major federal project and objected to the placing of the MX racetrack missiles within the state. By the mid-eighties many also criticized locating a high-level nuclear waste dump in the open spaces northwest of Las Vegas. However, after working for years to attract high-tech industries, Nevada enthusiastically requested the atom-smashing supercollider with its Star Wars space-based missile defense system. And the 1987 opening of the Great Basin National Park near Ely was widely applauded. It seems Nevada's ambiguous and often uneasy partnership with the federal government has matured into a more normal and perhaps healthy love-hate relationship. Civil-military issues, the Sagebrush Rebellion, atomic wastes, and Indian rights now spark open controversy. The state seems to have achieved Bernard DeVoto's characterization of the western attitude toward Washington: "Get out and give us more money."

Spirited environmentalists argue that Nevada should remain part of a great, unspoiled stretch of nature with both capitalistic developers and the federal government being barred from gaining a further foothold. Throughout this century, from John C. Van Dyke and Mary Austin to Edward Abbey and Charles Bowden, a group of desert writers has contended that America needs its vast empty spaces as a respite from civilization. Historian and visionary Donald Worster has suggested that "the small community simply cannot afford massive intervention in the environment." Therefore, communities should rely upon their own capital and knowledge and free themselves from distant and impersonal structures that have reduced democracy in the American West to little more than a meaningless ritual. Worster's design is for less domination of nature and more accommodation with nature. He believes that the self-managed community, as the "Mormons initially did in Utah," is still a viable approach.[8]

In reality, it is unlikely that any community in Nevada can free itself from distant and impersonal capitalistic and government influences. Nevada, more than most states, participates in the broad marketplace and draws on distant sources for its commodities, its labor force, and its tourist trade. Since the beginning of the industrial revolution, man has looked over his shoulder to the pristine, agrarian "good old days." Every generation has produced rhetoric about the return to nature, but few of us would remain long by Walden Pond. Bigness and organizational hierarchy are not likely to disappear.

Yet thousands of people have thought they saw or could create in Nevada a type of society similar to what Professor Worster suggests. The planners and missionaries sought isolated, economically viable valleys where the desert would bloom like the rose. A sampling of the two score colonies planned or established in the western Great Basin suggests the strange appeal of the empty wilderness.

In the eastern part of the state, the Mormons with some success created the United Order on the Virgin River, the Nevada Land and Livestock Company at Georgetown, near Ely, and settlements along White River in White Pine and Nye counties. In 1892 a thousand Danes planned to settle along the Walker River; in 1907 Father T. W. Horgan was to locate one thousand Irish in Carson Sink. In 1907 some four hundred Polish families considered old Fort Halleck as a potential home; in 1911 the Italians planned extensive vineyards at Unionville; and in 1915 the Russians inspected Elko County for farming possibilities. The Dunkards almost left Muncie, Indiana, to take over Spanish Springs in Washoe County, and The House of David, under George L. Studebaker of the famous wagon-automobile family, considered leaving Benton Harbor, Michigan, for Rhyolite. Well over a hundred Eastern European Jews arrived in Smith Valley in 1897–98; some three hundred to four hundred persons, of the twenty-five hundred who bought land, actually located in the cooperative settlement of Nevada City, near Fallon, during the years before World War I. By the 1970s and 1980s medicine men like Rolling Thunder attracted hundreds of people to wigwams near Carlin, while at the same time a millenarian group, The Builders, has been operating a large ranch, known as "Oasis," near Wells.

The rural experiments have generally failed, and the hopes of thousands of devout, idealistic, and often unsophisticated people have been dashed. Nevada's great interior clearly has not been a place where the disaffected could rush to free themselves from a contaminated world. (With atomic testing, it is the open spaces that have proved to be most contaminated.) Rather, one of the most urban states in America, with 86 percent of its land still in the hands of the federal government, has become the home for active battalions of rootless consumers just in from California and Texas and elsewhere. By late twentieth century, it is off-road bikes, flimsy trailer courts, and melancholy suburban sprawl, not visions of wilderness utopias, that make up one of Nevada's major settlement patterns.

In the assessment of Nevada, however, social and cultural criticisms have often overshadowed the economic and technological issues. During the mid-century decades, a series of conventional and derogatory half-truths was routinely applied to the state by both journalists and scholars. Walter Prescott Webb, often declared "the West's leading historian," typified the scholarly approach. He compared Nevada's casinos and their rows of slot machines to Utah's Mormon research centers and their rows of microfilm readers. According to Webb, the people of the Great Basin were like musicians who performed on instruments with many of the strings missing. As a result, two societies strangely out of tune had emerged, "one good and one bad." The good society was that of the Mormons in Utah. The bad society with little to recommend it was Nevada. The state "solved its problems by creating an oasis of iniquity and license in a sea of moral inhibitions. . . . Nevada is what it is today because of what it did not have yesterday. In compensating for what the desert denied it, it has created the most bizarre society in the nation."[9] Reporters of the same period commonly referred to Nevada's visitors as "suckers" trying to escape from their drab lives or as divorcées trying to escape from wayward husbands.

By the 1980s, however, much of the bite has gone. Nevada exposés are no longer a popular or lucrative endeavor. The sensational stories about salted mines, divorced movie stars, and assassinated gangland leaders have faded. Even Steinbeck's caustic wisdom in *East of Eden*, "You can boast about anything if it is all you have," could not be applied to late-twentieth-century Nevada. Instead, thoughtful and serious visitors now probe into the artistic promise of the cities, the psychological stability of the institutions, and the social consciousness of the society.

Commentators wonder if the standardization of glitz and the excess of glitter have undermined the best in artistic expression. Clearly, gargantuan signs, lavish design, and excessive imagery may sap man's capacity to respond. The glitz seems to ignore the idea that there is more to perception than obvious sensory reality. The visual arrogance suggests that we see what we are told to see, what is easy to see, what residents and tourists must see if Nevada is to remain a popular attraction. Someone has said that we see the most where there is the least to see, presumably because nothing gets in the way of inner vision. In Nevada's urban centers there is so much that is gaudy-artificial that perhaps there is too little room left for refined imagination by the sensitive observer.

A related question is whether Nevada's unrepentant dedication to fast-paced amusements, to diversion and fun, is absorbed into the human appetite and helps to stimulate and feed the "me" mentality. The French historian of ideas, Michel Foucault, argues that the cult of sexuality and the alienation into "self" probably first evolved in the "twilight age" of Rome. He further suggests that with the collapse of Victorian-inspired socioreligious standards, a similar frantic search for independence and immediate satisfaction has become a declared objective of our era. According to Foucault, in the latter decades of imperial Rome people feared the loss of personal autonomy, purpose, and individual control over their lives. Therefore, they developed an intense preoccupation with self-realization, with internalization, and with escape from the controls of priests, bureaucrats, governors, and the community. Some observers have found these characteristics basic to our understanding of today's human behavior in casino cities like Las Vegas and Reno.[10]

Although an overworked cliché, the Romans and the Americans are often seen as cousins, "imperial, a bit Philistine, mildly venal, petulantly self-absorbed" and quick to follow the fads of fashion. Nevada may resemble the Eternal City of two thousand years ago in the cultivation of "self," as well as in the architectural symbolism of Caesar's Palace. Like the Romans, we may suffer from a culture of narcissism; we seek health and happiness and a kind of salvation through an obsession with social freedom. Even Roman attention to marriage, dream interpretation, exclusiveness while living in a pulsating society and notions of sexual fidelity confused with wild permissiveness may remind one of Nevada's wedding chapels, divorce courts, prostitution, and the luxurious entertainment.

Nevertheless, we have been taught that an excess of social options allows for the weaving of a broader fabric than an excess of social controls. In Nevada those endorsing an altruistic and tolerant order have generally woven themselves into the same edifice as those supporting a pragmatic and expansionistic society. Under many names—openness, liberalism, practicality, progress—much has been permitted and much achievcd. The individual and personal freedoms that thinking men, from Pericles to Jefferson and from the Pilgrims to the Cowboys, viewed as great virtues, have in Nevada inspired both entrepreneurs and progressives, businessmen and humanitarians, to envision and to build a new Gilded Age.

Nevada seems to fit George Catlin's assessment of the American West of a century and half ago. "Phantom-like it flies before us as we travel." As a vehicle in the propagation of the western myth, part of Nevada has tried to maintain the fiction of a perennial frontier. But beyond the portrait of the Marlboro Man the new Nevada has overwhelmed the old. New money, social democracy, easy morality, ready mobility, and consumer technology have completely reshaped the state since World War II. Nevada's brand of technological cosmopolitanism has freed society from the physical drudgery of life and, in part, from the desert, as well as from provincial prejudices. It has made the state a new crossroads for humanity. Conversely, rapid urbanization has weakened the dependence on history and rural culture, eroded old courtesies, and initiated conceit. As James Reston of *The New York Times* has noted, our frontier history taught us "to deal with adversity," but in Nevada we "have not learned to deal with prosperity."

The Nevada genre—with its distinctive art forms, its premier showmanship, its sparkling virtuosity, its secluded mines, ranches, and ghost towns—is an American original. We have helped to populate an empty quarter and at the same time taught the world that professional entertainment and luxurious life-styles are not merely for the elite. Will the desert island sink back into the sea of sand when the magician leaves? Or is it a land that man has been searching for since the dawn of democracy, a fantasy where there is no sovereignty and yet where all can be king?

NOTES

1. Tom Wolfe, *The Kandy-Kolored Tangerine-Flake Streamline Baby* (New York: Farrar, Straus and Giroux, 1965, xv–xvii.

2. See book-review article by Aleka Chase, "Motion Pictures and the Freudian Script," *San Francisco Chronicle*, Review Section, August 8, 1987, 5.

3. Lawrence Stone, "Resisting the New," *The New York Review of Books*, De-

cember 17, 1987. Reference is from a review of Gertrude Himmelfarb's *The New History and the Old.*

4. Eric J. Hobsbawm, *The Age of Empire: 1875–1914.* See comments on "the plebeian arts" by James Joll in *The New York Review of Books,* April 14, 1988.

5. Horace Freeland Judson, "The Public Interest in Science," *Maryland Humanities,* Winter, 1987, 6. Also see Herbert Butterfield, *The Origins of Modern Science* (New York: The Free Press, 1965).

6. John M. Findlay, *People of Chance: Gambling in American Society from Jamestown to Las Vegas* (New York: Oxford University Press, 1986). Note Findlay's reference to Tom Wolfe, 144.

7. Eugene Martin Christiansen, "The Company's Town," *Journal of Gambling Behavior,* Spring, 1988. Reference is from a review of James W. Hulse, *Forty Years in the Wilderness.*

8. Donald Worster, *Rivers of Empire: Water, Aridity and the Growth of the American West* (New York: Pantheon Books, 1985), 332.

9. Walter Prescott Webb, "The American West: Perpetual Mirage," *Harper's Magazine,* May 1957, 31.

10. Mark Poster, *Foucault, Marxism and History,* (Oxford: Basil Blackwell, 1984). Poster shows how Foucault's *The History of Sexuality* can be used to develop a critical theory for today's societies.

Contributors

William A. Douglass, social anthropologist, is Coordinator of the Basque Studies Program, University of Nevada-Reno. His books include *Death in Murelaga: The Social Significance of Funerary Ritual in a Spanish Basque Village, Amerikanuak: Basques in the New World,* and *Emigration in a South Italian Hill Town: An Anthropological History.* A native of Nevada, he is part owner of two casinos in the Reno area and a pathological fly fisherman.

Russell R. Elliott is Professor Emeritus and Honorary Doctor of Letters at the University of Nevada-Reno. He and many members of his family were once employed in the copper smelters at McGill. After teaching in Nevada public schools, he served as longtime chair of the History Department, UNR. His major publications include *Nevada's Twentieth-Century Mining Boom, A Political Biography of Senator William M. Stewart,* and a *History of Nevada.*

Charles R. Greenhaw spent several years in Texas and Oregon as a printer-journalist before becoming a college English instructor. He is now dean of instruction at Northern Nevada Community College in Elko and writes essays about people and places in rural Nevada. He has published often in *Halcyon* and is working on a book called *Nevada People,* dealing with the collapse of traditional Nevada life-styles.

James W. Hulse is a member of an old mining family from Pioche. As a faculty member at the University of Nevada-Reno, he has for over two decades divided his time between researching European revolutionary movements and western American themes. His best-known local study is *The Nevada Adventure,* and his most controversial work, *Forty Years in the Wilderness: Impressions of Nevada, 1940–1980,* was issued in 1986.

John Henry Irsfeld has published three novels, *Coming Through, Little Kingdoms,* and *Rats Alley,* as well as numerous short stories, essays, and poems. He was born in Minnesota, raised mostly in Texas, and is an authority on and collector of police and military sidearms. He was longtime chair of the English Department, University of Nevada-Las Vegas, and is currently Deputy to the President at UNLV.

William Kittredge has published essays in *Atlantic, Harper's, Paris Review, Rolling Stone,* and other magazines. His book *The Van Gogh Field* won the 1980 International Fiction Award. Among his most recent works are *Owning it All,* 1987; the soon to be published novel *Sixty Million Buffalo;* and *Hole in the Sky,* a forthcoming autobiography. Kittredge is recipient of the Neil Simon award for his work on the film *Heartland* and has completed the script for Norman Maclean's *A River Runs Through It.* He was born and lived until thirty-five years of age on a ranch on the Oregon-Nevada border and is currently Professor of Creative Writing at the University of Montana.

Robert Laxalt is the son of a Basque sheepherder and operator of his small ranch. He is also a writer and professor at the University of Nevada-Reno. Laxalt has been an overseas United Press correspondent and a major contributor to the *National Geographic* and other magazines. His seven books and many short stories have won numerous awards like the *Tambor de Oro* bestowed by the city of San Sebastian, Spain. Laxalt was the first living inductee into the Nevada Writers Hall of Fame, declared a Distinguished Nevadan by the University System, and selected to write *Nevada* for the American bicentennial series.

Eugene P. Moehring is Chair, Department of History, University of Nevada-Las Vegas. A native of Brooklyn and an urban historian, he is author of *Public Works and the Patterns of Urban Real Estate Growth in Manhattan* and coeditor with Arthur M. Schlesinger, Jr., of the multivolume series *Foreign Travelers in America, 1810–1935.* His *Resort City in the Sunbelt: Las Vegas, 1930–1970* is now being published.

C. Elizabeth Raymond is a student of the history and perception of

landscape and has written about sense of place on the agricultural prairies of her native Midwest. Her interest in the Great Basin grew out of a summer seminar for college teachers sponsored by the National Endowment for the Humanities at Notre Dame University. Professor Raymond, now at University of Nevada-Reno, is currently working on a biography of Nevada's political and economic magnate, George Wingfield.

Ann Ronald is a student of western writers from John Muir and Zane Grey to Wallace Stegner and Edward Abbey. Indeed, her best-known work is *The New West of Edward Abbey,* and her most recent study is *Words for the Wild* published by the Sierra Club. Ronald is Acting Dean of the Graduate School, University of Nevada-Reno, and an avid hiker, backpacker, and friend of the wilderness.

William D. Rowley comes to academics from a family background of western coal mining and Northwest ocean fishing. At the University of Nevada-Reno he is a historian of natural resources and the urban scene. His recent books include *Reno: Hub of the Washoe Country* and *U.S. Forest Service Grazing and Rangelands: A History.* Rowley is the longtime administrator of the Western History Association.

Wilbur S. Shepperson has divided his time for almost four decades between teaching European history, editorial work, and service to the state. His best-known Nevada publications are *Retreat to Nevada* and *Restless Strangers*. Shepperson is a founding member and sometime Chair of the Nevada Humanities Committee and longtime member of the State Board of Museums and History. He holds the Grace A. Griffen Chair in History at the University of Nevada-Reno.